CENTRAL ASIA AND KASHMIR
A STUDY IN THE CONTEXT OF ANGLO-RUSSIAN RIVALRY

CENTRAL ASIA AND KASHMIR

A STUDY IN THE CONTEXT OF ANGLO-RUSSIAN RIVALRY

K. WARIKOO

GIAN PUBLISHING HOUSE
New Delhi-110002

CENTRAL ASIA AND KASHMIR

A STUDY IN THE CONTEXT OF ANGLO-RUSSIAN RIVALRY

ISBN : 9788121202657

Rs. 750

Published in 2014 in India by
Gyan Publishing House
23, Ansari Road, Daryaganj,
New Delhi - 110002
Phones : 23261060, 23282060 Fax : 23285914
e-mail : books@gyanbooks.com
website : gyanbooks.com

Laser Typesetting at : Vinayak Printers, Delhi
Printed at : Salasar Imaging System, Delhi

Preface

Due to its geographical proximity to Central Asia and the existence of overland caravan routes linking the two regions, Kashmir played an important role in the process of Central Asia's intercourse with India in the political, commercial and cultural domains both in the ancient and medieval times. But in the modern times the Anglo-Russian rivalry lent a new dimension to these contacts. From the early nineteenth century onwards when Britain and Tsarist Russia emerged as the main contestants in Asia, Central Asia became an object of colonial rivalry. By the middle of the nineteenth century, Britain had assumed paramount power in India after she annexed Punjab in 1849. This brougtht her empire in India into direct contact with Afghanistan and Central Asia. Likewise, Russia too after consolidating its position in the Kazakh Steppes was moving ahead in Central Asia. As a result, Central Asia was turned into the venue of Anglo-Russian rivalry which also had its roots in their earlier antagonism in Europe. When Russia found her forward movement blocked in Europe after her defeat in the Crimean War (1854-56), she focussed her attention on its expansion in the southerly direction towards the Central Asian Khanates which offered least opposition. Thus the two Great Powers expanded from two opposite directions without engaging themselves in any direct military confrontation. Towards the end of the nineteenth century the two empires found themselves face to face in Asia separated only by a thin wedge of the Pamirs. Although the Pamir Boundary Agreement of 1895 helped in diluting the intensity of this two-power rivalry, yet it did not bring an end to it. However, with the emergence of a common German threat, the two powers began to cooperate in the changed circumstances. But with the establishment of Soviet power in Russia the whole region was once again drawn into the centre of world attention. The British consolidated their hold on the North-West Frontier Province and the area in and around Kashmir with a view to using it as a springboard for intervention in Central Asia. They took pains in strengthening the military establishments in this whole frontier belt. In the process the normal intercourse between Central Asia and India via Kashmir was greatly disrupted. The British authorities in India sought to justify these measures as steps to prevent the spread of Bolshevism.

Throughout the nineteenth and early twentieth centuries, the extent and pattern of political, commercial and cultural exchanges between Central Asia and Kashmir was conditioned by the state of diplomatic relations existing between the three empires of the world – Britain, Russia and China. When in mid-nineteenth century Central Asia and Kashmir had become parts of Russia and Britain respectively,the process of mutual exchanges between the two regions was largely inhibited as a result of various restrictions imposed by the two rival powers. Due to its strategic location vis-a-vis Central Asia, Kashmir came to occupy a pivotal position in the British strategy of checkmating Tsarist Russia. Though Russia perceived India as the sensitive nerve of the British empire, which when touched would put a brake on the British interference with the Russian interests in the Balkans in Europe, Britain was more concerned with the possible psychological impact of the Russian predominance in Central Asia over the disaffected chiefs and people in India. This explained the strategic importance of Kashmir and its frontier territories which commanded the overland routes from Central Asia to India. Besides, this area provided to the British convenient bases wherefrom the Russian movements in Central Asia were monitored. The geographical contiguity and cultural affinity of Central Asia with Kashmir were important factors which influenced the formulation of British policy towards Kashmir and its frontier dependencies.

The 'great game' has been the theme of several studies, most of which assign a central place to Afghanistan or Central Asia or both. This study aims at breaking a new ground by making a critical analysis of the political contacts, trade relations and cultural exchanges between Central Asia and Kashmir in the light of the 'great game' played by Britain and Russia during the nineteenth and early twentieth centuries. It not only discusses the impact of the Anglo-Russian rivalry on the conduct of these bilateral contacts but also examines ramifications of the 'great game' and its implications for developments on and around Kashmir frontiers during this period. The study is rounded off by an investigation of the British policy towards Kashmir in the wake of the establishment of Soviet power in Central Asia.

This book is the first part of a multi-volume study of Central Asian relations with Kashmir in modern times. Its scope is limited to the territories lying within Soviet Central Asia, that is, the former Western Turkestan, Khanates of Khiva, Kokand and Bukhara on the one hand, and the Dogra State of Jammu and Kashmir including Ladakh, Gilgit, Baltistan and the frontier districts of Hunza, Nagar, Yasin, Punial, Chilas, Chitral, Kuh-Ghizar, Ishkoman and Dir on the other. Presently this area corresponds approximately to the Soviet Socialist Republics of Tadjikistan, Uzbekistan, Kirghizia and Turkmenia on the one side and the Indian State of Jammu and Kashmir which also includes the area under the occupation of Pakistan and China on the other. And the relations between Kashmir and Kashgaria or Xinjiang, that is, Chinese Central Asia shall be discussed in the subsequent volume.

The work is based on primary sources such as the records of the National Archives of India including the 'Secret Consultations,' 'Proceedings of the Foreign and Political Department of the Government of India' and also the diplomatic exchanges between British, Russian and Chinese governments on Central Asian affairs. Besides, the secret diaries, memoranda and political reports submitted by a number of British officials and agents employed in remote parts of Central Asia, Afghanistan, Punjab, Kashmir and its frontier outposts have also been extensively used. The annual trade reports of Ladakh and Chinese Turkestan and the administration reports of Jammu and Kashmir and Punjab have provided the data relevant to the study of Indo-Central Asian trade that passed through Kashmir. The old English and Persian records that are preserved in the State Archives Repository, Jammu and the local unpublished histories and travel accounts of Central Asia by Kashmiri authors, which are preserved in the Research Department Library, Srinagar provided a deep insight into the developments from a local point of view. Mitchell's translations of important articles in Russian newspapers and journals and also the travelogues of Danibegov, Yefremov and Abdul Karim helped in understanding the Russsian and

Central Asian viewpoint. In order to cross-check or corroborate the information derived from the British Indian sources, the author has also used the works of leading Soviet and pro-Soviet writers and scholars. Besides, the microfilms of Russian archival records, that are available in the National Archives of India, have also been consulted.

I am deeply grateful to Dr. Devendra Kaushik, Professor of Soviet Studies, Jawaharlal Nehru University for his inspiring guidance and encouragement in the course of my research studies. He not only stimulated my interest in this study but also helped me to better visualise and understand numerous issues relating to it.

I feel obliged to Prof. N.N. Raina, a freedom fighter and nuclear physicist, Sh. B. P. Sharma, a veteran journalist and President of Dogri Research Institute, Jammu and Prof. M.K. Teng, Head, Department of Political Science, Kashmir University for their valuable Suggestions. My thanks are also due to Dr.K.N.Pandita, ex-Director, Centre of Central Asian Studies, University of Kashmir, Srinagar and Dr. S.S.Deora of the School of International Studies, Jawaharlal Nehru University for their help.

I gratefully acknowledge the courtesy and cooperation received from the staff of the National Archives of India, Nehru Memorial Museum and Library, Indian Council of Affairs Library, Jawaharlal Nehru University Library and Central Secretariat Library, all in New Delhi; State Archives Repository, S.R.S. Library, and Jammu University Library, all in Jammu; Oriental Research Library, and S.P.S.Library both in Srinagar, where I studied the materials used in this book. I am especially indebted to the Director, National Archives of India and the Ministry of External Affairs, Government of India for granting me access to the 'closed period' records of the Ministry.

I am grateful to my parents and my wife for their encouragement without which this work could not have been completed in time.

K. Warikoo

Abbreviations

Comp.	Compiler
Ed.	Editor
Extl.	External
Frontr.	Frontier
GOI.	Government of India
Intl.	Intelligence
J&K.	Jammu and Kashmir
JKA.	Jammu and Kashmir State Archives Repository, Jammu.
KW.	Keep with
NAI.	National Archives of India, New Delhi.
n.d.	No date
N.W.	North West
OER.	Old English Records, J&K State Archives Repository, Jammu
OS.	Old style
OSD.	Officer on Special Duty
PR.	Persian Records
Pol.	Political
P.C.	Political Consultations
Pseud.	Pseudonym
RDL.	Research Department Library, J&K Government, Srinagar.
Rev.	Revenue
Sec.	Secret
S.C.	Secret Consultations
S.H.	Secret Home
S.I.	Secret Intelligence

Contents

1

Political Connections

(1) EARLY CONTACTS

At the close of the eighteenth century some Russians did find their way to Central Asia, Eastern Turkestan and Kashmir. Though not on any political mission yet they were the pioneers in opening up to the Russians the way to Ladakh and Kashmir via the barren deserts of Central Asia, Kirghiz Steppes and Chinese Turkestan. The importance of their travels in this period cannot be under-estimated because the Russians had very scanty, if any, knowledge of the territories traversed by these travellers. This was more true of the route via Kokand-Yarkand-Leh-Srinagar-Jammu towards the heartland of India.

Filip Yefremov, a soldier by profession, when posted at a Russian outpost of Dongus lying beyond Orenburg fell a prisoner to the Kirghiz tribals in 1774, who finally sold him off to a Bukharan as a slave[1]. Yefremov subsequently managed to escape from his new master's hold to Kokand wherefrom he continued his strenuous journey through Kashgar, Yarkand, Leh, Srinagar, Jammu and the

---

1. P.M Kemp, ed, *Russian travellers to India and Persia 1624-1798, Kotov. Yefremov, Danibegov.* Delhi, 1959. pp.53-54.
The Kirghiz marauders used to capture the Russians to sell them off at the slave markets in Bukhara and Khiva. Yefremov was bartered away in exchange for four dressed hides only.

Indian mainland. In his narrative he mentions about the kingdom of Ladakh being ruled by a local Raja and also about the Afghan rule in Kashmir with Karim Dad Khan as its Governor[2]. Yefremov's travels in Ladakh, Kashmir and Jammu bear some political importance due to the fact that after sailing from Calcutta to London, he reported about his experiences to the Russsian Ambassador there and also to count Alexander Bezborodko at St. Petersburgh. Yefremov was even honoured with an audience before the Russian Empress on November 5, 1782[3]. He can safely be described as a pioneer for bringing to the notice of the then Tsarist government the state of affairs in Ladakh, Kashmir and Jammu during the later years of the Afghan rule.

It was in March 1795 that King Irakly II (1720-1798) of Georgia despatched one Georgian namely Rafail Danibegov on a commercial mission to Madras where an Armenian merchant had established his trade. Danibegov travelled to Madras by a circuitous route through Turkey, Muscat, Bombay and Pondicherry. There on learning about the death of this Armenian, he decided to return to Russia. Accordingly he left Madras for Calcutta wherefrom he proceeded to Kashmir via Murshidabad, Patna, Garhwal and Delhi. Danibegov made his return journey to Russia overland via Ladakh, Yarkand, Aksu, Turfan, Semipalatinsk, Omsk fort, Makaria (Novgorod) and Moscow. Among other things Danibegov's travelogue touches upon the political situation in Kashmir and Ladakh. His estimate of the revenue collected by the then Afghan Governor of Kashmir from the Shawl-weavers[4] must have aroused some interest among the Russian official and commercial circles in the shawl production of Kashmir. He also referred to the subordination of the Kashmir Governor to the king of Kabul. Danibegov's explicit statement that Chinese frontier in southern part of East Turkestan was

2. *Ibid.*, pp. 79, 82.
   Karim Dad Khan was the Afghan Governor of Kashmir during the years 1777-83.
3. *Ibid.*, p. 63.
4. *Ibid.*, p. 119.
   Danibegov's estimate of the annual income of the Governor of Kashmir amounting to about one million rupees a year on account of the duties levied by the Afghan rulers on the Kashmir shawl weavers is yet another proof of the intense exploitation of Kashmiri artisans during this period. In 1836-37, when Sikhs ruled Kashmir, the revenue derived from the shawl indutry alone was twelve lakh rupees. See *Foreign. S.C.* 18 Nov. 1843. 17.

at Kokiar[5], is too important to be missed. Danibegov's statement that *Kahlon* or the Prime Minister of Ladakh was subject to the Governor of Kashmir[6] throws light on the nature of political relations between Kashmir and its adjoining territories during this period.

Inspite of their being strangers to the territories of Central Asia and Kashmir, both these travellers have given a vivid picture of the area they passed through. While Yefremov described the route from Russia to Ladakh, Kashmir and India via Bukhara, Kokand, Kashgar and Yarkand, Danibegov returned to Russia via Kashmir, Ladakh, Eastern Turkestan, Semipalatinsk (then the Russian frontier facing Central Asian Khanates), Omsk fort, Novgorod and Moscow. He bypassed the intervening Central Asian Khanates obviously due to the turbulent conditions there and acts of brigandage by the Kirghiz nomads. However, both these travellers proved to the Russian official and commercial circles that neither of these two routes was inaccessible for any determined traveller. They also highlighted the shawl trade in Kashmir. Yefremov's narrative was published in Russia in as many as three editions (in 1786, 1794 and 1811). Danibegov's account was translated from Georgian into Russian and published in 1815 from Moscow. Both Yefremov and Danibegov attracted considerable interest in the Russian academic and official circles.

Round about the same period, that is the late eighteenth and early nineteenth century, when Kashmir suffered under the Afghan yoke, one Abdul Karim, resident of Bukhara, travelled through Afghanistan, Bukhara, Khiva and Kokand to Kashmir. It is believed that he belonged to a Syed family of Bukhara and that he was also in the service of Shah Mahmud of Afghanistan[7]. Abdul Karim,

5. *Ibid.*, p. 120.
This confirms the statements of other contemporary sources that the Chinese frontier (in southern Sinkiang facing India in Ladakh sector) was at Kokiar, that is even beyond Shahidulla. According to Frosyth, Henderson, Earl of Dunmore and others who travelled in this area during the late nineteenth century Shahidulla constituted the Indian frontier facing Chinese Turkestan. Even as late as 1860s, there was a Chinese frontier post at Kokiar, where a frontier guard of Chinese soldiers used to check the entry of unauthorised travellers into Eastern Turkestan from the direction of India through Ladakh. See R. H. Davies, *Report*...Lahore, 1862. Appendix XXIV. p. cclvi.
6. *Ibid.*, p. 121.
7. Charles Schefer, ed. and tr, *Histoire de L'Asie Centrale par Mir Abdoul Karim Boukhary*. Paris, 1876. p. II.

basically a poet had also the distinction of having acted as the Manager of Ala-ud-Din, the Ambassador of the Khan of Bukhara at the Russian court[8]. In his travelogue Abdul Karim states that he visited Kashmir twice, first at the age of just sixteen coming via Herat, Kandhar, Kabul, Peshawar and Muzafffarabad. His second visit to Kashmir was at the close of the eighteenth century, when he was still in Russia. This time he had taken the route of Semipalatinsk, Ili, Aksu, Kashgar, Yarkand and Leh[9].

In his description of Kashmir, Abdul Karim has laid stress on its shawl industry explaining the weaving methods, extent of taxes levied on shawls and the trading pattern. He also reveals that one Haji Muhammad Hussain Khan of Merv in Central Asia after selling his property there, fled to Kashmir via Kokand, Kashgar and Leh[10]. This further strengthens the belief that due to turbulent conditions in the Central Asian Khanates and the internecine wars between the ruling chiefs, numerous princes, nobles and even common people used to migrate to safer places when power changed hands from one faction to another. As regards the approximate period of arrival of Haji Muhammad Hussain he might have come to Kashmir in the early years of the nineteenth century. Kashmir appears to have fascinated many among the Central Asian elite. Thus the court physician of Omar Khan, the then ruler of Kokand, arrived at Ladakh in 1821, in the company of Mir Izzet Ullah (a British Indian agent sent to Central Asia). Though no specific political motive can be ascribed to his visit, yet he was used by Moorcroft (then in Leh preparing for his journey to Central Asia) to facilitate his passage through Yarkand and Kashgar[11].

During 1830s another Bukharan, Abdul Rahim, stayed in Kashmir in connection with his shawl business. His agility and wit attracted the attention of Captain L.M. Wade (then British Political Agent at Ludhiana). Besides forwarding all important information regarding the state of affairs in Kashmir, Abdul Rahim also used to

8. *Ibid.*, p. III.
9. *Ibid.*
10. *Ibid.*, p. 149.
1. *Foriegn.Political.* 20 Sept. 1822. 67.

feed the British government with intelligence pertaining to the events in Kokand Khanate and Chinese Turkestan[12]. The political influence wielded by this Bukharan in the Sikh administration of Kashmir can well be gauged by the manner in which he demanded and secured a "seat as the company's agent" alongside Vigne, a Britisher, and the Governor of Kashmir[13]. On another occasion in 1835 an Austrian traveller, Baron von Hugel, was introduced by Abdul Rahim to Mehan Singh, then Sikh Governor of Kashmir[14], during his visit to the valley.

(2) AGHA MEHDI'S MISSIONS TO LADAKH

The presence of Russian and Central Asian merchants in Kashmir during the eighteenth and nineteenth centuries for purposes of shawl trade is testified by such eye-witness accounts as that of Bernier, Yefremov, Abdul Karim of Bukhara, Forster[15], Moorcroft[16] and other Russian sources. It is not surprising that as early as the first quarter of the nineteenth century, the Russian government had begun to evince interest in opening up its commerce with Kashmir. Since the shawls of Kashmir sold well in Russia, the Tsarist government was also keen to rear pashmina goats in Siberia. The setback suffered by Russia in its foreign trade with European countries during the Napoleonic wars and the continental blockade, induced the Tsarist government to pay attention to the extension of Russia's land trade with its neighbours in Asia. As an off-shoot of this policy, the Russian

---

12. *Foreign Political.* 25 July 1836. 14-16.
The then Governor General of India sanctioned a remuneration of nine hundred twenty four rupees in favour of Abdul Rahim for his map of Kashmir and other reports. See *Foreign P.C.* 1 August 1838. 32-33.
13. B.C. Hugel, *Travels in Cashmere and the Punjab.* Translated into English by T.B Jervis. London, 1846. p. 152.
14. *Ibid.* p. 115. Mehan Singh was the Governor in Kashmir during the period 1834-1841.
15. George Forster, *A journey from Bengal to England.* London, 1789. Vol. 2, p.24. He had met a Georgian merchant in Kashmir in 1783.
16. W.Moorcroft, *Travels.* Vol.2, p.195. See also Moorcroft's letter to John Adam, Political Secretary, GOI, 7 Sept. 1812. *Foreign Political* 18 Dec. 1812. 29.

Foreign Ministry assigned to I.F. Kruzernshtern the task of visiting ports of India[17]. Simultaneously Lt. Gaverdovsky led a large Russian caravan to Bukhara[18]. Serious attention also began to be paid to the study of trade routes to India. About the same time, Russian envoys were despatched to the Khans of Kokand and Bukhara for facilitating commercial intercourse and to ensure a steady check on the Turkoman and Kirghiz nomad raids on the caravans. They also sought the removal of excessive customs duties levied on Russian merchants in these territories. Russia did succeed in persuading the ruler of Kokand, Omar Khan, to provide safe convoy to the Russo-Chinese caravans through his territories[19]. Such mutual agreement paved the way for a freer movement of trading caravans from Russia through Kokand to Kashgar.

While Russia was making all efforts to remove various obstacles in its trade with Bukhara, Kokand and Eastern Turkestan, the British too had cast their eyes on the shawl-wool resources of Kashmir. They contemplated import of shawl-wool goats to England for breeding so that shawls could be manufactured there[20]. Acting under the instructions of the Court of Directors, the Governor General in Council (Bombay) wrote to the then Resident at Delhi, C. Metcalfe, on March 21, 1812 asking him to "endeavour to procure some of the sheep from the wool of which shawls are manufactured"[21]. In the same year Moorcroft was sent to Gartok[22] (in Tibet) to procure shawl wool. It was during his stay at Gartok that Moorcroft learnt about the arrival of some Russians in Kashmir disguised as merchants and carrying gifts for the local chiefs[23]. Taking an alarmist view of this information, which was provided to him by a Kashmiri trader named Ahmed Khan

17. O. F. Solov'yev, " K voprosu obotnoshenii tsarskoy Rossiik Indii v XIX nachale XX veka" *Voprosy Istorii* 1958, No. 6, pp. 96-109.

18. *Ibid.*

19. *Foreign. Political.* 9 Jan. 1824.33.

20. The court of Directors in its despatch dated 10 Oct. 1810 to the Governor General in Council, Bombay conveyed the desire of the British Board of Agriculture to rear the Kashmir sheep in England. See *Foreign Political.* 8 May 1812. 52.

21. *Ibid.*

22. Also called by the names of Garo, Gardokh or Gartope, it was one of the trading stations where natural produce of China and Tibet was bartered with the products of Kashmir.

23. Moorcroft to John Adam, Political Secretary, GOI, 7 Sept. 1812. *Foreign. Political.* 18 Dec. 1812. 29.

then purchasing shawl-wool in Gartok, Moorcroft cautioned his government against the Russian threat to the British political and commercial interests in the north and north-western frontiers of India[24]. The arrival of the Russian agents disguised as merchants in Kashmir is corroborated by the Russian sources. According to a Russian scholar, O.F. Solov'yev, the Russian Foreign Minister, Rumantsev, had commissioned in 1808, Mehti Rafailov, a native of Kabul (the same Agha Mehdi as described by Moorcroft), Zakhar Shargilov, a native of Tiflis and an Armenian, Egor Artemov, to ascertain the trade routes from Russia to India[25]. Apparently, Russia sought to prepare the ground for opening its commerce with Ladakh and Kashmir via Kokand, Kashgar and Yarkand.

The circumstances of the despatch of the Russian missions under Agha Mehdi(Rafailov) to Ladakh and also the British efforts to procure the shawl-wool goats (from Tibet, Sikkim and Ladakh) lead to the conclusion that both these powers had started to expand their commercial and political activity beyond their respective domains. Their interests naturally clashed in Central Asia along the frontiers of India. Whereas the British had sent Izzet Ullah (in 1812) and Moorcroft (1819-25) on fact-finding missions to Central Asia via Kashmir and Ladakh, Tsarist Russia too had her plans. Moorcroft reported on his arrival in Bukhara in 1825 that he had been preceded there by an accredited Russian ambassador (in about 1822) for seeking reduction of customs duties on goods carried by the Russian merchants through Bukharan territory and also to ask the Khan of Bukhara to reprimand the Oorgunj raiders involved in plundering the Russian caravans[26]. It was here in Bukhara in 1825, that Moorcroft claimed to have learnt about the Russian plans to despatch secret agents to Kashmir via Kokand, Kashgar, Yarkand and Leh for obtaining intelligence[27]. This is how the early phase of the Anglo-Russian rivalry in Central Asia started with a clash of their expanding commercial interests.

It was the astute and ever vigilant Moorcroft, who during his

24. *Ibid*
25. O.F. Solov'yev, *op cit.*
26. W. Moorcroft to George Swinton dated Bukhara, 6 June 1825. Sec *Foreign. Political*. 14 Oct. 1825. 27
27. *Ibid.*

stay at Leh in 1821 discovered that the Russian government had despatched an envoy named Agha Mehdi with a complimentary letter addressed to the Raja of Ladakh[28]. Moorcroft claims to have seen this letter through the courtesy of the Prime Minister of Ladakh[29]. Signed by a Russian Minister and addressed to the Raja, Mahmood Khan Nazim of Tibet[30], the letter expressed the Russian desire to "establish a friendly intercourse between the people of Russia and Thebet, and to open trade"[31]. It was clarified that though Chinese territory (Chinese Turkestan) intervened between Ladakh and Russia, yet such physical obstacles in the way of commercial intercourse could be removed if "goodwill and friendly disposition exist on both sides"[32]. Tsarist government was also keen to receive an envoy from Ladakh with full honours[33].

According to Moorcroft this Russian envoy Agha Mehdi was son of a Jew settled in Kashmir who had lost his parents at an early age. He started his career early in life as a mere peddler[34] and rose to be one of the leading shawl traders, well established in Russia and operating from Kabul. After embracing Christianity, his access to the ruling circles in St. Petersburgh was facilitated[35]. All these circumstances coupled with his intimate knowledge of the people and languages of Turkestan, Kashmir and Punjab made him fit to be employed as an agent for obtaining both topographical information and also to further Russian commercial interests in Ladakh and Kashmir. Agha Mehdi is reported to have been duly honoured by the

---

28. Moorcroft, *Travels*. Vol. 1, p. 383.

29. *Ibid.* For substance of this letter see appendix I.

30. The actual name of the Gyalpo (King) of Ladakh was Tonduk Namgyal. But he continued to be known as Akabat Mahmud Khan. Even the Dogra soldiers accompanying Zorawar Singh called him by this name. During the seventeenth century, the then Gyalpo had nominally embraced Islam in exchange for military aid received from the Mughal Governor of Kashmir for repelling the Tartar invaders. Obviously the Russians addressed the Gyalpo by his Muslim name. See A. Cunningham, *Ladakh*. London, 1854. p.338.

31. Moorcroft to C. T. Metcalfe, Political Secretary, GOI dated Leh 1 Jan. 1821. *Foreign. Political*. 10 Oct. 1823. 23-24. The word 'Thebet' mentioned in Nesselrode's letter refers to Ladakh, which was also known as 'Little Tibet'.

32. *Ibid.*

33. *Ibid.*

34. Moorcroft, *Travels*. Vol. 1, p. 385.

35. *Ibid.* In his letter sent through Agha Mehdi, Nesselrode introduced him as one of the court Counsellors of the State of Russia.

Tsar Alexander I with presents of gold chain and a medal for his successful mission to Ladakh[36]. The visit of a Russian envoy to Ladakh is fully corroborated by the Russian sources, which clearly state that Mehdi Rafailov alongwith two other companions left Semipalatinsk in 1808 via Chinese possessions of Aksu, Kuldja, Kashgar and Yarkand for Ladakh and Kashmir[37].

Soon after the Sikhs acquired their control over Kashmir in 1819, Russia decided to send Agha Mehdi Rafailov in Janurary 1820 on yet another mission to Ladakh and Punjab via Chinese Turkestan. Under orders of the Russian Emperor, he was to deliver friendly communications to the Raja of Ladakh and Maharaja Ranjit Singh at Lahore[38]. This mission appears to have been carried out after careful deliberations and preparations at St. Petersburgh, which is clearly borne out by the following information left to us by Moorcroft[39] :

(a) That Agha Mehdi had been tutored at St. Petersburgh for about a year by a trained British artist in the use of various dyes for applying to shawl goods.

(b) He was provided with several packages of dyes such as cochineal, indigo wood, berbery root and other mordants like acetile of lead, aluminic potash, soda lime etc. for use in Kashmir.

(c) He was equipped with several emeralds[40] and rubies meant as presents for the chiefs of Ladakh and Punjab, besides gold ducats in considerable

---

36. *AVPR, F. Spb. Glav. Arkhiv.* (USSR) 11-26, 1811. D. 4. L. 11-12. Citied in D. Kaushik, *India and Central Asia*. New Delhi, 1985. p. 83. See also Moorcroft, *Travels*. Vol. 1, p. 386.

37. O. F. Solov'yev, opcit. On his return jouiney, Mehti Rafailov along with him a considerable quantity of Kashmir shawls to St. Petersburgh. Apart from opening up of this new route to Russian merchants, Rafailov drew a rosy picture of the commercial viability of Kashmir, which further stimulated the Russsian interest. He was awarded the title of Counsellor of Commerce by a decree of the Senate on 27 Jan. 1817, and elevated later as Nadvornyy Sovetnik(Court Counsellor) with a civil rank of seventh class.

38. Moorcroft, *Travels*. Vol. 1, p. 387.

39. Moorcoft to Metcalfe, 6 May 1821. *Foreign. Political.* 10 Oct. 1823. 25.

40. Moorcroft was much impressed by the size and polish of these emeralds, some of which were set in gold. According to him, even Maharaja Daolat Rao Scindia had not worn such large emeralds.

See *Ibid.*

quantities.

(d) He was escorted across the Kirghiz Steppes to the borders of Chinese Turkestan by a troop of Russian cavalry.

The timing and compositon of this mission and also the tone of Nesselrode's letter to Maharaja Ranjit Singh suggest that Russia wanted to establish a regular commercial intercourse with Ladakh, Kashmir and Punjab. Though Moorcroft could not lay his hands upon the letter meant for the Raja of Ladakh, he did forward a true copy of the original letter signed by Nesselrode, the then Russian Foreign Mininster (dated St. Petersburgh 1820) in the name of Raja Ranjit Singh of Punjab, alongwith its English translation to the British Indian Government.* However, from the Russian sources we learn that Nesselrode had signed this letter on January 17, 1820.[41] Written in Russian language and transcribed in golden ink, the letter introduced Agha Mehdi, the son of one "Rafail, the agent for the affairs of the merchants of Persia and Tartary trading to Russia" as one of the "aulic counsellors of the State of Russia".[42] Nesselrode had conveyed the Russian Emperor's desire to open the "gates of friendly intercourse" and to clear "the road to traffic between the merchants of Russia and the Punjab from all impediments".[43] Ranjit Singh was further assured that any of his subjects whether merchants or travellers would receive the "most friendly manner and a consideration exactly proportionate to their rank and station"[44] on their visit to Russia.

If we are to believe what Moorcroft claims to have been told by Izzet Ullah after his return from Yarkand,[45] we cannot dismiss this mission as a purely commercial one. Agha Mehdi Rafailov is reported by Izzet Ullah to have encouraged the Khoja rebel Chief of Kashgar to rise against the Chinese by assuring them full Russian support.[46]

---

* See Appendix II

41. O.F. Solov'yev, *op cit.*

42. Moorcroft to Metcalfe, 6 May 1821.

43. *Ibid.*

44. *Ibid.*

45. Izzet Ullah had been sent by Moorcroft to Yarkand to prepare the ground for his passage through Eastern Turkestan to Kokand and Bukhara. He arrived at Yarkand on 25 Sept. 1821.

46. Moorcroft to G. Swinton, Political Secretary, 17 Oct. 1821. *Foreign. Political.* 26 July 1822. 56.

He is also believed to have been provided with money sufficient to meet the travel expenses of the Khoja Chief of Kashgar and also of the envoys from Ladakh and Punjab to St. Petersburgh.[47]

But Agha Mehdi Rafailov was not destined to fulfil his assignment. The news of his death near Karakoram pass whilst on his way to Ladakh reached Moorcroft in April 1821 when Agha Mehdi's deputy, Mohammad Zahoor, arrived at Leh carrying dyes and other articles.[48] Though Soviet scholars attribute Rafailov's death to illness,[49] it can more probably be assigned to treason rather than natural circumstances. Some of his fellow travellers must have been tempted to appropriate the treasure (charged to Agha Mehdi in the shape of gold ducats, emeralds etc.). The noted Hungarian orientalist and traveller, Alexander Csoma de Koros's statement made to one Englishman, W. Murray, that the Russian Ambassador was murdered by his followers at a pass several days' journey from Leh and his property plundered,[50] further substantiates this view. Besides, Agha Mehdi's companion Mohammad Zahoor was seen by Moorcroft selling off the dyes, emeralds and rubies, which he later invested in the purchase of shawls for resale in Bukhara.[51]

After sifting and analysing all the available evidence as provided by Moorcroft's secret despatches which also incorporate Izzet Ullah's findings in Yarkand and also the Russian sources, one can safely conclude that Agha Mehdi Rafailov was commissioned by Russian government to explore the possibility of establishing a friendly political and regular commercial intercourse between Russia and Ladakh, Kashmir and Punjab via Chinese Turkestan and also to make a study of the trade routes passing through these territories. The inference drawn by R.K. Parmu that "Yarkandis and Kashgaris had endeavoured to use Agha Mehdi's good offices to prevail upon the Raja of Ladakh and Ranjit Singh to send envoys to Russia",[52] is evidently wide off the mark. The fact of Agha Mehdi having been

47. *Ibid.*
48. Moorcroft to Metcalfe, 6 May 1821.
49. O.F. Solov'yev, *op cit.*
50. *Foreign. Political.* 7 Jan. 1825. 32.
51. Moorcroft to Metcalfe, 6 May 1821.
See also Moorcroft, *Travels.* Vol. 1, p. 391.
52. See his "*A History of Sikh rule in Kashmir*". Srinagar, 1977. p. 304.

trained in the art of dyeing besides being equipped with dyes for use in Kashmir shawls points to the keen Russian interest in the promotion of their trade with Kashmir. That he was required to procure a number of shawl-wool goats for purpose of rearing in Russia,[53] is proved beyond doubt by the Russian academician V. Bartold's statement that "in 1820, in connection with the project to breed Kashmir goats in Siberia the Commercial Counsellor Mekhti Rafailov was sent from Semipalatinsk to Tibet".[54] To facilitate the safe carriage of these animals through Kirghiz Steppes to Russia, a Russian cavalry escort continued to wait at Ili (in Chinese Turkestan) for the return of Agha Mehdi from Ladakh.[55] The despatch of Moorcroft and Agha Mehdi missions to Kashmir and Ladakh only underlined the importance attached during this period to Kashmir shawl-wool goats in both the British and Russian official and commercial circles. It is, however, necessary to put the mission of Agha Mehdi in its proper perspective. It would be absurd to use this circumstance as evidence of Russian imperial designs over Ladakh and Kashmir. It was too early for Russia to think in terms of conquest of northern India, as the Chinese possessions in Eastern Turkestan and independent Khanates of Kokand and Bukhara intervened between the two regions. Besides, Agha Mehdi's occupation as a regular merchant and his official position of commercial Counsellor in Russia point out to the peaceful nature of his mission. The main motive of Tsarist Russia in sending this mission was obviously commercial. But to expand trade and commerce between the two distant regions, it was also necessary to forge cordial political relations with the then Sikh State of Punjab under Maharaja Ranjit Singh and his dependency in Ladakh. However, Agha Mehdi's complicity in instigating the rebel Khoja Chief of Kashgar against the Chinese rule in Eastern Turkestan under orders of the Russian

---

53. *Foreign. Political.* 10 Oct. 1823. 25.

54. V. Bartold, *Istoriya Izucheniya vostoka v Europe i v Rossii.* (History of the study of the Orient in Europe in Russia). Moscow, 1925. p.228.

55. Moorcroft to Swinton, 18 April 1822. *Foreign. Political.* 20 Sept. 1822. 76. During his visit to Yarkand in 1821, Mir Izzet Ullah (Moorcroft's trusted assistant) too had learnt about the presence of some Cossack troops, who had escorted Agha Mehdi across the Steppe, in the neighbourhood of Yangi Turfan (in Chinese Turkestan) waiting for the return of Agha Mehdi. See *Foreign Political.* 26 July 1822. 56.

Foreign Ministry as was reported by Izzet Ullah, requires further substantiation from the Russian and Chinese sources.

(3) KOKAND ENVOYS VISIT LADAKH AND KASHMIR (1837, 1854)

In 1837 Capt. Wade, the British Political Agent at Ludhiana received authentic information about the arrival in Leh of an envoy of the ruler of Kokand enroute to India[56].This envoy was forced to adopt the guise of a merchant through Yarkand owing to the hostile relations existing between the ruler of Kokand and the Chinese in Eastern Turkestan. He had been deputed by the Khan of Kokand to present a pair of rubies and horses to the Governor General of India with a view to establishing friendly relations with the British government[57]. It was a strange coincidence that at about the same time one Haji Mohammad Ali of Yarkand had been maltreated by Raja Gulab Singh's representative at Leh for his friendly conversations with Vigne-a British traveller[58]. The Dogra Chief was keen to prevent the friendly intercourse of the British travellers with any visitors from the neighbouring Central Asian Khanates. Alarmed at the treatment meted out to the Yarkandi visitor, the Kokand envoy sold off his property in Leh and burnt the letter charged to his custody, returning to Kokand through Yarkand and Kashgar without attaining his object[59]. Thus Raja Gulab Singh's political prestige in the neighbouring Central Asian Khanates as a ruler powerful enough

56. *Foreign P.C.* 1 Aug. 1838. 32-33. Wade had received this information from Abdul Rahim, the Bukharan news-agent in Kashmir. Before forwarding it to the Government of India, Wade took care to confirm it from other sources including Dr. Falconer (the Supdt. of Company's Garden at Saharanpur), who was then at Leh.

57. *Ibid.*

58. *Ibid.*
Vinge had openly aligned himself with the cause of Ahmed Shah, the Chief of Skardo, naturally against the interests of Raja Gulab Singh. Vigne's attempts to explore the roads to Yarkand through Nubra were also thwarted by Gulab Singh. See G.T. Vigne, *Travels*. London, 1842. Vol. 2, p. 350.
Soon after, Wade complained to Maharaja Ranjit Singh against the supposed ill-treatment of Vigne at the hands of Gulab Singh and his representative at Leh.

59. *Foreign P.C.* 1 Aug. 1838. 32-33.

to reject the requests of British travellers like Vigne rose high.

Finding himself unable to resist the Russian occupation of fort Ak-Masjid[60],. the ruler of Kokand, Khuda Yar Khan, began his efforts to obtain succour from the British so as to enable him to safeguard the remaining portion of his territory. It was in August 1854 that an accredited envoy from Kokand, namely Shahzada Sultan Mohammad Khan, arrived at Peshawar bearing letters for the Governor General of India and the Commissioner of Peshawar Division, H.B. Edwardes[61]. The Kokand ruler wished the British government to loan the services of some of its officers for training his undisciplined forces to withstand any future Russian onslaught[62]. This envoy came to India through Oxus, Badakhshan, Zebak, Chitral and crossed the Malakand pass to reach Peshawar. He chose to return via Abbottabad, Kashmir, Ladakh and Yarkand, preferring it to the usual Kabul route on account of its being safe and free from turmoils and robbers.

Shahzada's visit to Kashmir while enroute to Kokand enabled Maharaja Gulab Singh of Kashmir to establish direct rapport with the Kokandi ruler and also to make a show of strength before his Central Asian guest. When Sultan Mohammad Khan arrived at Srinagar on September 10, 1855, he was not only received personally by the Kashmir ruler but also presented a purse of five hundred rupees[63]. Besides twenty rupees were sanctioned as daily allowance for each day of the envoy's stay in the valley[64]. The British government had attached a trained local surveyor Baboo Shuja to this envoy on his homeward journey for exploring the route to Kokand and ascertaining the position of Russians on the Kokand border[65]. But in his anxiety to keep his territory free from British influence, Gulab Singh managed to distract Baboo Shuja from his mission. This is borne out by Shahzada Sultan's letter to H.B. Edwardes, Commissioner, Peshawar Division, sent after his arrival at Kokand in August 1856. The envoy informed Edwardes that it was due to inducement of Ranbir Singh

60. The Kokandian fort on the Syr Darya-Ak Masjid (later Perovsk and now Kyzl-Orda) was captured in 1853.

61. *Foreign S.C.* 24 Nov. 1854. 1-25.

62. *Ibid.*

63. Ahmed Shah Nakshbandi to John Lawrence, Chief Commissioner, Punjab. *Foreign. S.C.* 30 Nov. 1855. 33-34.

64. *Ibid.*

65. *Foreign. S.C.* 30 Nov. 1855. 27-34.

(son of Maharaja Gulab Singh) that Baboo Shuja was dissuaded from accompanying him to Kokand[66], so that the British remained ignorant about the routes through Ladakh to Eastern Turkestan and Kokand. This is further corroborated by a letter received by Edwardes from his peon Mohammad Ali who had escorted the envoy back to Kokand. In this letter sent from Kokand on July 1, 1856, Mohammad Ali complained about the conduct of the Maharaja's agent at Leh named Bullajoo, who was alleged to have misrepresented the facts pertaining to Kokand envoy[67]. Bullajoo was reported to have informed the Yarkand authorities that the envoy's caravan comprised troops carrying arms and ammunition sufficient to subjugate that country[68]. On receipt of this news the Yarkand authorities were naturally obliged to take the precaution of detaining the envoy alongwith his companions at the frontier until after the real position was ascertained from the ruler of Kokand[69]. Gulab Singh's policy was to maintain direct and friendly intercourse with neighbouring Central Asian Khanates and to prevent any type of British activity in the frontier regions in and around Ladakh.

(4) KASHMIR'S OVERTURES TO RUSSIANS IN CENTRAL ASIA

When the British transferred to Gulab Singh the independent possession of the newly carved State of Jammu and Kashmir, they desired to have a say in the internal affairs of the State. On one pretext or the other British officers began to be deputed to Kashmir. The agreement of the Kashmir ruler to the temporary posting of a British Officer on Special Duty in Kashmir during summer months did not satiate the British thirst for a firm control over the internal and external affairs of Jammu and Kashmir through a full-fledged Resident. The anti-Dogra attitude of the English language press in India which played up the misrule in Kashmir was another cause of annoyance. All these factors led to a certain bitterness and resentment in the

66. *Foreign. Secret.* 27 March 1857. 21-22.
67. *Ibid.*
68. *Ibid.*
69. *Ibid.*

hearts of both Gulab Singh and his successor Ranbir Singh, who resisted all such moves politely but firmly. Both these rulers tried to keep their bosses in good humour by despatching grandiloquent letters which only amused the ruling British elite. Similarly the extravagant State reception accorded to every British visitor to the valley only helped them in winning over but a few personalities with little or no weight in the British Durbar. The Dogra rulers provided generous assistance by way of men and materials to the British for quelling the 1857 uprising[70]. Simultaneously they were trying their best to keep the British at an arm's length. With the Anglo-Russian rivalry in Central Asia gaining in intensity after the Russian penetration of the Kokand Khanate, the British temptations to use Kashmir as a listening post for monitoring developments in the neighbourhood increased. But Ranbir Singh was too scared to allow any British officer to reside in Kashmir permanently, as it would not only impinge upon his authority but also bring him disgrace among his loyal and complacent subjects. Dogra rulers wanted to be supreme within their territory. Complete and independent control over the affairs of the State, including the conduct of its foreign relations with the neighbouring territories in Afghanistan, Eastern Turkestan and other Central Asian Khanates, was most dear to both Gulab Singh and his heir Ranbir Singh. Ranbir Singh even toyed with the idea of establishing a direct and friendly intercourse with the Russians in Central Asia. Easy access of the Kukas to the Jammu Durbar and their employment by Ranbir Singh as carrier of his messages to the Russians in Central Asia, are now well established.

Before discussing the despatch of Kashmiri missions to Central Asia, it would be relevant here to throw some light on certain anti-British activities of the Dogra rulers. Maharaja Gulab Singh's crude diplomatic manoeuvre to prevent the passage of a British trained surveyor through Leh and Karakoram pass to Yarkand in the company of the Kokandi envoy has already been mentioned. A careful study

70. Recent researches have shown that it was Lawrence, the Chief Commissioner of Punjab who first secured Maharaja Gulab Singh's help in the siege of Delhi. On his part the Dogra ruler of Kashmir offered all his resources and despatched a contingent of 3000 troops including 2000 infantry, 200 cavalry with six guns to Delhi to help the British there. See S.S. Charak, *Life and times of Maharaja Ranbir Singh, 1830-1885*. Jammu, 1985. pp. 42-45.

of the documents pertaining to Bhai Maharaja Singh[71], an-anti-British Sikh fighter during and after the second Anglo-Sikh war, shows the indirect role played by Maharaja Gulab Singh and his son Ranbir Singh in his resistance against the British.

Bhai Maharaj in his struggle for saving the Sikh kingdom from extinction was allowed by prince Ranbir Singh, the then Governor of Jammu, to obtain supplies of food, forage and wood from Jammu[72], which proved to be one of the important supply centres in his operations. His followers could move freely within Jammu till the fall of Gujarat, when Bhai Maharaj was advised to shift his supply base from Jammu[73], obviously because the strength of the Sikh army had been broken in this battle. H. Vansittart, the Deputy Commissioner of Jullunder, informed his government that Bhai Maharaj had moved to Devi Batali[74] (near the Jammu hills in Gulab Singh's territory) after the defeat of Attariwalas in the battle of Gujarat and had stayed there for several months with the connivance of Maharaja Gulab Singh[75]. This is also borne out by the depositions made by numerous followers of Bhai Maharaj Singh such as Gurmukh Singh, Kanh Singh and Narain Singh after their arrest[76]. All these episodes suggest that the Dogra rulers aimed at checking the extension of British influence towards their territories, using any means whatsoever.

First mission from Kashmir, 1865

Now it is established beyond doubt that Maharaja Ranbir Singh despatched a mission to Central Asia soon after the Russians occupied Tashkent. Soviet scholar, N.A Khalfin, has on the basis of Russian

71. Bhai Maharaj alias Nihal Singh struggled hard to organise resistance against the British soon after the second Anglo-Sikh war (1848-49). He participated in anti-British campaigns alongside Dewan Mulraj, the Governor of Multan, Chattar Singh Attariwala, the Governor of Hazara, Bedi Bikram Singh of Una and others. He succeeded in keeping up this resistance even after Punjab was annexed in March 1849, till his arrest in December 1849. Bhai Maharaj died as a State prisoner at Singapore on July 5, 1856. See Nahar Singh, comp, *Documents relating to Bhai Maharaj Singh*. Ludhiana, 1965.

72. D.F. Mc Leod, Commissioner and Superintendent, Trans-Sutlej States to P. Melvill, Secretary to Punjab Board of Administration dated 11 Oct. 1850.

73. Nahar Singh, *op cit.* p. xxv.

74. Devi Batali is a village near Chamb Jaurian, Jammu.

75. Naher Singh, *op cit.*. p. 257.

76. *Ibid.*, pp. 207-10.

archival records, given details about this mission and also the Russian response to Kashmir overtures. According to him, two emissaries named Abdul Rahman Khan and Sarfaraz Khan *ibn* Sikandar Khan arrived in Tashkent on November 24, 1865[77]. They came via Peshawar, Balkh and Bukhara. The Kashmir emissaries were accorded a kind reception by the Russian Governor of Turkestan oblast, Major General M.G. Cherniaev[78]. They are reported to have informed Cherniaev that two other members of their mission including its leader were killed enroute and the letter from Ranbir Singh to the Russians was stolen[79]. Drawing the Russian attention to the general Indian discontent with the British rule, the Kashmir emissaries told Cherniaev that the Maharaja had commissioned them to convey his declaration of friendship and also to explore the prospects of developing the Russo-Kashmir relations[80]. They also informed him about the intention of the Kashmir ruler to send another mission to Russia via Leh-Yarkand-Ferghana route[81]. Cherniaev promptly reported the arrival of Kashmir emissaries to his superior, N.A. Kryzhanovsky, the Governor General in Orenburg[82]. On his part Kryzhanovsky instructed Cherniaev to obtain information about the political situation in the East and cautioned him not to make any commitment before the envoys. While transmitting the news of the arrival of a Kashmiri mission at Tashkent to the Russian Foreign Minister, A.M. Gorchakov on December 30, 1865, Kryzhanovsky observed that it would not be in the Russian interests to cold-shoulder any request for help from such people as could prove useful later especially for trade contacts[83]. But his remark that "a positive promise of aid with no means to proffer it to the populations of countries cut off from us by the Himalayas would be pointless and merely injure Russia's prestige in Central Asian eyes"[84] was an open

77. N.A. Khalfin, *Angliyskaya kolonialnaya politika na srednem Vostoke (70-e-gody XIX v.)*, Tashkent, 1957. pp. 136-142. See also his *Russia's policy in Central Asia, 1857-1868*. Translated from Russian into English by Hubert Evans. London, 1964. pp. 67-68.

78. *Ibid.*

79. *Ibid.*

80. *Ibid.*

81. *Ibid.*

82. *Ibid.*

83. N A. Khalfin, *op cit.*

84. *Ibid.*

admission of the Russian inability to go beyond the Himalayas. Besides Kryzhanovsky's advice to Cherniaev not to make any hostile remarks against the British in his talks with the Kashmir envoys[85], indicated the Russian desire to be inoffensive to the British. Not wishing to jeopardise the Anglo-Russian relations, Kryzhanovsky proposed to reply to the Kashmir envoys or similar other missions that might arrive in future, in the following terms :

> 'The Emperor of All the Russias is on terms of complete amity with the Queen of England, and so long as no hostile gesture is made by the British Government it is not proposed to move our troops to the banks of the Amu-Darya'.[86]

That both the Tsar Emperor and his Foreign office approved the proposals made by the Governor General of Orenburg[87], showed that Russia did not want to pick up any trouble with the British. But for treating the Kashmir envoys well and allowing them to stay at Tashkent for another six months, the Russian authorities in Central Asia promised nothing in return[88] for Maharaja's offer of friendship.

The Kashmir envoys were put under surveillance during their stay in Tashkent. On June 23, 1866, the new Governor of Turkestan oblast, D.I. Romanovsky, reported to his superiors that he had no reason to suspect the genuine desire of the Kashmir emissaries to be the first of the inhabitants of India to congratulate Russia on her military successes[89]. Romanovsky had met the envoys several times and found them intelligent and devoid of any shady connections[90]. They had also assured the Governor at Tashkent that trade could easily be developed between Kashmir and Tashkent via Kokand, as the Kashgaria Khanate was already under the influence of Maharaja Ranbir Singh[91]. It would not be pointless to mention here that it was a usual practice for Ranbir Singh to exchange his envoys with Yakub Beg, the ruler of Kashgaria (Chinese Turkestan 1865-77). During this period, the political prestige of the Kashmir ruler was

85. *Ibid.*
86. *Ibid.*
87. *Ibid.*
88. *Ibid.*
89. *Ibid.*
90. N.A. Khalfin, *op cit.*
91. *Ibid.*

so high in Kashgaria that his agents could travel freely through that territory to Kokand, Tashkent and Bukhara. Kashmiri agents trading in Yarkand and Kashgar had succeeded in thwarting certain British attempts to reconnoiter the areas lying on Kashmir frontiers and also in Eastern Turkestan by instigating the Kashgar authorities. So it can be safely surmised that the Kashmir envoys represented to the Russian Governor at Tashkent that Kashmiris could trade freely with Tashkent since the intervening territory of Kashgaria was on friendly terms with the Kashmir ruler. The Kashmir envoys left Tashkent around June 1866 for their return journey to Kashmir[92]. They were fairly successful in impressing the Russian authorities in Central Asia about Maharaja Ranbir Singh's sincere intention to develop Kashmir's cordial relations with Russia, which in their view would have greatly enhanced the political importance of Kashmir and facilitated direct trading between Kashmir and Central Asia much to the benefit of Kashmiris[93].

The records preserved in the National Archives of India and the Jammu and Kashmir Government Archives too confirm that political missions from Kashmir visited Russian Central Asia in the 1860s. The first report about the despatch of certain agents to Kabul by the ruler of Kashmir for obtaining intelligence from the neighbouring Central Asian Khanates reached the Punjab government from its news-agent posted in Kabul in September 1865[94]. Three such Kashmiri agents were claimed to be making preparations for their onward journey (from Kabul) to Turkestan in the guise of mendicants (*fakirs*)[95]. But for the routine circulation of this news diary, it did not attract any serious notice at the hands of the British Indian government.

Two years later, Dr. Cayley, the British Officer on Special Duty in Ladakh reported in his diary for October 1867, the arrival at Leh (from Yarkand) of one Sher Singh, an agent of the Maharaja and his departure for Jammu in a secret manner[96]. According to Cayley, this agent had been sent by the Maharaja some two years ago, that

92. *Ibid.*

93. *Ibid.*

94. *Kabul Diary* dated 26-28 Sept. 1865. *Foreign. Political A.* Oct. 1865. 95.

95. *Foreign. Secret.* March 1880. 251.

96. *Foreign. Political A.* Nov. 1867. 64-67.

is in about 1866, to Bukhara, Samarkand and Khodjent via Kabul and Badakhshan in the guise of a Muslim[97]. Though Cayley's information was correct, his presumption that Sher Singh acted as Maharaja Ranbir Singh's emissary to the Russian Governor at Khodjent[98], is not borne out by facts. Mehta Sher Singh was actually deputed by the Kashmir ruler at the behest of British Indian government to Russian Central Asia for obtaining political intelligence. That Mehta Sher Singh travelled incognito in Russian Central Asia without attempting to contact the Russian authorities there, disproves Cayley's contention. Cayley also reminded the Secretary to Punjab government that Dewan Jawala Sahai, Minister at Jammu Durbar, had in February-March 1867 brought two Kashmiris, Ahmad Khan and Mohammad Khan to Lahore from Jammu for passing on to the British authorities the information they had picked up during their visit to Bukhara[99]. These two agents were also believed by Cayley to have met the Russian Governor at Khodjent[100]. Obviously Cayley was trying to impress upon the British Indian government that Maharaja Ranbir Singh was indulging in anti-British activities by communicating with the Russian authorities in Central Asia.

Apart from Kabul and Ladakh diaries, the Punjab government too received similar intelligence reports from its own agents who operated in Kokand and Bukhara. One such agent Jalal Khan, a native of Kokand, reported to the Punjab government on May 7, 1867 about the arrival at Bukhara of a Hindu mendicant accompanied by three followers on 15 Zilhaj corresponding to April 21, 1867 and their subsequent departure for Tashkent and Kokand[101]. Jalal Khan believed this *fakir* to be a messenger from the Raja of Kashmir having come to Bukhara, Tashkent and Kokand for collecting intelligence. He further alluded to the visit of two Kashmiris including Mohammad Khan to Kokand and Bukhara via Leh and Yarkand[102], which tallies with Cayley's report of the visit of two Kashmiris to Central Asia.

---

97. *Ibid.*
98. *Ibid.*
99. *Ibid.*
100. *Ibid.*
101. *Foreign Political A*. Oct. 1867. 24-25.
102. *Ibid.*

Mehta Sher Singh's report of his travels in Central Asia[103], which was submitted by him to Maharaja Ranbir Singh soon after his return to Kashmir, throws interesting light on the nature of Ranbir Singh's policy towards Central Asia. The Kashmir ruler had sent Sher Singh on a secret fact-finding mission to Central Asia. The Kashmiri agent left Kashmir on 16 Sawan 1923 *Samvat* corresponding to July 28, 1866, to travel through Muzaffarabad, Hazara, Attock, Peshawar, Kabul, Balkh, Bukhara, Samarkand, Tashkent and Kokand[104]. Mehta Sher Singh who remained away from Kashmir for about sixteen months, spent about a fortnight in Bukhara during November-December 1866 and more than a month (March-April 1867) in Tashkent[105]. He returned to Kashmir on 12 Katak 1924 *Samvat* which corresponds to Octorber 24, 1867, via Kashgar, Yarkand and Leh route[106]. Whereas Cayley's report that Mehta Sher Singh returned to Ladakh in October 1867[107] lends confirmation to what Sher Singh has recorded about the date of his return to Kashmir in his tour diary, the *Kabul diary* for 26-28 September 1865 seems to confirm the movements of other Kashmiri agents in Kabul enroute to Central Asia, as reported by Khalfin. Mehta Sher Singh who followed Abdul Rahman Khan and Sarfaraz Khan, the first Kashmiri emissaries to the Russians in Central Asia (November 1865), was sent to assess the political situation in that region. In his report, Sher Singh has reproduced the contents of a letter addressed by the British Indian authorities to the Maharaja of Kashmir, whereunder the latter was asked to collect detailed information about the Russian movements in Central Asia, the strength of Russian troops, conditions of Kokandi defences, arms, ammunition and fortification on the two sides, relations between the rulers of Kokand and Bukhara etc[108]. The Maharaja was impressed upon to get the said intelligence collected through "a most trusted person who should take extraordinary care in verifying the reports obtained".[109] That explains as to why Sher Singh avoided any contact with the Russian officials during his travels

103. *Safarnama Mehta Sher Singh*, Samvat 1923-24. (Urdu MS, JKA). An abridged copy of this MS is also available in the Research Department Library, Srinagar.

104. *Ibid.*

105. *Ibid.*

106. *Ibid.*

107. See his *Ladakh Diary* 15 October 1867. *Foreign. Political A*. Nov. 1867. 64-67.

108. Mehta Sher Singh, *Safarnama*. folios 75-77.

109. *Ibid.*, folio 76.

within Russian parts of Central Asia. After his return to Kashmir in October 1867, Sher Singh submitted his report to the Maharaja in which he gave a detailed account of the Russian troops, their arms, positions and fortification. He even forwarded a sketch of the Russian fort in Tashkent.

Some conclusions drawn by Soviet scholars, Khalfin and Rasulzade, about the British comlpicity in the murder of two members of the first Kashmiri mission to Central Asia[110] are open to question on several counts. The disclosures of Pachino, a Russian who wanted to visit Kashmir, made in the course of his meeting with the Secretary to Punjab Government, Lahore in 1874[111], disprove this assumption. Pachino confirmed that soon after the occupation of Tashkent by Cherniaev two emissaries named Abdul Rehman Khan and Sarfaraz Khan, arrived at Tashkent to congratulate the Russian General for his success[112]. Pachino quoted the two envoys as having informed the Russians at Tashkent that their leader Ghulam Rasool Khan had been robbed alongwith his papers at the Khyber pass, due to which they could not show their credentials to the Russian General[113]. So far Pachino's statement corroborates the story recorded in the Russian archives, on the basis of which both Khalfin and Rasulzade hold the British Indian authorities responsible for the murder of two members of the mission including its leader and also for the theft of the letter of Ranbir Singh addressed to the Russians. But Pachino's disclosure made before Thornton at Lahore, that he had seen Ghulam Rasool Khan, the leader of this mission alive at Sialkot[114], changes the perspective altogether. The story of the murder of Ghulam Rasool Khan and the theft of his papers appears to be a sheer fabrication floated by these two Kashmiri agents in Tashkent. It is quite probable that in order to avoid any detection by and the consequent involvement with the ever vigilant British Indian authorities, the Kashmir ruler might have resorted to oral rather than any written

110. N.A. Khalfin, *op cit.* P. Rasul Zade, "Political relations between India and Central Asia in the second half of nineteenth century". *Central Asian Review* Vol. 12, 1964, p. 220.

111. For details of Pachino's interview with T.H. Thornton, Secretary, Punjab Government on March 29, 1874 at Lahore, see *Foreign. Secret.* May 1875. 156-158.

112. *Ibid.*

113. *Ibid.*

114. *Ibid.*

communications with the Russians. Since a British Resident was not posted in Kashmir during Ranbir Singh's time, there was no question of his involvement in the murder, as has been assumed by the Soviet scholars. To say that "the Resident in Srinagar almost got wind of what was in the air and took steps to intercept the message"[115], is thus not borne out by facts. But for getting some tit-bits of information from their agents, the British were generally ignorant[116] about the trans-frontier activities of the Kashmir ruler.

Kashmir Durbar's subsequent contacts with Russia

A second mission from Kashmir led by one Baba Karam Prakash was despatched in October 1869 and it reached Tashkent in June 1870[117]. According to the Russian archival records, Karam Prakash was commissioned by Maharaja Ranbir Singh to ascertain whether the Governor General of Turkestan was the proper authority to correspond with the ruler of Kashmir and as to which route would be advisable for Kashmir's commercial and political intercourse with Russia[118]. The Maharaja also wanted to convey his desire to establish friendly ties with Russia as his relations with the British were not satisfactory. The Kashmiri envoy informed the Russians that Maharaja Ranbir Singh did not comply with the British suggestion to attend the Amballa conference held in March 1869, when Lord Mayo (Viceroy) met Sher Ali Khan, the king of Afghanistan[119]. According to Khalfin, this mission failed in evoking any response from the Russian ruling circles[120].

Though the British Indian authorities failed to keep timely track of this mission, yet they learnt about it soon after. A party of Beluchis

115. N.A. Khalfin, *op cit.*

116. When the news of the arrival of such emissaries at Tashkent for offering Maharaja's support to Russia "for a joint action against the English" was published by *Russkiy Mir*, a Russian paper on March 7, 1877, it was dismissed by Lord Augustus Loftus, the British Ambassador at St. Petersburgh as a "pure invention" circulated deliberately to "create alarm in the public mind of England and India as to the present internal state of India". See *Foreign. Secret.* August 1877. 127-132.

117. N.A.Khalfin , *op cit.*

118. *Ibid.*

119. *Ibid.*

120. *Ibid.*

despatched by one Captain Grey[121] in 1869 to acquire some news about the Russian activity in Central Asia, learnt from a travelling Bukharan merchant that the Raja of Kashmir had sent an envoy to the Russian Governor of Samarkand[122]. This envoy who had been first treated "magnificently" was stated to have fallen in disgrace after he assumed "airs of royalty and refused to meet Governor", as a result of which his allowances were stopped, plunging him into utter poverty[123].

As per records available in the National Archives of India, the Punjab Government did learn afterwards about Karam Prakash's mission to Samarkand. He was reported to have presented a shawl to the Russian Governor General on which was inscribed a Persian couplet to the effect: "Every person looks out for a big tree in order to obtain rest under its cool shade"[124]. Ranbir Singh had reportedly desired Karam Prakash to enquire from the Governor General at Samarkand, as to when the Russians would be advancing towards India, in which case he had offered his whole-hearted assistance and asked for Lahore State in return[125]. This information cannot be taken at its face value and requires further corroboration from the Russian sources.

Ḳaram Prakash was reported to have returned to Jammu in 1872 (Asauj of Samvat 1929) bringing a message from the Russian Governor-General which read as :

> if the Governor received a letter from the Maharajas of Kashmir, Nepal and Gwalior, and the Amir of Kabul by Samvat 1931 or 1932 (1874-75 or 1875-76 AD) acknowledging the supremacy of the Czar, Russian troops would march on India a year after the receipt of the letter. If it were not received by Samvat 1932 the Russians would invade

121. Lord Mayo, the Viceroy had soon after the conclusion of the Amballa Durbar in 1869 assigned to Captain Grey, the Officer on Special Duty the task of deputing organized parties of natives to collect information about history, geography and the political situation in Central Asia. It was Party No. 5 which disclosed the above quoted information.

122. *Foreign. Secret.* 1872. 47-54.

123. *Ibid.*

124. *Foreign. Secret.* March 1880. 251.

125. *Ibid.*

> Turkey, where they would be occupied for two years, after which they would rest for a year, and then invade India via Kabul and Kandhar, Yarkand and Ladakh, and Kashmir [126]

Although one may have reservations about the authenticity of such a report, it is a fact that Maharaja Ranbir Singh did employ Karam Prakash as his secret emissary to Gwalior and Nepal.[127] That Karam Prakash submitted a report of his experiences in Nepal to the Maharaja provides fool-proof evidence to substantiate this conclusion.[128] Besides, the Maharaja's communication with the ruler of Kabul through similar other envoys cannot be disregarded as meaningless.

Karam Prakash occupied a respectable position in the Jammu Durbar and he held the post of *Adhishtata* (manager) at the Godawari *tirath* (place of pilgrimage).[129] It was in August 1874 (Bhadoon 1931 Samvat) that Karam Prakash set out from Ayodhya on a secret mission to Nepal.[130] A copy of his hand written report of journey to Nepal is preserved in the Jammu and Kashmir Government Archives. In his report Karam Prakash has thrown interesting light on the frantic preparations made by the British authorities for launching a military expedition against Nepal from the side of Gorakhpur. In order to escape detection by the British, Karam Prakash travelled in the guise of a mendicant taking the Nainital - Gorakhpur route towards Nepal,[131] where he was received well by Maharaja Jang Bahadur. He was honoured by the Nepal ruler by offering a seat which stood elevated than that was occupied by the son of Maharaja Jang Bahadur. [132] The Nepal ruler is reported to have enquired about the welfare of the Maharaja of Kashmir and also about the purpose of Karam Prakash's visit.[133] When Karam Prakash referred to his previous visit to Nepal for obtaining a *lingam* (image of Lord Siva) which had been much

126. *Ibid.*

127. According to Lepel Griffin, Secretary, Punjab Government, Karam Prakash was well known to the Punjab administration as a secret emissary of the Kashmir ruler to Gwalior and Nepal.
See *Foreign. Secret.* March 1880. 251.

128. Baba Karam Prakash, *Report of a journey to Nepal*, Samvat 1931. (Persian MS, JKA).

129. *Ain-i-Dharmarth*, J & K State. Jammu. p. 40.

130. Karam Prakash, *Report.* folio 1.

131. *Ibid.*, folio 2.

132. *Ibid.*, folio 11.

133. *Ibid.*

praised by the Kashmir ruler, the king of Nepal obviously taking the coded hint, dismissed his courtiers and engaged in private conversation with the Kashmir emissary.[134] Jang Bahadur complained about the non-receipt of any reply from the Jammu Durbar to his messages sent through an envoy.[135] He also spoke about the despatch of his son Vir Jang to Jammu on similar secret mission.[136] The Nepal ruler assured Karam Prakash that all Indian princes were cooperating in his fight against the British.[137] He expressed his keen desire to enlist the cooperation of Jammu Durbar in this task and asked Karam Prakash to propose to the Maharaja of Kashmir to be in close touch with the kingdom of Nepal.[138] The Nepal ruler also desired Karam Prakash to obtain a reply to his message.[139] In his report Karam Prakash has stated that he had several meetings with the king of Nepal during his stay in that country. He also had informed the Nepal ruler about the nature of relations existing between the Maharaja of Kashmir and the British Indian authourities.[140]

Though Karam Prakash does not allude to his previous visit to Russian Central Asia in his report, he leaves little doubt regarding the friendly relations existing between the Maharaja of Kashmir and the king of Nepal, both of whom stood on a common ground against the British. But Ranbir Singh appears to have been more cautious in planning his strategy and he refrained from any open confrontation with the British. During his visit to Nepal, Karam Prakash not only surveyed the internal situation in that country but also made a personal assessment of the British armed might vis-a-vis the defences of Nepal. After his return Karam Prakash gave his assessment to the Maharaja of Kashmir and conveyed the messages from the Nepal ruler. Ranbir Singh's attempts to make a common cause with other anti-British kingdoms naturally caused great concern to the British authorities who continued to receive reports about the exchange of envoys between Nepal and Kashmir.[141]

134. *Ibid.*, folios 11-12
135. *Ibid.*, folio 12.
136. *Ibid.*
137. *Ibid.*
138. *Ibid.*, folio 13.
139. *Ibid.*
140. *Ibid.*, folio 14.
141. In October 1880 Punjab government was informed by their news-agent at Peshawar that an envoy (*Motamid*) of the chief of Nepal had arrived at Jammu along with four attendants and that a number of furs had been purchased by an employee of the Jammu Durbar at Peshawar to be sent to the Nepal ruler as presents through the said envoy. Contd....

Alarmed at the receipt of such news reports from its agents posted in Kashmir, Punjab and the neighbouring Central Asian States, the Government of Punjab warned Lord Northbrook, the Viceroy, in early 1873 about the dangers involved in Maharaja's direct communications with the Russian authorities at Tashkent. This alarm was mainly based upon the intelligence gathered by Rahim Bai and Mohammad Sultan from Yarkand, who reported in July 1872 that the :

> Maharaja of Jammu had addressed a letter to the Russians to the effect that : the Russians should look upon the Maharaja's country as their own; that if the Russians were desirous of waging war with the British Government, they should first take Sarikol from the Yarkand ruler and avoid the Afghanistan route .[142]

As late as 1883, important disclosures were made by one Syed Khan, a Russian official at Katta Kurgan, on his arrival at Peshawar. According to him, one Karam Prakash Udasi carrying a letter from the Maharaja of Kashmir had come to meet General Kaufmann, the Governor General at Tashkent in 1871[143]. As per the same source, Kaufmann conveyed his readiness to treat the Maharaja as friendly to the Russians and that Karam Prakash was given a ruble note as a proof of his arrival at Tashkent, to be shown at Jammu[144]. Though the news report creates some confusion about the exact year of the arrival of the second Kashmiri mission at Tashkent, yet it further corroborates its existence particularly when Syed Khan alludes to Karam Prakash's stay with him at Samarkand after his return from Tashkent. As for the date, more reliance can be placed on Russian archives. Ranbir singh's keenness to clinch some deal with the Russians is evidenced by the despatch of yet another emissary, Ganga Ram[145], in 1870 to Central Asia, more probably to ascertain the cause of delay in the return journey of Karam Prakash.

W.M. Young, Secretary, Punjab government to A.C.Lyall, Secretary, Foreign Deptt. GOI, October 29, 1880. *Foreign. Secret.* Nov. 1880. 114-115.

142. *Foreign. Secret.* March 1875. 19.

143. *Foreign. Secret. E.* Jan. 1884. 40-95.

144. *Ibid.*

145. *Ibid.* Ganga Ram is believed to have stayed at Samarkand for a few years to learn Russian language. After his return to Jammu in about Samvat 1933 (1876-77), Ganga Ram was rewarded with an appointment as Tehsildar. See also *Foreign. Secret.* March 1880. 251.

The startling disclosures made by one Gulab Khan[146], which earned him much distinction in the British ruling circles provide specific instances of the anti-British postures made by the ruler of Kashmir before Russia. Gulab Khan communicated his reports during the years 1881-84 from Katta Kurgan to the Punjab Government through his couriers named Ghulam Mohy-ud-din, Sharaf-ud-din (both Indians but residing in Katta Kurgan) and Mulla Ikram, a Tajik of the same place[147]. Gulab Khan also conveyed the purport of a letter said to have been delivered by Karam Prakash to the Russian Governor at Tashkent, as :

> We obey the English because Russia is far off, when you come to Hindustan we will serve you with heart and soul. All the notables throughout India are disaffected to the English as we are [148]

The report of D. Mc Cracken, the Assistant to Inspector General of Police, Special Branch, Punjab Government dated January 26, 1882 that Sardar Attar Singh was incharge of the secret intelligence department in Jammu Durbar and that Baba Karam Prakash was employed in confidential missions[149] lends authenticity to Gulab Khan's version. In fact, Gulab Khan's mention about the death of Attar Singh gives an unimpeachable character to his report, since Mc Cracken also alluded to the same. Moreover, Gulab Khan clarified that Karam Prakash's mission to Russian Central Asia was preceded by another Kashmiri mission led by Sher Singh, a Brahman of Rajouri and *Hakim* (Tehsildar) of Sopore (in Baramulla circle of Kashmir)[150]. Gulab Khan also reported about the despatch of one Ganga Ram, a Brahman of Danisal (in Riasi, in Jammu circle) to Samarkand after

146. Gulab Khan, a native of Rawalpindi and formerly employed in Government Telegraph Department, Punjab had in June 1881 shifted to Katta Kurgan (situated between Samarkand and Tashkent) in search of better fortunes. Here he came in contact with the Russians through one Syed Khan (formerly in 24th Regiment of Punjab Native Infantry) and later an official in the Russian service. Gulab Khan's reports about the activities of Kukas in Russian Central Asia helped the British Indian authorities to apprehend Gurcharan Singh - a leading Kuka fighter. Gulab Khan's report about the interchange of emissaries between the Maharaja of Kashmir and the Russians in Central Asia, receive confirmation from other sources.

147. *Foreign. Secret.* Aug. 1882. 349-359.

148. *Ibid.*

149. *Ibid.*

150. *Foreign. Secret.* Aug. 1882. 349-359.

Karam Prakash and his stay there for a period of four years for learning Russian language[151].

In another report dated January 26, 1882 sent from Katta Kurgan, Gulab Khan disclosed the contents of a letter supposed to have been sent by the Maharaja in around 1880 to the Russians at Tashkent through one Jiwan Mal Dogra. The purport of this letter is stated to have been to the effect :

> you are preparing for war with China; when you have conquered them and intend to occupy Kashgar and the country close to my borders I will do whatever you tell me. You have not crossed your border, how then can I raise a disturbance till you advance ? We have a saying *ab na didah, mosah kashidah*. (he has taken off his shoes before he even saw the water) [152]

There is every likelihood of this report being nearer the truth, since the probable date of the despatch of this message coincides with the period when both Russia and China were at the brink of war on account of the Ili crisis. Besides, this letter reflects Maharaja's desire to take up his cudgels against the British only at the right moment, that is when Russia succeeded in occupying Kashgar and Yarkand in Chinese Turkestan. In a separate report, Gulab Khan referred to the agreement between Russia and China on Kuldja (Ili) and also about the Chinese consent to allow Russia to open its consulates in Chinese Turkestan at twelve places[153], which lends credibility to his information. During his visit to Lahore in 1883-84, Gulab Khan mentioned about the visit of some Kashmiri agents named Kale Khan, a Muslim and two Hindu employees of the Jammu Durbar to Tashkent in the company of Mansukh and Dharm Das (the Jammu agents posted in Russian Central Asia) carrying a sapphire cup and other jewels as Maharaja's presents for the Governor General of Turkestan[154]. Gulab Khan claimed to have received from Mansukh letters of introduction to the Kashmir ruler, which could enable him to earn favours at Jammu Durbar in return for any news about Central Asia[155]. But he could

151. *Ibid.*

152. *Ibid.*

153. *Ibid.*

154. *Foreign. Secret.* July 1884. 109-116.

155. *Foreign. Secret E.* Jan. 1884. 40-95.

not produce these letters as he was allegedly compelled to burn his papers at Kabul[156].

In February 1883 the British authorities of Punjab apprehended one Shankar Rai, a suspected Russian spy, soon after his arrival at Peshawar from Central Asia and seized some papers from his possession[157]. These papers included a letter in Persian bearing the seal of the Russian Governor at Katta Kurgan and addressed to the "Government of Hill Country in the East"[158]. The translation of this letter is reproduced below:

"In the name of God
By order of Higher Authority
To the Government of the Hill country in the East.

An answer to numbers 3, 5, and 7 will speedily be given. The disposition of the West is favourable. Be pleased to accept the message sent. Know this to be strictly true.

(Seal)
Wasakhawich,
Hakim, Katta Kurgan".

Testimonies of Syed Khan (an official in Katta Kurgan) and Gulab Khan during their visit to Peshawar led the British authorities to believe that this letter meant for "The Government of Hill country in the East" was intended for the ruler of Kashmir and not that of Nepal. The circumstance of Mansukh, a Dogra agent residing in Katta Kurgan for several years, further lent support to this suspicion. Three years later, Aziz-ud-Din's disclosure that the Governor General of Turkestan had deputed Shankar Rai to India for the Purpose of meeting the Amir of Kabul and the Maharaja of Kashmir[159], seems to confirm the assumption that the letter found in the possession of Shankar Rai was required to be delivered to Maharaja Ranbir Singh.

In 1878 one Mohammad Khan Effendi, formerly employed under Yakub Bég in Kashgar, informed the Secretary to the Punjab

156. *Ibid.*

157. *Ibid.*

158. *Ibid.*

159. *Foreign. Secret F.* Aug. 1887.390-406.

Government about his conversations with Maharaja Ranbir Singh at Jammu. He attributed to the Maharaja an open admission of the receipt of letters from Kaufmann[160]. According to Effendi, a Bukharan, then present at the Jammu Durbar, was proposed by Ranbir Singh for employment as a carrier of messages to the Russians[161]. Though Effendi's statements were not ignored, yet these were considered by Henderson, Officer on Special Duty in Kashmir, to have been exaggerated[162].

Such individual statements about the Maharaja's efforts to establish political relations with the Russians get confirmation from the casual remarks made by the Amir of Kabul in his Durbar from time to time. In 1880, the ruler of Kabul was reported to have informed a select gathering of his nobles that "during the last five years out of eleven years he passed at Samarkand, General Kaufmann received at least four letters from the Maharaja of Kashmir sent through Hindu agents"[163]. The Kashmir agents preferred to travel to Russian Central Asia via Kabul, either in the guise of beggars or in the company of travelling caravans, to avoid detection at the hands of the British agents posted at Ladakh and other stations within Punjab. The reports that were received by the British from their secret agents planted within Kabul Durbar, further substantiate this view.

Similar intelligence was received by J.T. Christie in 1880-81 from one Mian Rahat Shah Kaka Khel[164], a British mole in the court of Chitral ruler. According to Rahat Shah his father-in-law, Amanul Mulk, the ruler of Chitral had himself provided a safe passage as far as Faizabad to Maharaja's agents during their journey to Russian Central Asia[165]. He further affirmed that in 1880 two agents of the Kashmir ruler had gone to meet the Russians and that in their correspondence Russians were code-named as "Ahmad Khan-Turki

160. *Foreign. Secret.* Dec. 1879. 829-830 A.

161. *Ibid.*

162. *Ibid.*

163. *Foreign. Secret Supplement.* Nov. 1880. 127-128.

164. L.Griffin had employed Mian Rahat Shah, a member of the ruling family of Chitral for feeding news about Afghanistan, at a monthly salary of six hundred rupees. Rahat Shah proved indispensable to Captain Biddulph in his dealings with Amanul Mulk, the Mehtar of Chitral. Though his services were dispensed with effect from 15 July 1882, yet he was kept in hand through an annual gift-allowance of five hundred rupees.

165. *Foreign. Secret.* Jan 1882. 736-737.

merchant'' and the Maharaja as "Mirza Ishaq''[166].

The Kashmir ruler's frequent communications with the king of Kabul and his employment as news-agents of certain traders who used to travel regularly between Kashmir and Kabul led the Punjab Government and F. Henvey, the British Officer on Special Duty in Kashmir, to doubt the Maharaja's motives. In his letter dated August 7, 1879 to the Secretary, Foreign Department, Henvey identified two Kashmiris, Rasul Shah and Kamarud-Din, as agents sent to Kabul for such purposes[167]. He also suspected one Mohammad Nasim, a native of Herat, then living in Srinagar,as being a regular Russian spy[168]. Soon after Colonel T. Gordon of the Guide Corps got confirmation of Henvey's misgivings through his own sources[169]. Three years later, Henvey communicated to the British authorities additional details of the trading-cum-spying adventures of the Kashmir ruler. In his letter dated March 2, 1882 to C. Grant, the Secretary, Foreign Department, Henvey underlined the role of one Mian Laldin as being one of the sources of such intrigues. Laldin used to conduct Maharaja's agents to Central Asia from such far off stations as Bombay and Calcutta where he had his business establishments[170]. He further identified Abdul Raza Khan, a trader of Kabul, Rajab Ali, a horse dealer, Ahmad Daraz of Kashmir stationed in Kabul, Mohsin Shah, a Kashmiri trading between Srinagar and Bukhara, Sadik Mir of Kashmir operating in Yarkand, as the main agents employed by the Maharaja of Kashmir for obtaining news from and also for conveying messages to Kabul, Yarkand and Russian Central Asia[171]. Besides, one Rahim Shah Malik of Kashmir was alleged to have introduced certain Russain spies into the Jammu Durbar[172]. Mian Laldin was reported to have drawn as large an amount as fifty thousand rupees from the Jammu Durbar for trade purposes, out of which he spent twenty thousand rupees for sending spies to Kabul and Bukhara[173].

---

166. *Ibid.*
167. *Foreign. Secret.* Dec. 1879. 829-830 A.
168. *Ibid.*
169. *Ibid.*
170. *Foreign. Secret.* March 1882. 268.
171. *Ibid.* See also *Foreign. Secret.* April 1882. 9-10
172. *Ibid.*
173. *Ibid.*

From the above reports it becomes clear that the Kashmir ruler possessed a regular establishment of foreign intelligence network. He was astute enough to take adequate care in keeping his agents undetected by the British. Mostly he preferred to convey his messages by words of mouth rather than in writing. This assumption is strengthened by the fact that both L. Griffin and Henvey failed to seize any incriminating evidence even after apprehending some of these agents.

The contemporary evidences like intelligence diaries, official proceedings and reports of the British Indian and Tsarist Russian governments available in the Indian and Russian archives, provide a sound basis for the assumption that Maharaja Ranbir Singh was keen to establish friendly political ties with the Russians in Central Asia. His persistent efforts to maintain close contact with Russia by sending special envoys are self-explanatory. Karam Prakash's mission to Tashkent for meeting Kaufmann is confirmed both by the Russian and the British Indian sources. That the Russians desired the Kashmir ruler to form a joint anti-British front along with the disgruntled chiefs of Gwalior and Nepal cannot be dismissed off hand. In fact, the Russian Consul at Ili (in northern part of Chinese Turkestan) had in 1860 persuaded the Chinese government that the British warlike postures against China could be embarrassed by encouraging Nepal to attack British India from the north-west[174]. The recorded statements of Gulab Khan, Syed Khan, Aziz-ud-Din, Mian Rahat Shah and others leave no doubt about the frequent trips of Ganga Ram, Mansukh (both natives of Jammu) and also of Jas Ram and other Kuka fighters to Russian Central Asia as emissaries of the Kashmir ruler. Secret diaries received from Kabul, which quoted the Afghan ruler as being a witness to the passage of such agents through his territory, provide an additional corroboration.

The motives of the Kashmir ruler behind his overtures to the Russians can be better understood against the backdrop of Anglo-Russian rivalry for ascendancy in Asia. Though Russia was not strong enough to move beyond the Oxus in the south and Pamirs to the east

---

174. This proposal of the Military Governor of Ili was negatived by the Chinese Emperor by an Imperial decree issued on the Keng-Yin day of the Ist Moon (Feb. 1860). For full text of this decree see Appendix III.
Foreign . *Secret*. Sept. 1876. 129-133.

yet its military successes in Central Asia had earned it a definite advantage in respect of the psychological influence created on Asian peoples. The weak and uncertain position of the British in Afghanistan offered a total contrast to the Russian consolidation in Central Asia. The British Russophobes, actually felt concerned over the psychological impact of the Russian presence in Asia over their Indian subjects. The disgruntled ruling princes of India derived a sort of moral encouragement from the appearance of Russia close to the British Indian frontiers which stimulated their anti-British aspirations.

The pressure tactics employed by the British for exacting various concessions from Ranbir Singh had in course of time turned him bitter. They had not only secured his agreement to the reduction of customs duties on goods exported through his territories to Central Asia but also to the posting of a British officer at Leh. In 1870 the Maharaja was bound by a Treaty to abolish all duties on trade with Central Asia. While this resulted in some loss of revenue to the Jammu Durbar it also paved the way for greater interference in Kashmir's domestic affairs. The British Officers on Special Duty posted at Srinagar, Leh or Gilgit were instrumental in eroding the Maharaja's authority. Since the State officers could not compete with their British counterparts in both the administrative and political acumen, they found their power on the wane. To make matters worse, the British officers would highlight the alleged inefficient or corrupt methods of the Maharaja's officials. All such provocations further shaped his attitude towards the British. Ranbir Singh's role as Governor of Jammu during 1848-49, in helping Bhai Maharaj Singh to use Jammu as a supply base for his anti-British operations, has already been mentioned. When the Maharaja's repeated pleadings to the British Indian Government seeking the withdrawal of British officers from the State failed, he became convinced that the British were determined to whittle down his authority and autonomy as a prelude to their total annexation of his kingdom. However, it goes to the credit of Ranbir Singh that he stood like a rock against the posting of a regular British Resident in Kashmir until his death.

The reported offer of Ranbir Singh to provide his support to Russia and his advice to the Russians to seize Sarikol first, that is to come via Yarkand rather than Kabul, in the event of their advance towards India, though subject to doubt, cannot be dismissed out of hand. In this connection we may take note of the reported establishment of a regular regiment of 175 Kukas at Jammu in about 1868[175], which speaks of the Maharaja's embittered relations with the British. Though the Kashmir ruler disbanded this regiment in 1871[176] for fear of the British yet he continued to play host to the Kuka emissaries going to Russian Central Asia. In fact, the anti-British Kukas found it congenial to carry on their operations in Jammu rather than in Punjab where they were hounded out and watched closely. The Maharaja on his part did not fail in utilizing this opportunity to employ them as a medium of his communications with the Russians in Central Asia. It appears that both the Kukas and the Jammu Durbar had identical views about the British rule in India. This is also borne out by the reference of Baba Budh Singh about Ranbir Singh in one of his letters to the Governor General of Turkestan that "the hill raja is our friend"[177].

By the end of 1879 the India Office at London received a report from the British Charge d' Affaires at Constantinople relating to the exchange of letters between the Kashmir ruler and General Kaufmann, the Governor General of Turkestan. Convincing proof to this effect was provided by one Alim Mirza who claimed to have been in the employ of Gen. Kaufmann for conducting his Persian correspondence[178]. Alim Mirza had furnished to the British Ambassador at Constantinople a letter supposed to have been written by Kaufmann in 1877 to the address of Maharaja Ranbir Singh[179]. Though the letter dealt with the affairs of Beg Kuli Beg, the ex-ruler of Kashgaria and successor of Yakub Beg, Kaufmann's observation reflecting upon the nature of friendly ties existing between

---

175. Bajwa, Fuja Singh, *Kuka movement.* Delhi, 1965.pp. 66, 131. The Kuka movement led by Guru Ram Singh against the British holds a prominent place in the annals of the liberation struggle in India. The British authorities (L. Cowan, Dy. Commissioner of Police, Ludhiana and T.D Forsyth, Commissioner of Amballa) employed savage methods to suppress the Kuka uprising of January 1872 in Malerkotla, Punjab.

176. Bajwa, Fuja Singh, *Kuka movement.* p. 133. Only those Kuka recruits were enlisted at Jammu who possessed a certificate from Guru Ram Singh. See also *Home. Judicial.* Aug. 1872. 273-284. This Kuka regiment is reported to have spent about a year in the Batmaloo cantonment at Srinagar.

177. *Ibid.*, p. 134.

178. *Foreign. Secret.* March 1880. 251.

179. *Ibid.*

the ruler of Kashmir and the Russian empire are important. He wrote:

> I have always had at heart to strengthen the bonds of amity and union between the Russian empire and the powerful ruler of the country of Kashmir....It is noteworthy that the powerful Russian government is a beneficent ruler whose friendship furnishes incalculable advantages .[180]

Regarding the genuineness of this letter, it should be noted that it was written by Kaufmann to the Kashmir ruler for getting the property matters of Beg Kuli Beg settled. It may be recalled that Beg Kuli Beg while fleeing towards Kokand after the re-occupation of Kashgaria by the Chinese in 1877, had made over his treasure to his trusted servants for safe custody in India. But one of his servants had mis-appropriated a large part of this treasure[181] thereby causing loss to Beg Kuli Beg. There is little room for any doubt about the authenticity of this letter since the same Alim Mirza had in 1879 furnished two other letters purported to have been written by General Kaufmann to Amir Sher Ali and by General Stoleitov to Wazir Muhammad Shah Khan at Kabul, which were later found to correspond exactly with two letters discovered by F. Roberts at Kabul[182].

In 1886 equally important disclosures indicating the existence of close ties between the Kashmir ruler and the Russians were made by one Aziz-ud-Din after his return to India from an extensive tour through Persia and Russian Central Asia during the years 1884-85[183]. Basing his information upon the statement of one Muhammad Isan who

---

180. *Ibid.*

181. One Haji Nur Mohammad arrived at Leh from the direction of Yarkand on January 19, 1878 bearing about 800 silver *Yambus* (12000 pounds) as the money belonging to Beg Kuli Beg, who had wished this treasure to be kept safe in India during the disturbances in Kashgaria. He gave a written statement at the office of the Joint Commissioner, Leh giving details of the property valued about 1,32,600 rupees that was entrusted to him by Beg Kuli Beg for safe custody. See *Ladakh Diaries* 1-16 Jan. and 15-28 Feb. 1878. *Foreign. Pol. A.* May 1878. 256-275.

182. *Foreign. Secret.* March 1880. 251.

183. *Foreign. Secret F* August 1887. 390-406. Aziz-ud-Din, popular as L.M. or Lambert's Man in British circles had worked with J. Lambert, the Dy. Commissioner of Police at Calcutta during the years 1879-84 as a secret agent. He had proved his worth by breaking the Kuka communication passing between Punjab and Rangoon, in the seizure of 'seditious' books in Calcutta

Contd.....

had served as a native Aid-de-Camp to General Effamavitch at Samarkand, Aziz-ud-Din reported that soon after the receipt of news of Ranbir Singh's death, General Rosenbach conveyed a condolence message to the new ruler of Kashmir through special couriers named Gurditta of Amritsar (then residing at Tashkent), Mansukh of Jammu (then living in Katta Kurgan) and Dharm Dass of Kangra (then living in Dawal situated between Katta Kurgan and Samarkand)[184]. Aziz-ud-Din also affirmed to have himself seen this letter in the hands of Dharam Dass at Bukhara in the third week of October 1885[185]. This information may be nearer the truth as the purported Russian letter coincides with the date of the death of Maharaja Ranbir Singh[186]. He further disclosed that the Russian Governor General at Tashkent had deputed Syed Khan, Gulab Khan and Shankar Rai to India with a mission to meet Amir Abdul Rahman of Kabul and the Maharaja of Kashmir[187]. This statement is corroborated by the fact of Shankar Rai having been apprehended at Peshawar in early 1883, at the instance of Gulab Khan. As stated earlier, Gulab Khan used to communicate to the British Indian authorities in Punjab all important information from Katta Kurgan.

In another report dated July 9, 1887, Aziz-ud-Din divulged that about fifteen years ago, that is in about 1872, one Gopal Singh, a cousin of the late Maharaja accompanied by a Punjabi servant had travelled to Tashkent via Kabul and after meeting Kaufmann had returned to Kashmir via the Kashgar route[188]. The Punjab Government got confirmation of this report from Lorinda Mal and Lila Ram, both residents of Amritsar who claimed to have themselves acted as interpreters between the Kashmir emissary and the Russian

---

belonging to Nawab Mahammad Sadik Hussain of Bhopal and printed at Constantinople etc. In May 1884, Aziz-ud-Din was commissioned to go to Persia and Russian Central Asia to obtain intelligence. He succeeded in visiting Teheran, Meshed, Ashkabad, Geok Tepe, Kelat-i-Nadir, Tezan, Merv, Yulatan, Imam Baba, Charjui, Bukhara, Katta Kurgan, Samarkand, Tashkent and Karshi, collecting therefrom all important information. He returned to India via Kulab, Faizabad, Chitral, Dir reaching Peshawar on Dec. 10, 1885.

184. *Ibid.*

185. *Ibid.*

186. Maharaj Ranbir Singh died in Sept. 1885.

187. *Foreign. Secret F.* August 1887. 390-406.

188. *Foreign Secret F.* August 1889. 114-115.

General[189]. Their statement that Gopal Singh was in reality Ram Singh[190], casts a shadow of doubt on the authenticity of this information.

There is no doubt that Baba Karam Prakash's mission and Ganga Ram's and Mansukh's occasional visits to Russian Central Asia did take place. This leads us to the conclusion that an active communication network existed between the Kashmir ruler and the Russian authorities in Central Asia. Apart from conveying courtesy messages and greetings these communications also related to the disposal of individual cases like that of Beg Kuli Beg's mis-appropriated property. However, the reported offer of the Dogra ruler to provide all assistance to the Russians in the event of their attack on the British in India and his demand of Lahore State in return, the reports about the Maharaja sending presents of a shawl, a sapphire cup and other jewels to the Russian Governor General at Tashkent, the deputation of his own cousin brother to Russian Central Asia cannot be accepted unless proved right by the Russian sources. One thing is, however, clear that Maharaja Ranbir Singh by and large succeeded in eluding the well organised spy-ring of the Birtish and keep close contacts with the Russians. Ranbir Singh had even established a school for the teaching of the Russian language in the State with a view to train his agents in that language. This is borne out by a letter addressed by Ranbir Singh to his Chief Minister asking for "a person conversant with Russian language, who is willing to undertake a long journey"[191]. By doing so Ranbir Singh tried to overcome the language barrier in his free communication with the Russian authorities in Central Asia. Besides, his trusted agents were placed in a better position to make an independent assessment of the political situation in Russian Central Asia. Such mutual friendly liaison between any ruling Indian prince and the Russian authorities in Central Asia was not to be seen any more after Ranbir Singh's death.

---

189. *Ibid.*

190. *Ibid.*

191. According to B.P. Sharma, the Maharaja asked his Chief Minister "to send from the School of Russian language two students who are well acquainted with the language".
See his "Ranbir Singh, a princely freedom fighter". *Hindustan Times* 9 March 1969.
S.S. Charak, *Life and time of Maharaja Ranbir Singh*. p. 208. Both these scholars claim to have seen the document in the Archives Repository, Jammu.

(5) RUSSIAN RESPONSE TO KASHMIR OVERTURES

A critical assessment of all the available evidence on the exchange of emissaries between the Russian authorities in Central Asia and the Dogra ruler of Kashmir leads to the conclusion that Tsarist Russia though interested in promoting its commercial interests in Kashmir, was not prepared to run the risk of precipitating any crisis with the British in this region. The Russian interest in trade with Kahsmir and Ladakh was mainly due to the rich dividends gained by merchants dealing in Kashmir shawls. It was this lucrative shawl trade which in the early nineteenth century brought to Kashmir the missions of Aga Mehdi Rafailov. During the second half of the same century, both Britain and Russia were busy consolidating their gains within their respective spheres of influence whose boundaries were finally demarcated in 1895 by virtue of the Pamir Boundary Agreement. While measuring the Russian response to the overtures made by Maharaja Ranbir Singh of Kashmir, we should bear in mind that the Russian policy was not to cause any provocation to the British. The Russian authorities were not inclined to get involved in the internal affairs of India. In this context one may recall the British Indian Government's decision of not getting militarily involved in the internal affairs of Kokand and Bukhara when their rulers asked for armed assistance and exchange of envoys for checking the Russian advance in their territories.

Although the first Kashmir mission received a hospitable reception at Tashkent in November 1865, it did not succeed in obtaining any concrete answer to the Maharaja's "declaration of friendship" with the Russians in Central Asia. The Russian Governor General at Orenburg, N.A. Kryzhanovsky was alive to the importance of requests for help, particularly in matters of developing trade, from princes like the Maharaja of Kashmir[192]. At the same time he was against making a commitment for aid unless it could be carried out successfully in far flung areas lying "beyond the Himalayas"[193]. Kryzhanovsky was averse to putting Russian might to

192. N.A. Khalfin, *op cit.*

193. *Ibid.*

such a crucial test and running the risk of impairing its image in the Asian eyes. This line of action was endorsed by Gorchakov and approved by the Tsar Emperor, which points to the consensus in Russia so far as its policy towards India was concerned. The reply sent to the Kashmir ruler through his emissaries gives a clear insight into the extreme caution taken by Russia in being inoffensive to the British.

Although the attempts made by the Kashmir ruler to establish friendly relations with the Russians in Central Asia had no political fall-out, these did result in some positive developments in promoting the socio-economic intercourse between the two regions. This is what must have sustained Ranbir Singh's interest in continuing his communications with the Russian authorities in Central Asia until he died in 1885. As per Faiz Buksh's report made to the British authorities in Punjab in 1871, the Russian Governor at Tashkent, Cherniaev had agreed to transmit Kashmir shawls to Russian markets[194]. According to certain Russian sources Gorchakov too had consented to provide adequate protection to Kashmiri merchants in Russian territories[195]. Numerous Kashmiris began to reside in Russian Central Asia, some learning Russian language and some running shops. Thus the two sides succeeded in establishing a mutually beneficial understanding on the socio-economic plane which could not continue due to its disruption by the British. But the absence of any expansionist designs towards British India including the State of Kashmir at the given moment did not imply that Tsarist Russia adopted an indifferent attitude towards the Kahsmir ruler. It did try to reciprocate the Maharaja's sentiments by deputing some envoys in disguise. Since these emissaries could not penetrate the British fence to reach the Maharaja of Kashmir, any attempt to forge a political understanding between the two sides could not succeed.

The Yarkand meeting, 1872

In 1872 Russia did succeed in securing from Yakub Beg of Kashgaria the privileges of trading without molestation within his dominions subject to a maximum duty of two and a half per cent' on Russian goods entering Eastern Turkestan[196]. This was

194. *Foreign. Political A.* Dec. 1872. 592-93.

195. O.F. Solov'yev, *op cit.*

196. C.U. Aitchison, *Treaties, Engagements and Sanads*. Calcutta, 1909. Vol. 11, pp.297-298

accomplished by a high-power embassy headed by General Kaulbars which arrived in Kashgar in May 1872 and concluded a treaty to the effect with Yakub Beg. That this embassy had also tried to establish contact with the Kashmir ruler through the agency of various Kashmiri traders and agents residing in Yarkand, became known to the British Indian government in early 1873. A trader named Buniad Ali, who used to trade between Ladakh and Yarkand, reported to the Punjab government about the activities of this Russian embassy at Kashgar[197]. According to Buniad Ali a Russian officer attached to this embassy had come to Yarkand for making an on-the-spot assessment of the quantum of trade passing between Kashmir and Yarkand and particularly to find if any arms and ammunition were exported to Yarkand from British India[198]. This Russian officer was also reported to have made an unsuccessful bid to contact one Abdullah Jan, a trusted agent of the Kashmir ruler, then in Yarkand. Yet it did not deter the Russian officer to communicate his sentiments through another Kashmiri named Khaliq Dar, an established trader in Yarkand[199]. Such a piece of intelligence would have escaped serious British attention, had not Khaliq Dar himself revealed the same later in July 1873, on his arrival in Kashmir. Soon after his arrival in Kashmir he sought the audience of the Maharaja to convey the message of the said Russian officer. The Maharaja asked his Minister Kripa Ram to record the written statement of Khaliq Dar and forward it to H.L. Wynne, the British Officer on Special Duty posted in Kashmir. The Maharaja who had himself been sending emissaries to Russian Turkestan decided to convey this information about Russian interest in Kashmir affairs to the British to demonstrate his continued loyalty to them. According to Khaliq Dar, the Russian officer on arrival in Yarkand contacted him through the agency of a Bukharan merchant named Mir Balai Mirza who also acted as an interpreter between the two. After making enquiries about the state of affairs in Kashmir, the Russian officer was stated to have offered a "secret Russian alliance with Kashmir"[200]. It is important to note that Khaliq Dar visited Kashmir in 1873 after a prolonged stay of six to seven years in Yarkand where he had all along been acting as the

197. *Foreign. Secret.* April 1873. 59-60.

198. *Ibid.*

199. *Ibid.*

200. *Foreign Secret.* March 1875. 19-29 K.W.

Maharaja's agent[201]. His visit to Kashmir was not without any specific purpose, which was to transmit the message received from the Russian officer to the Kashmir ruler.

Instead of really appreciating the Maharaja's gesture, the British Indian authorities decided to strike the final blow to his authority by planting a permanent British Resident in Kashmir to "save the imperial interests". But due to the difference of opinion in the India Office, London on this issue, the permanent posting of a British Resident in Kashmir was postponed. The Maharaja was, however, made to agree to retain the British Officers on Special Duty in Kashmir and Leh for eight months and full one year respectively.

Pachino mission

The storm created by Khaliq Dar's statement was soon followed by another flutter in the British Indian ruling circles which was a result of the voluntary disclosures of a Russian officer named Pachino made before the Secretary to the Punjab Government, T.H. Thornton in 1873-74. A comparison of the statements of Pachino made at Lahore with the theme of his address delivered at a meeting of the Russian Geographical Society leaves no doubt about the authenticity of his claims. Possessing a long career in the Russian Foreign Service, Pachino's knowledge of Arabic, Persian and Turki languages had proved an asset to him on more than one occasion[202]. All these qualifications coupled with a wide experience of having travelled in Central Asia extensively made Pachino a suitable agent. So it is not surprising that he had been commissioned to meet the Maharaja of Kashmir. In the course of his interviews with Thornton[203], Pachino claimed to have travelled in the guise of a Turki merchant as far as Gilgit, Skardu and Leh via Kolab, Faizabad, Langar, Yasin and Bolar in about 1869-70 to convey a written message to the

201. *Foreign Secret*. April 1873. 59-60.

202. Pachino had served as Second Secretary to the Russian Legation at Teheran. He had accompanied Capt. Reinthall to Kashgar in 1864 and Major Romanovsky to Tashkent in 1866. He had also been to Kabul in 1868 after which he served in Tashkent. Pachino had made himself familiar with Kashmir by collecting information from the Kashmiri merchants visiting Tashkent, on the basis of which he wrote his "Stories about Kashmir".

203. These interviews took place at Lahore on 12 Nov. 1873 and 29 March 1874. *Foreign. Secret*. May 1875. 151-163.

Maharaja of Kashmir. But on learning that the Lt. Governor of Punjab was in Kashmir at that time[204], Pachino abandoned the mission midway at Leh.

Russian eagerness to respond to Kashmir ruler's overtures is manifest in the renewed attempt of Pachino to reach Kashmir. It was in 1873 that he had been commissioned by General Kaufmann, Governor General of Tashkent, to meet the Maharaja of Kashmir "en response de cette Ambassade". Leaving St. Petersburgh in June 1873 Pachino travelled via Vienna and Trieste to Alexandria where he adopted the guise of an Arab merchant and sailed to India[205]. Then he changed his garb to that of a Turkish physician to reach Jammu. Pachino's visit to Jammu took place at a time when the Maharaja was away in Kashmir. So he had to content himself with a meeting with Dewan Jawala Sahai and his son Lachman Das who were reported to have had a free and frank conversation with Pachino "upon all matters concerning the English and ourselves"[206] (Russians). Pachino was, however, advised to seek permission from the British authorities at Lahore for visiting Kashmir. This did not discourage Pachino from visiting Lahore where he tried all means within his power to get a permit for going to Kashmir. His attempt to secure a reply from the Maharaja through his agent at Lahore also did not click. Having failed in his object, Pachino returned to Russia. But he is reported to have repeated his visit to India and Lahore again in 1875 when the British Indian authorities prevented him from crossing the border towards Kashmir[207]. They also ensured that Pachino did not make an overland return journey to Russia via Chitral. Thus ended in failure a well-contemplated Russian move to establish direct diplomatic contact with the Kashmir ruler. Pachino's determination to reach Kashmir had further aroused the British suspicions. Apart from asking the Maharaja of Kashmir to

---

204. The visit of Captain Grey to Jammu in November 1869 to negotiate the terms of a commercial Treaty with the Maharaja of Kashmir, was followed by Forsyth's visit in early 1870 for purpose of concluding the discussions and signing the said Treaty. It is therefore possible that Pachino might have heard at Leh about the arrival of these British officers in Kashmir Durbar, which made him retreat to Russia.

205. *Foreign. Secret.* June 1874. 52-53.
See also "Russians in India". *Pioneer* 21 December 1886.

206. *Pioneer* 21 December 1886.

207. *Foreign. Secret.* May 1875, 151-163.

forbid Pachino from entering his territories, they also warned Pachino under the Punjab Frontier Regulations to desist from crossing the border towards Kashmir[208]. Simultaneously the India Office at London was kept abreast of these developments to enable them to meet any possible diplomatic challenge from the Russian Ambassador at London on this issue. Finally, Pachino had to leave Lahore for Bombay on March 9, 1875.

These two episodes of Khaliq Dar and Pachino lead us to the assumption that Russia did not entirely cold-shoulder the Kashmir ruler's friendly gestures, but did try to respond by sending accredited envoys to him, though in disguise. But due to the British barricades such attempts were doomed to failure. However, such episodes had a catalytic effect upon the British in future tightening of their grip over Jammu and Kashmir.

(6) RUSSIAN POLITICAL CONNECTION WITH HUNZA

Whereas the British activity in the northern Indian frontier region upto the Hindu Kush right from 1870s is evidenced by the despatch of reconnaissance missions of Gordon (1874), Biddulph (1874,1876), Elias (1885) and Lockhart (1886) to Hunza and even upto the Pamirs, the Russian presence in Hunza was till then generally absent except for the easy availability of Russian textile goods in its local markets. But the increasing British interest in and around Hunza was not hidden from the Russian Consul at Kashgar, N. Petrovsky, who used every means to collect all possible information about Hunza. Petrovsky's alarmist reports sent to the Russian Foreign Ministry must have raised the importance of this small principality in the Russian political circles particularly in the context of the Anglo-Russian rivalry in the Pamirs region. Finally the visit of the Russian soldier-cum-explorer, Captain Grombchevsky to Hunza in 1888 paved the way for direct Russian contact with the then Chief of Hunza, Safdar Ali.

First reports about the intended visit of a Russian officer to

---

208. *Ibid.*

Hunza reached the British Indian government through the Kashmir Durbar as early as 1887. Muhammad Akbar Khan, the then Deputy Governor of Ladakh, reported to the Prime Minister of Kashmir on September 7, 1887 about the wanderings of a Russian officer at Sarikol[209]. Similarly Bakshi Mulraj, the then Governor at Gilgit, received intimation from Safdar Ali himself through a courier, that the said Russian had arrived at Aktash in Sarikol district on his way to Hunza[210]. It was about a year later that the Jammu Council received confirmation from its Governor at Gilgit about the stay of a Russian officer at Hunza for four days[211]. According to Bakshi Mulraj, the Russian officer presented to Safdar Ali two horses, three breech-loading rifles and three boxes of cartridges receiving in return twelve home-made cloaks and four pieces of silken cloth[212]. Both the hospitable reception of the Russian party at Hunza and the exchange of presents between the two sides showed Hunza's eagerness to have friendly political contacts with the neighbouring Tsarist Russia.

Capt. Grombchevsky himself told his British counterpart, Captain Younghusband, when they met near Taghdumbash Pamirs on October 23, 1888, about his Hunza mission of 1888[213]. Grombchevsky claimed that Safdar Ali had conceded his demand to ride alongwith his Cossack escort right upto the Mir's court where he was received in full durbar as "an ambassador from the Great White Czar"[214]. Some letters exchanged between Safdar Ali and Grombchevsky during 1888 which fell into the hands of the British Agent at Gilgit during his search of the Hunza fort in early 1892[215], speak volumes about the friendly relations existing between the Russians and the Chief of Hunza at that time. These letters indicate that Safdar Ali had provided men and material assistance to facilitate the visit of a Russian envoy to Hunza in 1888. In one such letter, the Russian officer expressed his thanks to Safdar Ali for causing his party to be

209. T.C. Plowden, Resident in Kashmir to Secretary, Foreign Departmant, GOI dated 27 Sept. 1887.
Foreign. Secret F. Feb. 1888. 424-27.

210. *Ibid.*

211. Bakshi Mulraj to Jammu Council 14 Asauj 1945 Samvat (28 Sept. 1888).
Foreign. Secret F. May 1889. 544-47.

212. *Ibid.*

213. *Foreign. Secret F.* Feb. 1890. 59-77.

214. F.E. Younghusband, *Northern frontiers of Kashmir*. 1890. p. 64.

215. *Foreign. Secret F.* 1892. 396-472

entertained at every stage, as he was considered as a guest from "His Majesty the White Czar"[216]. That Safdar Ali was in regular touch with the Russian Consul at Kashgar even before 1888, is proved by the fact of Grombchevsky having been armed with an introductory letter for the Hunza chief by Petrovsky. Safdar Ali's action in providing a hospitable reception to the Russian officer in 1888 is in sharp contrast to Ghazan Khan's treatment meted out to Colonel Lockhart during his visit to Hunza in April 1886. Lockhart was then refused permission to pass through Hunza, until after he promised to assist in the evacuation of Chaprot, a fort held by Kashmir troops. The importance attached to Hunza by Russia, particularly in its continuing struggle for ascendancy over the Pamirs, is explained by the despatch of a responsible officer like Captain Grombchevsky who held the post of the Chief District officer at Marghilan. Speaking both Turki and Persian fluently, he was an accomplished explorer. His successful Hunza mission of 1888 was rewarded by a special audience of the Tsar Emperor and a gold medal from the Russian Geographical Society[217].

His first successful experience coupled with a liberal grant from the Russian Geographical Soceity[218] encouraged Grombchevsky to undertake yet another extensive and penetrating reconnaissance mission to the Pamirs, Hunza and Kashmir frontiers. His original plan to explore Shignan, Zebak, Ishkoman and Kafiristan in 1889 was thwarted by the Afghan ruler's refusal to permit him from passing via Zebak to Kafiristan[219]. The Russian officer was therefore obliged to retrace his steps from Darwaz towards Pamirs and Taghdumbash, where he met Younghusband and expressed his desire to proceed towards Shahidulla and Ladakh[220]. From Leh, he wished to take the route followed by Carey to the Mang-tse lake and thence into Tibet[221].

---

216. *Ibid.*

217. *Foreign. Secret. F.* Feb. 1890. 59-77.

218. While this Society paid the expenses of Grombchevsky's mission (5000 rubles), the Russian government provided him with an escort of six Cossacks and one non-commissioned officer. See F. E. Younghusband, *Northern Frontiers of Kashmir.* p. 60.

219. Amir of Afghanistan to General Ahmed Khan, Amir's Agent at Simla dated 8 Aug. 1889.
See *Foreign. Secret F.* Sept. 1889. 287-293.

220. *Foreign Secret. F.* Feb. 1890. 59-77. *Novoe Vremiya* Jan. 11, 1891 (O.S).

221. *Ibid.*

In fact, the Russian explorer meant to examine the Karakoram route to Leh and thence to Tibet. Grombchevsky's ambition of reaching Leh received a setback when his application dated October 28, 1889 to R.P. Nisbet, then Resident in Kashmir seeking permission to proceed to Tibet through Ladakh, was rejected on the grounds that even "British officers have not been permitted to enter Tibet"[222]. But in reality, the British Indian government soon after receiving information from the Afghan ruler about the intended visit of Grombchevsky to Kafiristan, had alerted its agents posted at Gilgit, Kashmir and Chitral. The Russian Geographical Society in its proceedings for the year 1890 gave an account of this expedition. Arriving at Raskam on 10 October 1889, Grombchevsky had moved forward towards Shimshal range with the intention of crossing over to Hunza. But he was reported to have been stopped at the Hunza outpost of Darband and refused permission to enter Kanjut[223], possibly under the psychological pressure of Captain Younghusband's presence nearby. It was during this adventure that Grombchevsky witnessed a band of Kanjutis going on their expedition to villages of Pakhpu and Chukshi with a double object of collecting yearly tribute and for capturing a Kirghiz named Turdi Kol[224]. According to him, the "Kirghiz of Aksu, Pamirs, Danginbash and the Tajiks of Sarikol pay tirbute to the Kanjutis" under advice from the Chinese authorities[225].

Nearing Shahidulla in November 1889, Grombchevsky advanced towards Karakoram where severe cold and the sight of a Kashmiri trader losing twenty seven ponies out of forty five, forced him to retreat to Suget[226]. During this journey the Russian explorer discovered that the Chinese prohibition on the export of grains from Sanju and Kilian to Shahidulla had forced the Kashmir garrison to abandon the fort there in the autumn of 1889[227]. This paved the

222. H.S. Barnes, Secretary to Foreign Department, GOI, to R.P. Nisbet dated 25 Nov. 1889. *Ibid.*

223. See *Proceedings of the Imperial Russian Geographical Society* Vol. 26, No. 1, 1890.
Foreign. Frontr. B. Sept. 1890. 128-129.

224. *Ibid.* Turdi Kol, a Kirghiz resident of Shahidulla had acted as a guide to Younghusband during his visit to that place.

225. *Ibid.*

226. *Ibid.*

227. *Ibid.*

way for the occupation of Shahidulla fort by Chinese, who after arresting the local Kirghiz Beg under employment of Kashmir, entrusted the job to another local Kirghiz. Obviously Grombchevsky was unaware of the British decision to prevent the Maharaja of Kashmir from re-occupying Shahidulla as part of their appeasement policy towards China. They wanted China to extend its authority onto the Pamirs and thus prevent the Russians from doing so. It was in early 1885 that the Foreign department of the British Indian government directed its Officer on Special Duty in Kashmir to "take a suitable opportunity of advising His Highness the Maharaja not to occupy Shahidulla"[228]. In fact when Ney Elias, the British Joint Commissioner in Ladakh sensed that the Kashmir Governor of Ladakh was determined to re-occupy Shahidulla, he "strongly advised the Wazir to do nothing towards occupying Shahidulla"[229]. With the result Kashmir government abandoned the move.

British refusal of permission to Grombchevsky for entering Ladakh via Shahidulla and Karakoram disappointed him and he referred to the great privations suffered as a result, publicly in a lecture at the Russain Geographical Society at St. Petersburgh[230]. In fact the British Ambassador at St. Petersburgh reported to Salisbury, the British Secretary of State for Foreign Affairs, on February 18, 1891 that "a very intense feeling of bitterness exists at St. Petersburgh in reference to the treatment by our Resident in Kashmir of M. Grombchevsky and his companions"[231]. His two expeditions to the Pamirs and Hunza made Grombchevsky thoroughly conversant with the state of affairs on the roof of the world and Hunza. In a paper read at the Academy of the General Staff in St. Petersburgh in 1891, Grombchevsky gave a vivid account of the British activities in Hunza and advocated the Russian occupation of the Pamirs[232]. While referring to the Kanjuti raids on the caravans plying between Kashmir and Yarkand, he gave a full account of Hunza raids on the Kirghizs of Shahidulla. He also noted that Younghusband was deputed by the British to meet the demands of these Kirghizs and get the Shahidulla fort occupied by a Kashmir garrison, after the Chinese had refused to exercise jurisdiction over that area[233].

228. *Foreign. Secret F.* Nov. 1885. 12-14.
229. *Ibid.*
230. *Novoe Vremiya* 11 (23) Jan. 1891.
231. *Foreign. Secret F.* April 1891. 145-155.
232. *Novosti* 20 Nov. (2 Dec.) 1891.
233. *Ibid.*

Russian connexion with Hunza does not end with the two expeditions of Grombchevsky. In Kashgar, Petrovsky continued to monitor closely the developments in Hunza. He even broached the subject of Hunza's dual loyalty to Kashmir and China before Captain Younghusband during the latter's visit to Kashgar in 1890[234]. It was during his stay in the Chinese Turkestan that Younghusband learnt about the despatch of emissaries by Safdar Ali, Mir of Hunza to the Governor-General of Russian Turkestan in mid-1891[235]. According to him, the Kanjuti emissary was received well in Russian Turkestan and provided with *Khillats* and money by the Governor General in addition to a complimentary letter for the Chief of Hunza[236]. This information was soon confirmed by Macartney, who reported about the return of Kanjutis from Russian Turkestan via Alai Pamirs and Tashkurgan to Hunza, bearing a gift of eight Russian rifles[237]. Russian Berdan rifles are reported to have been used by Hunza against the British during the 1891 campaign. Russian sources too confirm the reception given to Safdar Ali's envoys in August 1891, by General Vrevsky, the Governor General of Turkestan at Uch Kurgan[238]. According to same sources, the envoys were treated well but given a non-committal message[239]. This is borne out by the fact of Russia remaining a silent spectator to the British action in Hunza. Obviously, Safdar Ali was seeking Russian assistance to meet the impending British threat. Durand, the British Agent at Gilgit, later revealed that the Governor General of Russian Turkestan had in 1891 advised Safdar Ali to be on good terms with the British and remain quiet till the spring when "the Russians would come and build forts at Aktash, Soma and Bozai"[240]. And the Russians seem to

---

234. F.E. Younghusband to W.J. Cunningham dated Kashgar 28 Dec. 1890. See *Foreign. Secret F.* June 1891. 128-131.

235. Younghusband to Cunningham dated Kukturk, 5 Sept. 1891. See *Foreign. Secret F.* Oct. 1891. 253-305.

236. *Ibid.*

237. G.Macartney to Government of India dated Yangi Hissar, 24 Oct. 1891. See *Foreign. Secret F.* April 1892. 1-92. To quote Alder: "a Hunzakut mission was sent to Kashgar which ostentatiously ignored Younghusband, gave presents to Petrovsky, had a meeting with the Russian Governor General at Osh in great secrecy and then returned with presents including arms and ammunition." See his *British India's Northern Frontier* .pp.227-28.

238. N.A Khalfin, *op cit.*

239. *Ibid.*

240. *Gilgit Diary* 21-27 Feb. 1892. *Foreign. Sec F.* July 1892. 271-292

have kept their word as a Russian Cossack party led by Colonel Ivanov expelled Younghusband from Bozai Gumbaz in August 1891. The question of Safdar Ali's request for assistance to meet the British threat also figured in the official correspondence between the Russian Consul and the Chinese Taotai at Kashgar. Petrovsky on receiving a written request from the Hunza chief to intercede with the Chinese authorities at Kashgar for giving him aid, brought the matter to the notice of the Taotai[241]. The issue came up for discussion on 10 March 1892 at a meeting of John Walsham, the British Ambassador at Peking with the Chinese foreign office[242].

Durand's discovery of a bunch of letters addressed to Safdar Ali, in the Hunza fort in early 1892, furnished convincing evidence about the exchange of secret communications between the Hunza chief and the Russians. One of these letters believed to have been sent by Petrovsky to Safdar Ali is quite revealing. The Hunza chief was informed in this letter that his deputation had been sent to "the appointed place (in Russian Turkestan) to meet a person who is doing numerous favours to them"[243]. Besides, Safdar Ali was asked to provide a true copy of Hunza's agreement with the British about the annual payment of subsidy[244]. He was also entrusted with the task of intercepting letters exchanged between the British agent at Gilgit and Captain Younghusband at Kashgar, for onward transmission to Petrovsky[245].

Safdar Ali's deposition by force of British armed might in late 1891 and his consequent exile to the Chinese Turkestan drew him closer to the Russians. Friendship with Russia was the only alternative left to him in these circumstances. He was anxious to come under the Russian protection rather than continue to live in Chinese Turkestan[246], where his stay was rendered uncomfortable by Macartney who would act as a watch-dog over him. The exiled Safdar Ali still commanding a large following in Hunza and the reported desire of Mohammad Nafis Khan, half-brother of Mohammad Nazim Khan

---

241. *Foreign Secret F.* July 1892. 130-177.

242. *Ibid.*

243. *Foreign. Secret F.* Sept. 1892. 396-472.

244. *Ibid.*

245. *Ibid.*

246. *Gilgit Diary* 16 June 1898. *Foreign. Sec F.* Sept. 1898. 452-467.

(the new Mir of Hunza) to flee to Russia[247] are sufficient evidence to lead us to the assumption that the Russian influence had filtered down the rank and file of the ruling clan in this principality. The British Agent at Gilgit, when informed by the Hunza Chief in September 1901 about the possible defection of Nafis Khan to Russia,was so alarmed that he lost no time in rushing to Hunza and getting the landed property restored to the aggrieved Nafis Khan[248]. On finding a large party at Hunza still supporting Safdar Ali, the British Agent was perturbed. He convened an assembly of the local people and declared at an open durbar that "anyone who wished to join the Russians was quite at liberty to do so. They would be provided with Rahdaris (permits) if required"[249]. He cautioned his audience against Safdar Ali's attempt to re-establish himself in Hunza with the Russian support[250]. As Gurdon, the British Political Agent in Gilgit, put it, "a very exalted idea of the power of Russia" had perhaps influenced the psyche of the new Chief of Hunza, who was now suspected by the British to be friendly with the pro-Russian Safdar Ali[251]. So the British Agent at Gilgit asked Macartney at Kashgar to watch the movements of Safdar Ali in the Chinese Turkestan with particular attention to his possible correspondence with the Russian Consul at Kashgar or the Russian officer at Tashkurgan[252]. This resulted in the Chinese restricting Safdar Ali's movements to Kuchar only under pressure of Macartney.

The British occupation of Hunza in 1891, coupled with Younghusband's adventures in Chinese Turkestan, caused considerable alarm in Russia. The Russian Imperial Council convened an extraordinary meeting on January 12, 1892, where it was decided to send an intelligence expedition to the Pamirs[253]. The meeting also recommended to start negotiations with Britain and China

247. *Kashgar Diary* 21-31. Dec. 1901.
Foreign Frontr B. May 1902. 234-36.

248. *Ibid.*

249. *Ibid.*
About one hundred families in Hunza were believed to be still loyal to the ex-Mir.

250. *Ibid.*

251. B.E. Gurdon to G.Macartney dated 16 Nov. 1904. *Foreign. Sec. F.* May 1905. 150-153.

252. *Ibid.*

253. N.A. Khalfin, *op cit.*

for demarcation of frontiers in the Pamirs[254]. At another meeting of the said council convened in April 1892 to discuss the Pamirs issue, divergent stands were taken by the War Ministry and the Foreign Ministry, the former taking an extremist stand and the latter proposing a cautious policy[255]. Finally, it was decided to avoid any movement to the Hindu Kush passes and instead start negotiations for the demarcation on the basis of 1873 agreement[256]. *Novoe Vremya*, a paper believed to have the backing of the military circles in Russia, in its issue dated June 28, 1891 had expressed concern over Younghusband's dealings with the delimitation of the frontiers between Afghanistan and China. The paper feared a "complete seizure of the Pamirs" by Britain[257]. The same paper in its issue dated August 30, 1892 went to the extent of claiming Russian rights on the whole of Pamirs including Hunza as an inheritance of the Kokand Khanate's jurisdiction over these territories[258]. Grombchevsky's elevation as Governor of Osh in July 1892[259] and the issue of an Imperial *Ukase* on 13(25) March 1893 expressing the Emperor's thanks to Col. Ivanov, Lt. Col. Gribbe and M. Grombchevsky, for their "zealous and valuable services"[260], are sufficient evidence to show that Russia meant to possess control over the Pamirs in order to combat any possible British challenge from their newly acquired base in Hunza.

Russian dealings with Safdar Ali lent a new dimension to the Anglo-Russian rivalry on the Pamirs. The extension of British control upto the south of Hindu Kush was countered by Russia in assuming control over a large portion of the Pamirs including Bozai Gumbaz and Somataṣh. Commanding a better position at the Pamirs, Russia found itself face to face with Britain in Hunza in late 1891. So in a desire to maintain the status quo and settle the question once for all, Russia hinted to Britain in early 1893, its readiness to appoint "a Joint Commission for the Geographical investigation of ancient

254. *Ibid.*

255. *Ibid.*

256. *Ibid.*

257. Cited in Alder, *op cit.* p. 223.

258. *Foreign Secret F.* Dec. 1892. 337-392.

259. *Foreign Secret F.* Sept. 1892. 857.

260. *Foreign Secret F.* May 1893. 161-280.
The British Ambassador at St. Petersburgh expressed his government's displeasure to Chichkine, with the manner, Grombchevsky was honoured by the Russian Emperor for his 'intrigues in Hunza'.

limits (in Pamirs)''[261]. Petrovsky's enquiry from Macartney on July 2, 1895 regarding the northern frontier limits of Hunza[262] also indicates the Russsian anxiety to see the British influence checked at Hunza. Russian concern at the possible extension of British control towards Kashgar is reflected in their rigid stand on the issue of Hunza rights on the Raskam lands. In the eyes of Russia, any acceptance of these rights by China would enable Britain outflank the Russian position in the Pamirs. Even the Russian War Minister, General Kuropatkin, in the course of his conversation with a visiting British officer Lt. Col. Mac Swiney on 9 June 1899, gave vent to his distrubed feelings by saying : ''if your Kanjutis go into Raskam, we shall be forced to take Kashgar, Tashkurgan and C''[263]. Thus Russia saw to it that China did not allow Hunza to reclaim Raskam lands*. This only resulted in keeping in abeyance any final settlement and demarcation of the Sino-Indian broder between Hunza and Sinkiang, until after it was unilaterally done by China and Pakistan in 1963, under protest from India.

261. Earl of Rosbury to R. Morier dated 19 Jan. 1893. *Foreign. Sec. F.* May 1893. 161-280.

262. *Kashgar Diary.* 8-15 July 1895. *Foreign. Sec. F.* Oct. 1895. 150-173. This query was related to the Hunza claim over Raskam lands.

263. *Foreign Secret F.* Sept. 1889. 216.

* For a detailed discussion of the Russian stand on Raskam issue see Chapter 5.

2

Commercial Relations

The huge mountainous ranges of western Himalaya, Karakoram, Kuen Lun and Hindu Kush could not deter the overland trade communication that existed between India and Central Asia since ancient times. With the passage of time and after the establishment of urban cultures in Central Asia, this trade developed further. In effect the caravan traders not only became the instrument of transmission of culture between the two regions but also assisted in the process of urbanisation. So much so, many areas along the trade routes became famous for their specific products. For instance, Khotan was famed for jade, carpets and silken fabrics. Samarkand became known for its paper, cotton fabrics and hemp cords. Bukhara was noted for its carpets;Badakhshan for lapis-lazuli and rubies; Tibet for musk and paṣhm wool ; Turfan for pashm wool and Kashmir for its saffron, fine shawls and calligraphed books. In short, these areas developed into important trading centres in this east-west trade which was carried through the famous 'Silk Route'. Starting from the Chinese terminus, Luoyang, this trade route ran up to Dunhuang where it bifurcated into northern and southern routes in order to circumvent the Taklamakan desert to join again at Kashgar.[1] Several tracks branched off the

1. D.E. Klimburg-Salter, *The Silk route and the diamond path*. Los Angeles, 1982. p. 27.

southern route at Khotan and Yarkand towards the Karakoram or Pamir passes on the way to India through Kashmir territory.

Due to its geographical proximity to Central Asia and linkage with the old 'Silk route', Kashmir became a transit emporium in the bilateral Indo-Central Asian trade. The more frequented trade route which passed through Kashmir territory was via Srinagar-Leh-Yarkand-Kashgar-Kokand. This route presented enormous difficulties as several high passes like Zoji La, Khardong La, Sasser, Karakoram and Suget were to be crossed. Yet traders and travellers, thronged this route mainly because Kashmir was devoid of political turmoils and banditry. Such was the safety of this route that in the event of unfavourable weather or death of ponies, traders would march to a safe place leaving behind their goods which were fetched after the climate became favourable or substitute transport became available. That is why wealthy Central Asian Haj pilgrims and merchants, who carried sufficient quantities of gold and silver preferred this route to that via Bukhara-Afghanistan-Punjab because the latter side was comparatively risky. Those traders who conducted small business in Chitral, Gilgit, Hunza, Nagar, Skardu etc., thus bypassing Leh and the valley of Kashmir, used other caravan mountainous tracks--Ferghana-Kashgar-Tashkurghan-Hunza-Gilgit, Bukhara-Kabul-Chitral-Peshawar, Ferghana-Pamirs-Wakhan-Chitral. As regards the volume of Indian trade with Central Asia via the above noted channels, it was considerably lesser in value than what passed through Punjab-Afghanistan-Central Asia or the Bombay-Batum-Caspian sea routes. But the importance of the overland trade routes between India and Central Asia lies in the fact that these were important channels of communication between the two sides before the discovery of sea routes.

Though the caravan trade between Central Asia and India through Kashmir was handled by pedlars and trading agents either individually or collectively, there is sufficient evidence to suggest that the Russian ruling circles started evincing interest in this trade towards the end of the 18th century. By now part of the Indian caravan trade with Central Asia, which had earlier converged on Astrakhan, made for Orenburg.[2] When the Russian merchants experienced difficulties in their commercial dealings with Europe due to Napoleonic wars and continental blockade, they began to think of expanding Russian trade with Asia. Plans were

2. D. Kaushik, *India and Central Asia in modern times*. p. 21.

prepared for the establishment of a Russian commercial company which would exclusively deal with Asian States with its operations extending even up to Kashmir, Tibet and India. The proposal for establishing such a company was mooted by the President, Russian Board of Trade in a memorandum dated November 4, 1800, presented to the Advocate General of Senate[3]. He also proposed the abolition of customs duties on all Indian imports into Russia. In his report dated December 1800 to the Emperor Paul I, the Advocate General of the Senate not only endorsed the proposal of establishing the commercial company but also stressed the need to "enter into relations with Afghan Khans, who rule over independent Kandhar, Kashmir and other northern Indian provinces for securing them unlimited transit right for the Russian caravans through their kingdom"[4]. It was in the first quarter of the 19th century that Russia took active interest in developing commercial relations with Central Asia, Afghanistan, Punjab and Kashmir. Official diplomatic and trade missions were now sent to Kokand, Bukhara, Punjab, Ladakh and Kashmir with the object of establishing an understanding with the rulers of these territories to ensure safe transit of goods. In this context mention may be made of Agha Mehdi's missions to Ladakh and Kashmir.

The second half of the nineteenth century found both Britain and Tsarist Russia face to face in Central Asia separated by a thin wedge of the Pamirs. By now British empire in India encompassed the whole of Kashmir, Punjab and Sindh, which were regarded as the gateways to Central Asia and Afghanistan. Russia too had consolidated its control over Western Turkestan and reduced the Khanates of Bukhara and Khiva as vassals. Central Asia came into the sharp focus of the Anglo-Russian rivalry both in matters of politics and trade. As a sequal to this rivalry, Tsarist Russia imposed stringent curbs on the import of goods from British India into Russian Central Asia. Russia prohibited the import of all such goods excepting Indian tea, indigo and muslin which being not available locally, were essential commodities for the Central Asian population[5]. Since the Khanate of Bukhara received unusually large

3. Ts G.A.D.A, F. Kantselyariya general-prokurora senata, op. 3, 1800 AD., d. 2399,ff 79-846.
   Cited in Surendra Gopal, *Indians in Russia in the 17th and 18th century*. New Delhi, 1988. pp 239-41.
4. Ts G.A.D.A,F. Kommerts-Kollegiya, d. 187, ff. 2-9.
   Cited in *Ibid*. pp. 241-48.
5. *Turkestanskie Vidomosti* 21-22 August 1894.

supplies of Indian goods from the side of Kabul, it was decided to include Bukhara within the Russian Customs jurisdiction[6]. Military police inspection posts were established at the Oxus frontier line to guard against the import of Indian goods from that side[7]. In pursuance of the new regulations for the import of Indian goods into Russian Central Asia, which were published in *Kavkaz* dated 25 September 1894 (OS), fruits, spices, tea, leather shoes made in India, precious stones, corals, indigo, muslin, confectionary and jams were allowed to be imported subject to the payment of certain prescribed customs duty. The same customs tariff was applicable to such Indian goods imported into the Russian parts of Central Asia via Srinagar-Leh-Yarkand-Kashgar route. On their part the British Indian government thought it inexpedient to "lodge a protest against the prohibition of import of European and Anglo-Indian goods into Trans-caspia and Bukhara" with the Russian government. This was because the Indian trade with Russian Central Asia via Bombay-Batum sea route was faring better than that through Afghanistan-Bukhara route[8]. Under these circumstances the importance of Kashmir-Kashgar-Kokand route was relegated to a secondary position at the close of the nineteenth century so far as Indian trade with Central Asia was concerned.

(1) INDIAN EXPORTS TO CENTRAL ASIA VIA KASHMIR

Central Asian imports from India comprised tea, indigo, muslin, brocades, spices, indigenous medicines, Kashmir shawls, corals etc., for which goods there existed a good demand among the people of Central Asia. According to an estimate, Indian goods worth 54,75,000 rubles were exported to Bukhara annually[9]. Bukhara had developed into a transit emporium wherefrom Indian goods found their way to markets in Russian Turkestan and other parts of Russia. But for the direct export of its shawl produce to Central Asia, Kashmir's involvement in the Indo-Central Asian Trade was limited to being a transit station for the transmission of Indian goods such as tea, indigo and coral to Central

6. *Ibid.*
7. *Ibid.*
8. GOI to G.F. Hamilton, Secretary of State for India, London. 15 April 1896. See *Foreign. Frontr. B.* May 1896. pp. 1-16.
9. P.N. Rasulzade, *Iz istorii sredneaziatsko-induskikh svyazei posle prisoyedineniya kriia k Rossii.* Thesis, Tashkent, 1964. p. 13. Cited in D. Kaushik: *op cit.* p.101.

Asia through the Leh-Yarkand route. Hand-made books, mainly religious and historical in character, which were produced by Kashmiri calligraphists were also exported to Central Asia.

Tea

The people of Central Asia harboured a special liking for Indian tea, which explained the increasing export of this commodity from India to Central Asia via Punjab-Kabul-Bukhara and Kashmir-Kashgar-Kokand overland trade routes. A considerable portion of this trade was later diverted to the Bombay-Batum sea route after the extension of railway communication in Russian Turkestan. There is sufficient ground to believe that a part of the tea exported to Chinese Turkestan from India found its way to Russian Central Asia from Kashgar. When in the years 1887-88 the Chinese authorities imposed severe restrictions on the import of Indian tea for use within Sinkiang via Leh-Yarkand route, the traders from Russian Central Asia came personally to Leh to purchase tea for consumption in their markets[10]. This was because of the fact that the Chinese authorities in Sinkiang had imposed no such curbs on the Andijani traders if they imported Indian tea via Leh-Yarkand route but only for sale within Russian parts of Central Asia. Consequently the value of Indian tea exported from Ladakh to Yarkand fell from 1,04,600 rupees in 1887 to 12,000 rupees only in 1888[11]. And the whole was bought by Andijani traders for sale in Russian Turkestan. During the year 1889-90 Indian tea worth 37,500 rupees was imported into Chinese Turkestan from Leh, which was exclusively meant for Russian Central Asia[12]. The Chinese would detail a force to accompany such Russian traders carrying Indian tea upto the frontier at Irkishtam to ensure that no part from such consignment was sold in Chinese territory on the way[13]. This trade soon assumed considerable proportions. In 1890 the Russian customs authorities at Osh collected a revenue of 30,000 rubles on account of the duty levied on Indian tea imported via

---

10. See *Ladakh Trade Report*, 1888-89.
11. British Joint Commissioner, Ladakh to Resident in Kashmir, October 30.1888. *Foreign. Frontr.* A. Dec. 1888. 106-133.
12. *Ladakh Trade Report*, 1889-90.
13. *Note on Leh trade report*, 1893-94. By Macartney dated 16 March 1895.

Kashmir-Kashgar route [14]. Since this commodity could be exported to Russian Central Asia from India via Afghanistan and Persia routes at cheaper rates than was possible through Leh-Yarkand route, the export of Indian tea to that quarter via the latter route dropped to insignificance towards the end of the nineteenth century [15].

Indigo

Apart from its export to Central Asia via Kabul-Bukhara route, Indigo found its way to Chinese Turkestan from India via Kashmir. A fraction of this dye was later re-exported to Russian Turkestan from Kashgar. The Russian merchants are reported to have purchased a large quantity of indigo at Yarkand during the year 1874 [16]. Macartney, the British Consul at Kashgar reported in early 1895 that a large quantity of indigo imported into ChineseTurkestan via Kashmir was being exported to Russian Turkestan via Osh[17]. But when indigo began to reach Russian Turkestan from India via Persia in large quantities, the re-export of this dye from Kashgar to that side ceased in the closing years of the nineteenth century [18]. As per the data collected by the Russian Consulate at Kashgar, 1500 rubles worth indigo and 1000 rubles worth aniline dye were exported to Russian Turkestan from Kashgar during the year 1915 [19]. Such exports of Indigo to Russian Turkestan via long and indirect India-Kashgar route reached the high point of 52,500 rubles during the year 1916 [20]. But the import of indigo into Russian Central Asia from India via Kashmir-Kashgar route was far below the level of Indian exports of Indigo to Chinese Turkestan.

---

14. Macartney to N.Elias, dated Kashgar, 8 Feb. 1891. See *Foreign. Sec. F.* Sept. 1891. 176-77.
Turkestanskiye Vidomosti 9(21), 13(25), 16(28). October 1894. According to Petrovsky, the Russian Consul at Kashgar, the Russian Customs at Osh derived considerable revenue from the levy of duty on such tea. According to him 36 Kopeks per pound weight of tea imported via Leh-Yarkand-Kashgar route were charged as duty.
15. *Report on trade with Chinese Turkestan, 1897-98.* By Macartney. *Report on trade between India and Chinese and Russian Turkestan via Ladakh, 1898-99.* By Macartney.
16. *Ladakh Trade Report*, 1874 See also *Ladakh Diary*, 21-31 Dec. 1874.
17. *Note on Leh trade report of 1893-94.* By Macartney Dated 16 March 1895.
18. *Report on trade with Chinese Turkestan for 1897-98.* By Macartney.
19. *Indo-Yarkand trade report, 1915-16.* By Macartney.
20. *Report of trade of Eastern Turkestan with China, Russia and India*, 1916-17. By Macartney.

Slaves

That slaves belonging to Chitral, Hunza, Gilgit, Yasin and other adjoining frontier territories of Kashmir also formed an item of trade between Chitral, Badakhshan and numerous Central Asian Khanates, becomes clear from a study of several contemporary sources. Burnes, who travelled through Bukhara in 1830s, has mentioned about the sale of such slaves in Bukhara [21]. The Mehtar of Chitral, a Sunni Muslim himself, used to send such slaves who were Shia Muslims, to the Mir of Badakhshan as presents or in exchange with horses and guns [22]. These slaves were later sold by the Badakhshi ruler in the markets of Balkh, Bukhara and Kabul against payment in cash or in kind [23]. It was a usual practice with the Chief of Chitral to capture his subjects or kidnap others from adjoining territories for sale as slaves in the markets of Central Asia [24]. Similarly he used to punish his subjects involved in any criminal or political offence with enslavement [25]. Mac Gregor sheds important light on the state of this trade. To quote him:

> The slave trade forms one of the principal items of revenue of the Chitral rulers. The annual tribute which they pay to the chief of Badakhshan is made in slaves. The Chitral boys and girls are the most prized of all the different descriptions of slaves brought to the Turkistan market for their superior beauty, docility and fidelity. A boy or a girl can generally be purchased for some 100 to 500 rupees but the more comely of the females fetch high prices varying from 500 to 1000 rupees. Their price is generally paid partly in cash and partly in goods, and rarely wholly in cash .[26]

But soon after the establishment of Russian administration in Central Asia, such a feudal practice of slave trading was abolished. With the result the erstwhile Chitrali, Gilgiti or Kanjuti slaves working

---

21. A.Burnes, *Travels into Bokhara*. Vol. 2. p. 209.
22. Faiz Buksh, *Translation of a report on Badakhshan, Balkh and Bukhara*. Lahore, 1871, p.27.
23. *Ibid.*
24. C.M.Mac Gregor, Comp, *Topography, ethnology, resources and history of Afghanistan*. Calcutta, 1871. p. 215.
25. *Ibid.* p. 215
26. *Ibid.* pp. 215-216.

as manual labour for their Central Asian lords began to lead a free life. In fact an Indian agent, Shah Khushwakt who was sent by the British officer in Gilgit in May 1878 to collect information from Kabul, Bukhara, Samarkand and Kokand, saw many such slaves cultivating lands and owning shops[27].

Shawls

Shawl which signifies an intricately woven and embroidered dress material made of fine wool, continues to be one of the celebrities of Kashmir. Since there existed great demand for shawls in Europe, the British and Russian governments made serious efforts to acquire pashmina yielding goats for breeding in England and Siberia respectively. Used as a body-covering, scarf or a turban, the shawl formed the attire of the kings, queens and the nobility. As in the Western countries, shawls were popular among the affluent sections of society in Central Asia. Till lately there existed a tradition among the Central Asian ruling nobility to present Kashmir shawls to an honoured guest or to any superior in rank and authority as a mark of esteem. Central Asia which maintained close commercial ties with Russia acted as a transit station in the forward transmission of Kashmir shawls to markets in Russia, Persia and Constantinople. Whereas Kashmiris went as far as Orenburgh to trade their goods, Central Asians used to come personally to Kashmir for making on the spot purchases of the shawl goods.

During his visit to Kashmir in 1783 A.D, Forster noticed several merchants and commercial agents who had come to the valley from such far off places as Georgia, Turkey, Persia and Tartary [28]. One Abdul Karim, a Bukharan by birth, who visited Kashmir towards the close of the eighteenth century, was witness to several Kashmiri merchants travelling from Kashmir to Ladakh to sell their packages of shawls in Central Asia[29]. When Moorcroft visited Kashmir in 1820 he took extraordinary interest in the study of shawl industry in Kashmir. He saw numerous merchants of Turkestan, Kabul and Persia getting shawl-goods prepared in Kashmir in conformity with the requirements of their customers [30]. According to Moorcroft the demand for shawls in Russia

---

27. *Foreign. Secret.* Nov. 1879. pp. 152-191.
28. G. Forster, *A Journey from Bengal to England..* London, 1798. Vol. 2. p. 20.
29. C. Schefer, *op cit*. p. 233.
30. Moorcroft, to G.Swinton, 12 Nov. 1822. See *Foreign. Pol.* 10 Oct. 1823. 29.

was great at that time and a big trading house in Yarkand had sent its representative to Kashmir for the sole purpose of purchasing shawls suited to the Russian market [31]. By then the Russian ruling circles had started evincing interest in the development of Russian commerce with Kashmir and it was the shawl which had stimulated this interest. This is evident from the dispatch of a mission under Agha Mehdi Rafaelov to Kashmir by the Russian Foreign Ministry with an object of exploring the possibilities of developing the commercial intercourse between the two sides. [32] Agha Mehdi who was an established shawl trader was trained in the art of dyeing at St.Petersburgh. That he actually imported several loads of dyes, mordants and samples of dyed woolen fabrics in several designs for introducing the dyeing techniques in Kashmir[33], indicates the Russian earnestness in the development of Kashmir's shawl industry. At the same time the heavy consumption of shawls at home and the pressures of local industry induced the Russian government to commission Agha Mehdi to procure shawl-wool goats for rearing in Siberia[34]. When Agha Mehdi died near the Karakoram pass without fulfilling the assigned task, his deputy Mohammed Zhoor invested the funds entrusted to his mission in purchasing shawls at Kashmir for resale in Bukhara[35]. Similarly when Moorcroft arrived at Bukhara in 1825, he brought alongwith him a considerable quantity of Kashmir shawls for sale there [36]. This points to the great demand for shawl goods in Central Asia.

Meyendroff, who accompanied the Russian mission of De Negri to Bukhara in 1820, was informed by a Kashmiri trader there that about 2000 Kashmir shawls were exported to Russia each year[37]. According to Moorcroft these Russians had purchased Kashmir shawl goods at Bukhara for consumption within Russia [38].

All the available evidence suggests that Kashmir shawls used to be exported to Central Asia and therefrom to Russia mainly during the first

---

31. Moorcroft to G. Swinton 12 Nov. 1822. See *Foreign Pol.* 10 Oct 1823. 29
32. During his first mission to Kashmir in 1808, Agha Mehdi had taken back a consignment of shawls to St. Petersburgh. See O. F. Solovyev, *op cit.*.
33. *Foreign. Pol.* 10 Oct. 1823. 25, 28.
34. *Ibid.*
35. Moorcroft to C. Metcalfe, 6 May 1821. See *Foreign Pol.* 10 Oct. 1823. 25.
36. *Foreign. Pol.* 14 Oct. 1825. 27
37. David N.Druhe, *Russo-Indian relations*, 1466-1917. New York, 1977. p. 102.
38. Moorcroft to Swinton, 28 Nov. 1821. See *Foreign. Pol.* 30 March 1822. 97.

half of the nineteenth century after which such trade dropped in value considerably. Bukhara had developed into a main transit centre receiving shawls from the direction of Kabul and forwarding them for consumption in Russia. Such trading was further facilitated by the settlement of a large number of Kashmiri artisans and traders in Kabul, Peshawar, Lahore and Amritsar. Mohan Lal, who accompanied Burnes on his mission to Turkestan and Bukhara in 1831-32, noticed there a trader carrying shawls from Kabul to Moscow through Bukhara-Orenburg-Makria route [39]. He sold these goods in Moscow at double the cost[40]. According to Burnes an approximate number of 120 to 300 pairs of Kashmir shawls made of finest texture were annually exported to Russia through Central Asia [41]. He estimated that "two lac rupees worth of shawl goods have passed to Russia during 1832" [42]. To quote him again, "the passion for shawls among the Russian nobles is great and will account for the exhorbitant prices given for them"[43]. That the Kashmiri embroiderers used to travel long distances to Russia for assessing the actual requirements of their Russian customers and also to alter the designs of their shawl goods in accordance with the tastes of shawl buyers [44], indicates the flourishing state of shawl trade between Kashmir and Russia through Central Asia in the early nineteenth century. During the year 1836 the British Agent in Ludhiana, Captain Wade, received information from Kabul that three packages of Kashmir shawls had come from Peshawar for export to Bukhara [45]. A European traveller, who passed through Bukhara during the years 1834-36, has also mentioned Kashmir shawls as one of the mercantile commodities of Bukhara[46]. The incidence of frequent travels of shawl merchants between Kabul and Bukhara in connection with their business is further established by the report of Allahdad, a native agent employed by Burnes to collect intelligence from the Khanates of Khiva and Bukhara in 1840 [47]. He had actually travelled to Bukhara in the train of some of

39. Mohan Lal, *Travels in the Punjab, Afghanistan and Turkistan*. p. 84.
40. Ibid. This trader named Mullah Rahim Shah had purchased Kashmir shawls for 17000 rupees, which he later sold at Moscow for 34000 rupees.
41. A. Burnes, *Travels into Bokhara*. Vol.2. p. 435.
42. *Ibid.*
43. *Ibid.*
44. *Ibid.*
45. Mason to Capt. Wade, 30 Sept. 1836. *Foreign. S.C.* 30 Jan. 1837. 30.
46. J.M. Honigberger, *Thirty five years in the East*. London, 1852. p.74.
47. Allahdad to A. Burnes, dated Balkh 14 Jan. 1840. See *Foreign. S.C.* 30 March 1840. 42-43.

these shawl merchants[48]. Allahdad's report indicates that shawl traders were being troubled by the predatory tribes of the Khanate of Khiva. His revelation that

> some of the shawl merchants have made a resolution in case the Russian army has reached the neighbourhood of Khiva, they will go to their camp and will also go with them .[49]

indicates the extent of unsettled and turbulent conditions in Khiva at that time, which prevented the development of Indian trade with Central Asia.

Kashmir shawls reached the Central Asian markets through the Leh-Yarkand-Kashgar-Kokand and Srinagar-Amritsar-Kabul routes as well. According to an authoritative estimate, shawls worth 12,30,000 rupees were annually exported from Kashmir to Amritsar[50]. From there these goods were mainly exported to Europe and a small portion was also forwarded to Kabul. The same authority has mentioned that some merchants travelled through Srinagar-Leh-Yarkand-Kashgar-Kokand route to sell shawl goods at Irbit and Nijni Novgorod[51].

That Kashmir shawls were imported into Kokand, was revealed by the Kokandi envoy, Shahzada Sultan Muhammad Khan himself during his visit to India in 1854[52]. According to another eye-witness account, the Bukhara authorities used Kashmir shawls in *Khilats* and presents to the Russian authorities in Central Asia[53]. This created a reasonable demand for such goods in Central Asia.

The circumstance of lucrative shawl trade with Russia must have also been a factor with Maharaja Ranbir Singh's desire to establish friendly relations with Russians in Central Asia. When his emissaries arrived at Tashkent in 1865 they stressed the importance of such friendly relations for the development of Kashmir's trade with that

48. *Ibid.*
49. *Ibid.*
50. R.H. Davies, *Report.* p.72.
51. *Ibid.* pp. 22-23.
52. *Foreign.S.C.* 24 Nov. 1854. 1-54.
53. Nažir Ibrahim Khan, *Account of journey to Bukhara in 1869-70*. See *Foreign Pol. B.* Nov. 1871. 31.

region [54]. On their part the Russian authorities also encouraged the Kashmir envoys to discuss the issues relating to development of bilateral trade. The Russian Minister of Foreign Affairs, Gorchakov is reported to have recognized the advantage of "offering the Kashmir merchants those rights of trade with Russia which in general the Central Asian peoples enjoyed", on a reciprocal basis [55]. Since Kashmir could offer nothing but shawls and other handicrafts for export to Russia and Central Asia, Ranbir Singh must have been interested in developing this trade. This is further corroborated by a contemporary news-report sent by Faiz Buksh to the British Indian authorities. According to Faiz Buksh the Kashmir emissaries succeeded in "obtaining a letter from Cherniaev regarding the transmission of shawl goods to the Russian fair" [56].

Year	*Value in rupees*
1867	3416
1868	800
1869	1800
1870	24100
1871	44354
1872	5200
1873	2400
1874	6140
1876	4900
1877	10700
1878	650
1879	-
1880	680
1881	-
1882	-
1883	1275

A study of the annual Ladakh trade reports for the period 1867 to 1920 shows that the export of Kashmir shawls from Kashmir to Central Asia via Leh-Yarkand trade route became insignificant in quantitative terms after 1877, when the Chinese reoccupied Eastern Turkestan. Evidently shawls of Kashmir, which were used as turbans by Andijanis

54. N. A. Khalfin, *op. cit.* p. 141.
55. O.F. Soloyev, *op cit.*
56. *Foreign. Political A.* Dec. 1872. 592-93.

and Kokandis [57], were in demand in Kashgar during the rule of Yakub Beg there. A part of such shawl goods also reached Russian Central Asia from Kashgar. But such trade appears to have dwindled to nil after the extermination of Khoja rule in Eastern Turkestan in 1877-78. This is borne out by the figures quoted in the annual Ladakh Trade reports for the respective years, which are reproduced here. However, the Kokandi and Andijani merchants who came personally to Kashmir even up to the later years of the nineteenth century, used to take small quantities of Kashmir shawls for their own consumption.

Coral

A steady and sizeable demand for coral ornaments among the Central Asians was responsible for increased export of the coral beads to Russian Turkestan from India via Ladakh and Chinese Turkestan. Though coral was equally popular amongst the people in Ladakh, Tibet and Chinese Turkestan, its export to Sinkiang registered a sharp increase only after the bilateral Russo-Sinkiang trade was put on a regular and firm footing as a result of the signing of St. Petersburgh Treaty in 1881. This facilitated the export of coral to Chinese Turkestan from India for consumption in Russian Central Asia. Since the Russian authorities had imposed duties of 4 to 5 rubles per 1b on coral[58] imported into Russian Turkestan, as part of their policy to restrict Indian exports to that area, smuggling of coral into Ferghana through the mountain passes of Irkishtam and Osh flourished. About half of the total quantity of coral imported into Russian Turkestan was estimated to have been smuggled[59]. As per the data available with the Russian Consulate in Kashgar about 40,000 rupees were collected by the Russian Customs House as duty on coral worth about 1 lakh rupees exported to Russian Turkestan from Kashgar in the year 1901-02 [60]. Similarly 21,600 rubles were collected as duty on this item of trade alone during the year 1904-05 [61]. In view of the high duties realised by the Russian Customs authorities and the consequent smuggling of coral into Russian Turkestan coral export to Russian Central Asia from India via Kashgar was

57. See *Ladakh Trade Report* for 1874 by E.Molloy.
58. Macartney to Resident in Kashmir 31 March 1902. *Foreign. Frontr A.* Jan. 1904. 137-144. *Report on Indo-Yarkand trade via Ladakh 1907-08.* By Macartney.
59. *Report on trade with Chinese Turkestan for 1897-98.* By Macartney.
60. Macartney to Resident in Kashmir. 31 March 1902. *op cit.*
61. *Report on Indo-Chinese Turkestan trade 1904-05.* By Macartney..

actually more than what was recorded at the Russian Consulate in Kashgar. An idea of the quantity or value of coral exported form India via Ladakh to Chinese Turkestan and later to Russian Turkestan can be formed from an analysis of the data recorded in the annual Ladakh Trade Reports. Coral exports to Chinese Turkestan were unusually large in the years 1893 to 1898 and 1901 to 1908 after which an abrupt depression followed possibly due to increased supplies from Russia. This trade reached its lowest point in 1918 when coral worth 180 rupees only was exported from Ladakh to Chinese Turkestan[62]. It would be safe to assume that on an average half of the coral exported to Chinese Turkestan found its way to the markets in Russian Central Asia. It also needs to be recorded here that all such coral trade was entirely in the hands of British Indian traders who found it both profitable and easy to transport. This coral was imported from Italy into India where it was re-exported to Central Asia. Indian exported coral must have been selling at cheaper rates in Russian Turkestan than what was imported via a more direct route of Batum, for a higher duty of 10 rubles (per 1b) was chargeable on the latter route [63]. It is not insignificant to note that despite such heavy odds as the restrictive duties imposed by the Tsarist government and the circuitous and hazardous nature of the Leh-Yarkand-Kashgar-Ferghana route, coral exports from India to Russian Central Asia flourished for more than a quarter of a century.

ESTIMATE OF CORAL EXPORTS FROM INDIA TO CHINESE TURKESTAN VIA LADAKH.

Year	*Quantity*	*Value in Rupees*
1868	350 Tolas	1050.0.0*
1870	400 Tolas	800.0.0**
1873	1200 Tolas	3600.0.0**
1879	N.A.	3976.0.0**
1881	N.A.	38852.0.0**
1882	N.A.	36650.0.0**
1883	N.A.	39998.0.0**
1884	N.A.	22075.0.0**
1885-86	N.A.	18500.0.0**

62. *Ladakh Trade Report for 1918-19*.
63. Report on *Indo- Yarkand trade for 1905-06*. By Macartney.
* Aitchison: *Handbook of trade products of Leh*. p. 166.
** These figures have been taken from the Ladakh Trade Reports for respective years.

Year	*Quantity*	*Value in Rupees*
1887-88	N.A.	6800.0.0**
1888-89	N.A.	11230.0.0**
1889-90	N.A.	32200.0.0**
1890-91	N.A.	46330.0.0**
1893-94	147590 beads	147590.0.0***
1894-95	238012 beads	238012.0.0***
1895-96	219315 beads	219315.0.0***
1896-97	186405 beads	186405.0.0***
1897-98	113680 beads	113680.0.0***
1898-99	124995 beads	124995.0.0***
1899-1900	91220 beads	91220.0.0***
1900-01	48782 beads	48782.0.0***
1901-02	105 maunds	152646.0.0
1902-03	216 maunds	216170.0.0***
1903-04	140 maunds	148424.0.0***
1904-05	110 maunds	115088.0.0**
1905-06	103 maunds	129441.0.0**
1906-07	87 maunds	103625.0.0**
1907-08	181 maunds	281546.0.0**
1909-10	2 maunds	5570.0.0**
1910-11	7 maunds	6400.0.0**
1911-12	26 maunds	17228.0.0**
1912-13	8 maunds	2946.0.0**
1913-14	17 maunds	24675.0.0**
1914-15	9 maunds	10200.0.0**
1915-16	3 maunds	3080.0.0**
1916-17	6 maunds	4837.0.0**
1917-18	15 maunds	32631.0.0**
1918-19	N.A.	180.0.0**
1919-20	3 maunds	2265.0.0**

** These figures have been taken from the Ladakh Trade Reports for respective year[s]

*** Figures taken from the report of E. Le Mesurier(Assistant Resident at Leh) to Maj[or] A.F. Bruce(Assistant Resident in Kashmir) dated 26 August 1903. See *Foreig[n] Frontr. A.* Jan 1904. 143.

(2) INDIAN IMPORTS FROM CENTRAL ASIA VIA KASHMIR

Indian traders who conducted their business with Central Asia, found it lucrative to send their sale proceeds back to India in the form of gold coins and rubles. There was no other alternative product in Russian Central Asia that could have been imported by these traders for resale in India. However, Russian made cotton goods maintained a small but steady demand in the frontier territories of Kashmir.

Russian Cotton Cloth

Russian made cotton goods like drill-cloth, broadcloth and chintzes used to be imported into Kashmir and its frontier areas almost steadily during the nineteenth century, though in small quantities. These goods reached Ladakh through the medium of traders who operated on the Leh-Yarkand route. Russian made cloth was preferred by the Buddhist lamas of Ladakh to that made in England for being cheap and durable. It was even exported to Tibet from Ladakh for the same reason. The remark made by Captain H.Ramsay, the British Joint Commissioner in Ladakh, in his annual trade report for the year 1884, that a small trade between India and Leh in Russian piece goods sprung up only in 1883 [64], is not borne out by facts.

Moorcroft, who was present in Ladakh in early 1820s, has mentioned Russian broadcloth as one of the commodities imported by the trading caravans into Ladakh from the direction of Yarkand[65]. J.E.T. Aitchison who acted as the British Joint Commissioner in Ladakh during 1872, has recorded that Russian broadcloth, linen and longcloth, which were locally known as *Banat*, *Lanka* and *Latha* respectively, used to be imported from Yarkand into Ladakh wherefrom these were also exported to Kashmir and Kullu [66]. In the year 1868 Russian broadcloth

64. H. Ramsay to O.St. John (Resident in Kashmir) dated Leh, 4 January 1886. *Foreign. Frontr. A.* March 1886. 89-94.
65. Moorcroft. *Travels*. Vol. 1. pp. 356-57.
66. J.E.T. Aitchison ; *Handbook of trade products of Leh*. pp. 14, 16, 150, 152. Import of Russian made cotton fabrics into Leh is also corroborated by Henry Strachey and R.H Davies.

Contd...

valued at rupees seven hundred reached Leh from Yarkand[67]. The value of its import later rose to nine hundred rupees in 1869[68]. There is every likelihood that an increased quantity of Russian cotton goods might have been reaching Ladakh, than what is actually recorded in the annual Ladakh Trade Reports. Several factors lead to this assumption. Firstly, this type of cloth had carved for itself a steady but limited demand among Ladakhi and Tibetan Buddhist population. Secondly, from late 1870s an increased quantity of cotton manufactured goods were imported into Ladakh from Chinese Turkestan. Since the traders used to pack them one and the same pony-load irrespective of their being of Yarkand, Kashgari or Russian make, it was not possible for the authorities of Ladakh to specify the quantity representing the Kashgarian or Russian made cloth. This is further substantiated by the reports of G.Macartney, the British officer posted in Kashgar, who being on the spot possessed better means of ascertaining the nature and value of the Russian exports to Ladakh from Kashgaria. On one occasion the British Joint Commissioner in Ladakh, S.H. Godfrey, was perturbed at the increasing penetration of Russian made cotton cloth into Ladakh for local consumption and also for export to Lhasa (Tibet)[69]. In his opinion it represented "new and undesirable trade current which may tend to widen the sphere of antagonistic influences more effectively than armed exploration or scientific expedition"[70]. From late 1890s onwards Russian drill-cloth, which was locally called *Shaitan-Tari*, found a small but steady demand in Ladakh and Kashmir[71]. It was in 1897 that the Russian Consul General in Kashgar, Petrovsky, boasted before his British counterpart, Macartney, that *Shaitan Tari* was finding a ready sale in Kashmir[72]. Whereas few pieces of *Shaitan Tari* were imported into Ladakh during the year 1897-98 [73], the value of its export to Ladakh from Chinese Turkestan in the year 1901-02 stood at fifteen hundred

---

See H.Strachey ; *Account of Ladakh trade*. 5 July 1851. *Foreign* S.C. 12 September 1851. 153-56.

R.H Davies; *Report*. 1862. p 68.

67. *Ladakh Trade Report for 1868*.
68. *Ladakh Trade Report for 1869*.
69. S.H. Godfrey to D.W.K. Barr, Resident in Kashmir dated 14 December 1893 *Foreign. Sec F*. May 1894. 358-387. But Godfrey admitted that Russian cotton cloth was "fully equal to that of the average British import" in quality.
70. *Ibid*.
71. *Report on Indo-Chinese Turkestan trade for 1904-05*. By G.Macartney dated Kashgar, 22 May 1905.
72. *Kashgar Diary* 31 December 1897. *Foreign. Sec. F*. May 1898. 167-192.
73. *Report on trade with Chinese Turkestan for 1897-98*. Dated 31 March 1898.

rupees[74]. Few years later a Yarkandi trader furnished a sample of Russian *Shitan - Tari* to a commercial agent of a German firm in Amritsar for reproduction of a similar texture[75]. On his part this trade agent got a similar cloth, possibly German make, supplied to the markets of Kashmir and Ladakh thereby reducing the demand for Russian *Shaitan-Tari* considerably[76]. Despite the entry of this new competitor, the Leh market received a small quantity of *Shaitan-Tari* during 1907[77]. So much so, the average annual export of this cloth to Ladakh from Chinese Turkestan was about a decade later estimated to be worth five thousand rupees[78]. Such imports, however, decreased considerably due to the rise in prices of *Shaitan - Tari* in the Central Asian markets[79] caused by internal disturbances during and after the Bolshevik revolution.

All the available evidence indicates that Russian made chintzes and cloaks sold readily in the frontier areas of Kashmir like Gilgit, Hunza and Chitral. Whereas the Bajaori and Badakhshi traders operating between Chitral and Badakhshan via Dorah or Zebak passes brought these goods into Chitral [80], Kashgari, Yarkandi or Gilgiti traders imported the same into Hunza [81] and Gilgit through the Russian Pamirs, Tashkurghan and Kilik pass. According to Macartney, at least four thousand rupees worth Russian cotton prints were exported to Hunza from Yarkand via Sarikol during the year 1910-11 [82].

An analysis of the pattern of the import of Russian manufactured cotton goods into Kashmir shows that these textile goods being coarse, cheap and durable maintained almost steady demand in Ladakh, Gilgit, Hunza and Chitral, which territories were directly coterminous with

74. Macartney to Resident in Kashmir. Dated Kashgar 31 March 1902. *op. cit.*
75. *Report on Indo-Yarkand trade via Ladakh for 1905-06.* By Macartney.
76. *Ibid.*
77. *Report on Indo-Chinese Turkestan trade via Ladakh 1906-07.* BY Macartney.
78. *Indo-Yarkand trade report 1915-16.* By Macartney.
79. *Ladakh Trade Report 1917-18.*
80. In May 1897, B.E.M. Gurdon, the then Assistant Political Agent in Chitral brought to the notice of his government that seventy ponyloads of Russian goods mainly drill-cloth and chintzes used to be imported there annually. *Foreign. Sec. F.* August 1897. 216-251.
    See also *Chitral Diaries* 25-31 October 1899, 1-7 November 1899. *Foreign. Sec. F.* Feb. 1900. 10-11.
81. A Badakhshi merchant was reported to have arrived in Hunza on 19 March 1895 bringing Russian cotton-cloth. See *Gilgit Diary* 17-25 March 1895.
82. Macartney to Erakine 31 May 1911. *Foreign Frontr B.* 57-59.

those in Chinese Turkestan or the Pamirs. Since Russian cotton prints used to be sold openly in Badakhshan, these reached Chitral from there via the caravan track between Chitral and Badakhshan. Similarly the proximity of Gilgit and Hunza to the Pamirs facilitated the entry of Russian cloth into these areas via Kashgar-Tashkurghan-Hunza or Russian Pamirs-Tashkurghan-Kilik tracks. In the year 1903-04 a new Russian cloth made from horse-hair worth rupees 3675 was introduced into Ladakh from Chinese Turkestan[83], which however did not find any buyers. Whereas cotton prints were liked by the people in Hunza and Chitral, Russian drill-cloth and broadcloth were popular with Ladakhis. Though Russian *Shaitan-Tari* ceased to be imported into Kashmir by 1920, a cloth bearing the same name is still popular with Kashmiris for being a durable and coarse cloth fit for winter use. The *Shaitan-Tari* consumed by the masses in Kashmir as late as in 1940s was of English or German make rather than the Russian one. Though the import of Russian-made cloth into Kashmir territory was insignificant quantitatively yet its successful penetration into the British Indian frontier regions via a circuitous and hazardous route speaks of the traditional links between the two regions. The Russian cloth suited the requirements and tastes of the poor Kashmiri and Ladakhi masses. The German or English trade agents lost no time in exploiting the demand in Kashmir for such a cloth.

Silk Cloth

That a small quantity of fine silk cloth made in Bukhara, Kokand and Andijan reached Ladakh through its usual trade connection with Chinese Turkestan becomes clear from an examination of Ladakh Trade Reports. Among such silk imports may be listed soft thin silken handkerchiefs known as *rumals*, which were produced in Bukhara, *Darua*- a mixture of cloth and silk in various coloured designs and *Shahi*-fine silk cloth, both made in Kokand and Russian made silks like *Zarbaf-i-Kalab* (imitation brocades), silk velvets and satin [84]. According to an official estimate Bukhara and China silks worth about four to five hundred rupees a year used to be imported into British India via Yarkand-Ladakh-Kullu route during and before the year 1850 [85].

83. *Report on Indo-Chinese Turkestan trade 1903-04*. By P.J.Miles.
84. J.E.T Aitchison, *Handbook*. pp 10, 218-19.
85. T.W. Mercer to Secretary to Punjab Government, 12 July 1861. See R.H Davies, *Report*. Appendix C. p 39.

Aitchison has recorded that *Darua* worth about rupees three hundred and *rumals* valuing rupees 7,607 were imported into Leh from Yarkand during the period 1867 to 1872 [86]. In 1875, 200 pieces of Kokandi silks(*Darua and Shahi*) valuing about 1,125 rupees were imported into Ladakh from Chinese Turkestan [87]. There was a sudden spurt in the value of such imports from Yarkand during and after the year 1883. This was due to the fact that Kokandi and Andijani traders coming personally to Ladakh to buy Indian tea [88] for consumption within Russian Central Asia brought alongwith large quantities of silk cloth for selling purpose. Thus 1374 pieces of *Shahi* silk worth 6,870 rupees were brought into Leh during the year 1883 [89] as against worth 790 rupees only in the previous year [90]. In the following year(1884), 611 pieces of Kokandi silk valuing 3,055 rupees were imported [91]. The year 1885-86 was important in the sense that 2087 pieces of Kokandi silk (*Shahi*) worth 10,435 rupees brought into Ladakh [92]. The over-all import of silk cloth whether made in Khotan (in Chinese Turkestan), Kokand or Bukhara declined steadily in value from 1890 onwards [93]. Such small imports of Central Asian silk cloth into Kashmir, however, stood nowhere as against the large export of Indian silk goods like brocades, velvet, satin etc. to Chinese Turkestan and also to Russian Central Asia. The import of Bukharan and Kokandi silks into Ladakh and Kashmir was not only insignificant in value but also irregular and fluctuating. Such import was only due to the Kokandi and Andijani traders and pilgrims

---

86. Aitchison, *Handbook*. p. 218.
87. *Ladakh Trade Report* for 1875.
88. Chinese authorities in Sinkiang had in 1880s imposed a prohibition on the import of Indian tea for sale within Chinese Turkestan, in a bid to encourage the use of China tea there. Whereas the Kashgarian or Indian traders could not trade in Indian tea, the Kokandi, Andijani or Russian traders were free to import the same via Chinese Turkestan but for sale in Russian Central Asia. So these traders were obliged to come personally to Ladakh to purchase Indian tea required for consumption in their homeland. To ensure that no Indian tea was sold off partly or fully while in transit within Chinese Turkestan, the Chinese guards used to accompany such trading caravans up to the Russian frontier at Irkishtam.
    See G. Macratney, *Note on Leh trade report of 1893-94*. Dated 16 March 1895.
89. *Ladakh Trade Report* for 1883.
90. *Ladakh Trade Report* for 1882.
91. *Ladakh Trade Report* for 1884.
92. *Ladakh Trade Report* for 1885-86.
93. During the years 1893-94 and 1894-95, 399 pieces of Kokandi silk valuing 1,197 rupees and 841 pieces of Bukhara silk valuing 2,523 rupees were imported into Ladakh from Yarkand, respectively.
    See *Ladakh Trade Reports* 1893-94, 1894-95.

who brought this commodity for sale in Ladakh during their personal visits to that quarter. Besides, there was little demand in Kashmir for such costly fabrics due to the poverty conditions in the valley. The Indian silk brocades and velvets which were more readily available catered to the small local demand.

Russian Leather

Russian leather goods like shoes, belts, furcoats and skins which were locally known as *bulgar* in the Leh and Kashmir markets, were imported into Ladakh via the Kokand-Kashgar-Yarkand route but in very small quantities. It were only the wealthier and ruling classes in Ladakh who could afford to wear the shoes and coats made of *bulgar*. Due to their pleasant aroma and peculiar preparation [94] the Russian *bulgar* hides came to be used as gift articles on special occasions and for that purpose these were imported into British India from Ladakh via Lahoul, Kullu and Kangra[95]. That the fine Russian leather reached as far as Tibet through the hands of Kashmiri and Ladakhi traders, is evidenced from Moorcroft's findings during his mission to Tibet in 1812 [96]. Eight years later when Moorcroft arrived at Leh on his way to Central Asia, he was not pleased to find several affluent Kashmiris and Ladakhis in possession of Russian dress wares. Both Moorcroft and Cunningham, who stayed in Ladakh during the years 1820-22 and 1846-1847 respectively, mention Russian *bulgar* as one of the items of imports into Ladakh from Chinese Turkestan [97]. Whereas this commodity filtered into Ladakh more or less steadily during the first half of the nineteenth century, its imports dwindled to nil particularly after the extension of Russian control into Central Asia during the 1860s. According to a reliable estimate about fifty to sixty skins of Russian leather used to be imported each year into Ladakh from the direction of Yarkand before and during the year 1850 [98]. The traders derived a handsome profit by

---

94. J.E.T. Aitchison, *Handbook*. p. 6.
95. Capt. T.W. Mercer, Assistant Commissioner, Kullu, to the Secretary to Punjab Government 12 July 1861. See R.H. Davies, *Report*. Appendix C. p 38.
96. W.Moorcroft to J.Adam, Secretary, Political Department, GOI dated Niti, 7 September 1812. *Foreign. Pol*. 18 December 1820. 29.
97. Moorcroft, *Travels*. Vol.1.p 356.
A Cunningham *Ladakh*. p 242.
Strachey and Davies too have mentioned Russian leather as one of the items imported into Ladakh from Yarkand. See Davies, *Report*. p.34. H.Strachey, *Report on Ladakh*.21 May 1851. p 410.
98. Mercer to Punjab Government 12 July 1861.

selling each piece at the rate of twenty rupees in British India, whereas it cost them only twelve rupees [99]. During the year 1870 only two *bulgars*[100] were imported into Ladakh from Chinese Turkestan as against thirty-two Russian posteens(skin coats) valued at a total of rupees 812 during the preceding year(1869)[101]. The annual reports of Ladakh trade with Chinese Turkestan for the years 1871 to 1920-21 are silent about this item of import trade between the two sides, which means that no *bulgars* came into Ladakh and therefore into India after 1870. This however, does not rule out the possibility of Kashmiri and Ladakhi traders and carriers purchasing the Russian leather goods for their personal consumption during their occasional trips to various trading marts in Chinese Turkestan.

Silkworm Eggs

Whereas the mulberry plantation has existed in Kashmir since ancient times [102], the silk industry was modernised in Kashmir only in the nineteenth century during the rule of Maharaja Ranbir Singh [103]. By that time such Central Asian towns as Khotan (in Chinese Turkestan), Kokand, Andijan, and Marghilan (in Russian Central Asia) had attained a high degree both qualitatively and quantitatively in silk production. After the signing of St.Petersburgh Treaty in 1881 the Russo-Chinese trade in Turkestan flourished by leaps and bounds. Russia being the main buyer of raw silk from Sinkiang paid special attention to the development of silk industry in that area. Large quantities of silk worm eggs were supplied to Kashgaria in a bid to encourage sericulture in that country. It was in the year 1881 that a small quantity of ten seers of silkworm eggs valuing 1600 rupees [104] reached Kashmir through the traditional Yarkand-Ladakh channel of communication for use in the valley. The extensive damage caused to the Kashmir silk industry as

---

99. *Ibid.*
100 *Ladakh Trade Report for 1870.*
101. *Ladakh Trade Report for 1869.*
102. The use of mulberry twigs in Yagnopavita ceremony and the worshipping of mulberry trees by the Kashmiri Brahmans even up to present time testifies to the existence of this tree in Kashmir since the Vedic ages.
103. M.Ganju,*Textile industries in Kashmir*. Delhi, Premier, 1945. pp. 154-56.
J&K Government Sericulture Deptt, *Report on the investigations into the conditions of the sericulture industry in Jammu and Kashmir State*. Srinagar, 1942. p.6.
104. *Ladakh Trade Report* for 1881.

a result of the spread of the silkworm disease in 1878 [105] must have induced some enterprising Kashmiri trader to import silkworm eggs from Yarkand where these were abundantly available due to large supplies that came from Russian Central Asia. A few years later in early 1890 five seers of Bukharan silkworm eggs of high quality were imported into Kashmir through the medium of Government of India and the British agent in Kabul, Lt. Col. Ata Ullah Khan [106]. Though such import was too small in quantitative terms, it was sufficient for introducing high grade Bukharan silk in the Kashmir filatures.

Bukharan and Kokandi Gold Tillas

Precious metals like silver ingots and coins, gold in dust and coins were traditional item of import into Kashmir from Chinese Turkestan. Several factors were responsible for such import. Firstly, the Central Asians had much less to offer in exchange for the manufactured goods exported there by the Indian traders who found it convenient to import bullion as one of the means of transferring their sale proceeds back to India. Secondly, the hazardous journey over the high altitude and tedious Leh-Yarkand route made it incumbent upon the traders to carry such goods as were light and easily transportable. Thirdly, the Central Asian Haj pilgrims who annually travelled through India enroute to Mecca brought sufficient quantities of bullion for meeting their travel and other expenses. However, the quantum of gold imports into India via Ladakh and Kashmir varied in accordance with the nature of political and economic conditions prevailing in Central Asia from time to time. During the first half of the nineteenth century gold *tillas* (coins) of Bukhara [107] and Kokand flowed into Ladakh and Kashmir almost regularly. But with the extension of Russian control over the Central Asian Khanates this trade was seriously disrupted. Since this study is confined only to the import of such gold as originated from Russian Central Asia, the data contained in the Ladakh Trade Reports about the quantity and value of silver, gold dust and coins imported into India

---

105. M.Ganju, *op. cit*. p. 157.
106. *Foreign. Frontr. B*. Feb. 1890. 199-202
Foreign. Frontr. B. April 1890. 87-92.
107. Vigne who travelled through Kashmir and Ladakh, in late 1830s mentions gold coins of Bukhara as one of the imports from Yarkand into India via Ladakh. See his *Travels in Kashmir*. Vol.2. p 344

from Chinese Turkestan via Ladakh gives us an idea of such import trade existing between Kashmir and Central Asia.

Gold *tillas* of Bukhara and Kokand, each of which weighed about two-fifths of an Indian tola of nearly pure gold, bore the titles of Khans of Bukhara and Kokand [108].

Since such coins were abundantly available in Kashgaria mainly due to the free movement of Kokandi, Andijani, Bukharan, Kashgari and Yarkandi traders throughout Central Asia, these were consequently imported into Ladakh from the direction of Yarkand. According to a British officer, H.Strachey who was in Ladakh during 1849-50 in connection with survey work, the Kokandi gold coins were more numerous in Ladakh and that the Bukharan coins contained best gold[109]. All such coins were sold as merchandise rather than used as coins. According to Strachey these coins were sold in India at the rate of six and a half to seven Indian rupees [110]. That these were being valued at five and a half to six rupees in Ladakh market becomes clear from the value quoted for each coin in Ladakh Trade Reports. Yakub Beg, the independent ruler of Kashgaria, is reported to have issued his own gold coins in his Kingdom in 1874 [111]. That is why the gold coins imported into Ladakh via Yarkand from 1875 onwards were of Kashgarian[112] rather than of Kokandi or Bukharan origin. Because of these gold coins having been overvalued [113] by Yakub Beg their imports into Ladakh decreased considerably. But from 1883 onwards the imports of gold coins and dust registered a sharp increase which was due to the arrival of Shikarpuri merchants from Bukhara and other towns in Russian Central Asia via Kashgar-Yarkand-Leh caravan route. These traders, whose money-lending activities had been strictly restricted by the Russian authorities in Central Asia, were forced by the changed

---

108. H.Strachey, *Report on geographical and statistical information and commerce of Ladakh*, 21 May 1851. p 378.(NAI)
109. *Ibid.*
110. *Ibid.*
111. See *Ladakh Trade Report for 1874*.
112. It becomes amply clear from the fact that the value shown for each gold coin imported from Chinese Turkestan into Ladakh during the years 1875 to 1882 is shown as five rupees only as against five and a half rupees during the years preceding 1875.
113. These were rated at only five Indian rupees per coin in ladakh and were thus considered an unprofitable item for trade.

conditions there to return to India. So they brought their accumulated capital and profits earned during their long stay in Central asia in the form of gold coins and dust. Due to such increased imports prices of gold fell in Kashmir[114]. This phenomenon continued till 1900 from which years onwards the Russian gold and paper rubles substituted the earlier form of bullion imports.

An idea of the value of Kokandi or Bukharan gold coins imported into Ladakh from Chinese Turkestan during the years 1871-74 can best be formed from the following data that has been collected from the annual Ladakh Trade Reports for the years 1871, 1872, 1873 and 1874.

Year	*Number of gold coins*	*Value in Rupees-Annas-Paise*
1871	3275 Tillas	17194.0.0*
1872	4360 Tillas	23980.0.0
1873	2510 Tillas	13810.8.0
1874	2391 Tillas	13150.0.0

Russian Gold Thread

The tradition of using gold and silver thread in embroidering Kashmir shawls and other apparels persists even today. *Tilla-Kari*, the Kashmiri name for this type of embroidery work has derived its name from the term *Tilla* [115] that was used by the Punjabi traders for gold thread. Though the demand for gold thread in Kashmir was largely met by supplies from British India coming via Amritsar, yet the Russian-made gold and silver thread reached Kashmir in small quantities through the Bukhara-Kabul-Peshawar-Amritsar-Srinagar and Kokand-Kashgar-Yarkand-Leh routes. Both the pure and imitation types of Russian gold thread were imported. The Indo-Central Asian traders and Kashmir shawl embroiderers considered the Russian-made gold and silver thread

114. *Ladakh Trade Report for 1890-91.*
   * This information has been derived from *Aitchison's Handbook.* p. 251.
115. See Aitchison, *Handbook.* p. 113.
   As against this, the *Tilla* meant a gold coin in the Khanates of Bukhara, Kokand and Kashgaria.

as genuine in comparison to that imported from British India which was looked down upon as imitation [116]. The gold or silver wire twisted upon a silk thread that came from the direction of Russia was known in Yarkand and Ladakh as *Kalabatun* [117]. However in Leh and Srinagar markets the Russian gold thread was called as *Atnuf* [118] and the silver thread from the same country was known as *Seemgot* [119].

According to an authoritative estimate Russian gold, silver and imitation wire valuing about 7850 pounds sterling was annually imported into India via Kabul-Peshawar route in 1850s [120]. As per the same source gold thread and *Seemgot* (both Russian and Indian makes) worth about 20,000 rupees was annualy exported from Amritsar to Jammu and Kashmir [121]. *Atnuf* was imported into Ladakh from the direction of Yarkand for consumption in Kashmir but in small quantities[122]. During the year 1869 seven bundles of gold thread valuing 305 rupees are reported to have arrived in Leh [123]. It was during 1880s, when Shikarpuri merchants and money-lenders returned to India after their long residence in Central Asia, that a significant quantity of Russian gold thread was imported into Kashmir by them. Whereas the Annual trade returns registered at Leh in 1884 showed an import of 240 tolas of gold thread valuing 480 rupees [124] only (thus showing it to be of imitation), the figures registered during the year 1885-86 showed the imports of this commodity as one thousand tolas valued at 32,000 rupees [125] (thus testifying to its purity). By and large the Import of Russian gold thread into Kashmir was only occasional and not a regular feature of the Indo-Central Asian trade.

---

116. *Ibid.*
117. *Ibid.*
118. *Pari chap* quality of *Atnuf*, literally meaning as the Angel's Seal, was considered to be of best quality, whereas other type was usually imitation.
See *ibid.* p. 11.
119. *Ibid.* p. 113.
120. R. H. Davies, *Report*. p. 45
121. *Ibid* p.72.
Average annual trade turnover of Amritsar with Afghanistan and Turkestan and Jammu and Kashmir stood at 2,35,253 and 2,11,555 pounds sterling respectively, during this period. See Davies, *Report*. p. 75.
122. Aitchison, *Handbook*. p.11.
Captain Strachey has also listed this item as one of the Ladakhi imports from Yarkand. See his *Report on Ladakh*. 21 may 1851. p. 409.
123. *Ladakh Trade Report for 1869.*
124. *Ladakh Trade Report for 1884.*
125. *Ladakh Trade Report for 1885-86*

Russian Gold and Paper Rubles

The import of Russian gold ducats(rubles) and copper coins (kopeks) into the Leh market from Yarkand as a trading commodity was not only occasional but also insignificant during the nineteenth century. Vigne who visited Kashmir and Ladakh in late 1830s records that Russian gold ducats were brought into India via Yarkand and Leh as a part of the merchandise imported from that end.[126] Strachey, who happened to be in Ladakh in around 1850, found such gold ducats-locally named as *Budki* - being sold as merchandise.[127] The availability of *Budki* and *Bugh-i-Ruski* (copper coins) in Leh market has also been indicated by Aitchison.[128] But at the close of the nineteenth century Russian currency began to occupy an important place in the Indian imports from Chinese Turkestan. The tendency of the Indian traders to transmit their earnings in Kashgaria to India in the Russian currency continued, subject to minor fluctuations till 1919 when the British authorities in India prohibited such imports. Several factors like the easy availability of Russian rubles in Chinese Turkestan due to increased earnings from Sinkiang's exports to Rusia, the advantageous position held by rubles vis-a-vis the local Chinese currency in exchange value and the British Indian policy to restrict import of hemp drug into India by imposing high taxes on the same, were collectively responsible for the increased export of Russian rubles to India. The quantity and value of this import altered with the change in the overall trade climate brought in by any shift or alteration in any of the above noted operational factors.

The raw materials exported from Chinese Turkestan to Russia via Ferghana were paid back in Russian manufactured goods and rubles. Since Sinkiang's exports to Russia far exceeded the imports from that end,[129] the balance was met by ruble payments. As a result of the

126. G.T. Vigne, *Travels*. Vol. 2. p. 344.
127. See his *Report on geographical and statistical information and commerce of Ladakah*, 21 May 1851. p. 380.
128. Aitchison, *Handbook*. pp. 32, 249.
129. For instance, in 1854 Sinkiang exported raw materials worth 16,01,400 rubles to Russia importing therefrom goods valuing 6,52,100 rubles only. However, in 1890s this trade is reported to have become more or less balanced.
See M.I. Sladkovsky, *The Long road; Sino-Russian economic contacts from ancient times to 1917*. Moscow, 1981. pp. 228-231. This does not, however, mean that Russian exports to Sinkiang stood higher in value than its imports after 1893 and the Soviet
(contd...)

conclusion of the St.Petersburgh Treaty in 1881 [130] the Russo-Sinkiang trade scaled new heights thereby ensuring a regular and abundant supply of Russian rubles in the market of Kashgaria. Due to the unusually large Kashgarian exports to Russian Turkestan in the year 1900-01 the value of ruble dropped to seven *tengas* in Kashgar [131] which encouraged the Indian traders to make bulk purchase of rubles. Any slump in this bilateral trade produced an adverse effect on the Indo-Chinese Turkestan trade on the whole. So when in 1909 the export from Sinkiang to Russian Turkestan and Russia proper had decreased in value, that year (April,1909-March 1910) witnessed a corresponding depression in the export trade of rubles to India from Chinese Turkestan [132]. This was due to the fact that rubles had become scarce in the Kashgarian markets and their high prices [133] rendered them unprofitable as a commodity for the Indian traders. Similar situation had arisen earlier in the year 1905-1906 [134]

---

scholar has provided no figures to prove it otherwise. Several factors like the nature of backward economy in Sinkiang where people could not afford to buy foreign goods and continued with their tradition of using home made clothing, the cheap availability of rubles in Kashgaria which became only possible due to the abundant supply of the Russian currency there, are responsible for Sinkiang's exports to Russia being generally higher in value than the imports from that quarter though subject to certain fluctuations. In fact the then Russian Consul at Kashgar (M.Koloklov) in his report on the "*Economic review of Kashgaria*"(1906) has attested this fact by providing figures of Kashgarian exports to Russia and vice versa from 1882 to 1905.

See *Foreign. Sec.F*. June 1907.302.

This explains the huge influx of rubles into India from Kashgaria during the early twentieth centnry.

130. The Treaty of St.Petersburg allowed the Russians to trade free of duty in the towns and other places of Ili, Tarbagatay, Kashgar, Urumchi and other districts that lay both on the northern and southern slopes of the Tian Shah range, thus providing free access to the Russian traders in Kashgaria for the first time.

131. *Report on trade between India and Chinese Turkestan 1900-01*. By G. Macartney.

132. *Report on Indo-Chinese Turkestan trade for 1909-10*. By Macartney.
As per the Ladakh Trade Report for 1909-10 Russian gold coins valuing 78,279 rupees were imported into Ladakh from Chinese Turkestan in that year, whereas the quantity of Chinese silver *Yambus* and Khotan gold dust imported during the same period represented an amount of 1,68,815 and 93,997 rupees respectively. This shows that the Indian traders had preferred to remit their money to India in Chinese silver and gold dust rather than in rubles which were dearer.

133. Macartney reported that the exchange value of a ruble in Chinese silver had risen to 0.875 *Tael* during 1909 as against 0.6025 *Tael* two years ago.

134. The import of Russian gold coins into Ladakh during the year 1905-06 was valued at 2,43,335 rupees as against 4,27,505 rupees in the preceding year. See *Ladakh Trade Reports for 1904-05, 1905-06*. During the Russo-Japanese war India received little supplies of Japanese silk thereby raising its price. That is why Indian traders in Kashgaria brought bulk quantities of Khotan silk to earn more profits from its resale in India at exhorbitant prices.

due to the Russo-Japanese war and later in the year 1915-16 [135] on account of the world war.

The Russian institutions operating in Kashgar were actively encouraging the brisk trading in the Russian paper currency. Far from being a passive spectator, the Russian Consulate General used to wield its influence over the local Chinese authorities for ensuring that the ruble commanded a respectable price in the Kashgarian market. For instance during the year 1900 the local administration was reported to have been pressurised by the Russian Consulate into issuing a public notification whereby the value of a ruble was fixed at ten tengas[136]. Similarly the Kashgar branch of the Russo-Chinese bank [137] functioned as a regulator and helped in maintaining the higher price of the ruble in relation to the local silver currency. So whenever the value of ruble fell in Kashgar in terms of Chinese silver, this bank would import silver from Russia in large quantities with a view to lowering the value of the local Chinese currency in relation to the ruble [138]. Apart from this, the bank provided facilities to the Indian traders in Kashgaria for transmitting their money to India at the fixed exchange rate which in 1905 was 154 rupees per 100 rubles [139]. The Indian traders would deposit rubles with the bank in Kashgar and receive their payments in rupees in Bombay at approved exchange rates. Similarly, the Russian Post Office in Kashgar offered the telegraphic money order service to traders whereunder the money could be sent to India (Bombay) via Irkishtam and Samarkand [140]. Such measures not only helped in restricting the tendency to export Russian gold coins to India but also acted as a stimulant to the bilateral Indo-Yarkand trade by providing adequate means to the Indian traders to balance their increased imports into Chinese Turkestan with a corresponding export of their earnings

135. During the year 1915-16 gold rubles worth 22,784 rupees only were imported into Ladakh, which amount represented less than one-sixth of such import in the preceding year. See *Ladakh Trade Reports for 1914-15, 1915-16.*

136. *Report on Indo-Chinese Turkestan trade for 1900-01.* By Macartney. The value of ruble on this occasion had drifted to a low level of seven *Tengas* in local currency from that of twelve previously.

137. This branch was opened in the year 1900.
See Report by M. Lavrov (of Russian Consulate General, Kashgar) on Russian trade in Kashgaria. *Foreign. Sec. F.* June, 1907. 302.

138. Macartney to the Resident in Kashmir, 31 March 1902. *op cit.*

139. *Report on Indo-Chinese Turkestan trade for 1904-05.* By Macartney.

140. *Report on Indo-Yarkand trade 1907-08.* By Macartney.

without any risks. When the Russian Bank and Post Office ceased issuing drafts and money orders for India during the period 1914-16 (due to World War), there was a consequent spurt in the import of rubles into India through Ladakh. As against such Russian facilities, the British Consulate in Kashgar had no arrangements to offer to the Indian traders, whose interests the Consulate professed to look after, for transferring their capital to India in Indian rupees. That explains the preference given by the Chinese and Indian traders to the purchase of Russian paper rubles for transmission to Shanghai and of gold rubles for export to Kashmir and India respectively [141]. The Russian Consul in Kashgar (Kolokolov) has himself recorded that the price of gold rubles used to rise as much as by three to five kopeks at the time of their purchase by the Indian merchants for transmission to India [142].

The prevalence of barter transactions and lack of sufficient resources to suit the Indian requirements (both in raw and manufactured state) in the markets of Kashgaria left little option before the Indian traders but to send back their earnings to India in the form of a suitable commodity which could fetch good price. That is why they imported raw silk, hemp drug, silver or gold from Chinese Turkestan, not because these were in great demand in India, but only as a forced medium to transfer their earnings. In the process the import of hemp drug via Ladakh became an inalienable feature of the Indo-Chinese Turkestan trade causing much harm to the health of the common people in Punjab who consumed this drug. Following the recommendation of the Indian Hemp Drugs Commission in 1894 [143] the British Indian government imposed prohibitive duties [144] on all *charas* that was imported into India. Though such import did not cease altogether yet the Indian traders got discouraged to import *charas* from Chinese Turkestan and they

141. See a note on "The circulation of Russian coinage in Kashgar". By S.Kolokolv. 1906. *Foreign. Frontr. B.* Dec.1908. 132.

142. *Ibid.*

143. The Commission had proposed the levy of not less than 80 rupees per maund on all charas imported into Punjab.
W.M. Young(Chairman), *Report of the Indian hemp drugs Commission*. Calcutta, 1894. p. 360.

144. The Indian government imposed a tax of 20 rupees per maud on charas imports during the year 1896, soon raising this levy to 80 rupees per maund in 1897. This tax would yield a recurring revenue of 1,20,000 and 4,80,000 rupees a year to the government respectively.
See *Ladakh trade Report for 1895-96*.

began to search for alternative medium to send their capital to India from Kashgaria. Russian currency came in handy for this purpose and began to be imported in large quantities from the late nineteenth century (that is after the government's decision to charge high duties on *charas* imports).It was as late as the end of nineteenth century that the Russian currency had nearly substituted Chinese silver *Yambu* and Khotan gold dust as treasure imports into India mainly because of its higher profitability. One silver *yambu* which used to cost about 160 rupees in Ladakh till early 1870s dropped in value to about 110 rupees about two decades later. But the same silver *Yambu* would exchange in Kashgar for 94 rubles which would in turn be sold for 146 rubles in India[145]. One ruble was usually sold in Bombay at an average rate of one and a half rupees [146]. Thus the Indian traders instead of purchasing *yambus* for export to India imported rubles in large quantities. As and when the Kashgar exports to Russian Turkestan exceeded imports from that quarter, there occurred an unusual increase in the ruble supply in Chinese Turkestan thereby lowering its prices as low as 7 *tengas*. However in times of scarcity the ruble maintained a high price of up to 13 *tengas*.

The year 1897 appears to have been a cut-off point when the Russian currency began to be imported into India as a trade commodity. During that year rubles worth about 85,000 rupees were remitted to Bombay from Kashgar [147]. But for temporary periods of depression such import went on rising in value till it scaled the new height of about six million rubles in the year 1919-20.[148] Then came a sudden halt to this trading in Russian gold and paper currency as a result of the British prohibition imposed on any ruble imports into India as part of their anti-Bolshevik campaign. Even the possession of the ruble by any Indian would invite punishment. In the beginning only the Russian gold rubles were in demand with the Indian traders who sold them to the jewellers for making gold ornaments. During the period from 1901 to 1916 such gold coins were imported in considerable

145. Macartney to the Resident in Kashmir, 31 March 1902.

146. *Report on Indo-Chinese Turkestan trade for 1900-01*. by Macartney.

147. *Report on trade with Chinese Turkestan for 1897-98*. By Macartney. During this year the exchange value of the ruble had fallen from an average 10 *tengas* to seven and a half *tengas*.

148. During the year 1917-18 rubles were purchased in Kashgaria at about 25 rupees per 100 and sold in Bombay upto 30 rupees per 100. See *Ladakh Trade Report for 1917-18*.

quantities through the Yarkand-Leh caravan trade route. Besides, the Central Asian pilgrims desirous of making a *haj* pilgrimage through India brought in sufficient quantities of gold coins to meet their expenses, thus ensuring a regular supply of Russian bullion to the Indian market. But when the Russian government introduced effective measures to encourage dealings in paper rubles and to check the out-flow of gold currency, the Indian traders operating in Kashgaria found themselves lured by the facilities offered [149]. They availed of the services provided by the Russo-Chinese Bank and Russian Post Office in Kashgar to send money to India by drafts or money orders. Though no official estimate of the actual value of paper rubles imported through these channels is available, it is certain that the import of Russian currency into India far exceeded the estimates as shown in the annual Ladakh Trade Reports. An idea of this trade can be had by the fact that about three million rubles were deposited in the government treasuries at Srinagar and Leh in a short period of first three months of the year 1920 [150]. Besides, more than 26 lakh rubles were re-exported to Chinese Turkestan from Ladakh during the period April 1920 to March 1921 [151]. Yet there is no denying the fact that the increasing ruble imports into India was only a result of the depression in the export trade of Chinese Turkestan which did not possess the capacity to supply alternative goods to India. The ruble trade was in no way a part of any direct trade dealings between India and Russian Turkestan.

Estimate of Gold and Paper ruble imports into India via Ladakh.*

Year	*Rubles(Paper)*		*Gold Rubles*	
	Number	*Value in Rupees*	*Number*	*Value in Rupees*
1897-98	N. A.	85,000**	nil	nil
1898-99	N. A.	2,000***	nil	nil

149. At least four lakh of rupees worth rubles were delivered by the Indian traders to the Russo-Asiatic Bank and the Russian Post Office at Kashgar during the year 1910-11. See Macartney to Lt. Col. K.D. Erskine, Resident in Kashmir, 31 May 1911. *Foreign. Frontr.B.* Oct. 1911. 57-59.

150. *Ladakh Trade Report for 1919-20.*

151. *Ladakh Trade Report for 1920-21.*

* All these figures have been taken from the *Ladakh Trade Reports* for the respective years (except otherwise indicated).

** *Report on trade with Chinese Turkestan, 1897-98.* By Macartney.

*** *Report on trade between India and Chinese and Russian Turkestan via Ladakh, 1898-99.* By Macartney.

Year	*Rubles (Paper)*		*Gold Rubles*	
	Number	*Value in Rupees*	*Number*	*Value in Rupees*
1899-1900	N.A.	1,00,000****	(including gold coins)	
1900-01	125265	1,87,897.8.0	134615	201922.8.0
1901-02	4508	7,044.0.0	229875	359534.0.0
1902-03	1300	2,031.0.0	233950	365547.0.0
1903-04	nil	nil	174054	271958.0.0
1904-05	nil	nil	273603	427505.0.0
1905-06	nil	nil	156886	243335.0.0
1906-07	nil	nil	338572	529019.0.0
1907-08	nil	nil	360912	563925.0.0
1909-10	nil	nil	50098	78279.0.0
1910-11	nil	nil	93976	146938.0.0
1911-12	nil	nil	261195	408217.0.0
1912-13	nil	nil	97281	151960.0.0
1913-14	nil	nil	81851	127265.0.0
1914-15	nil	nil	96401	150626.0.0
1915-16	nil	nil	14583	22784.0.0
1916-17	N.A.	N.A.	948524	796188.0.0
			(including paper notes)	
1917-18	2397390	853727.0.0	115575	194362.00
1918-19	2262179	628111.0.0	98066	184355.0.0
1919-20	5844439	810484.0.0	30145	56022.0.0
1920-21	750	70.0.0	20230	31031.0.0

Since the territories of Russian Central Asia and Kashmir were not coterminous, no direct trade was possible between the two regions. Whatever commerce was transacted was through Punjab, Afghanistan or Chinese Turkestan via difficult and circuitous Srinagar-Punjab-Afghanistan-Bukhara and Leh-Yarkand-Kashgar-Kokand routes. Due to such geographical factors this trade was subjected to numerous

**** Macartney to Resident in Kashmir, 31 March 1902.

inhibiting influences like the state of unstable political conditions in the Central Asian Khanates and the hazardous nature of the mountainous trade routes. This trade was just an extension of the traditional and well established Kashmir-Kashgar trade. It came under the influece of the overland Russo-Kashgar trade. This was particularly so when the influx of Russian gold and paper rubles into Chinese Turkestan increased and when the Shikarpuri traders from Central Asia returned to India via Kashgar carrying with them their earnings in the form of gold after the Russian authorities imposed restrictions on their business activities. The Indo-Central Asian trade became the casualty of the Anglo-Russian rivalry over Central Asia. The British success in adopting various measures in Kashmir for promoting Indian trade with Chinese Central Asia was undone by the steps taken by the Tsarist administration for keeping British goods away from the Central Asian markets. Under such circumstances there existed no substantial trade dealings directly between Kashmir and Russian Central Asia except for small indigenous products of India like spices, indigo, books, tea, shawls and brocades which maintained steady demand among the Central Asians and the occasional import of Russian gold and paper currency. But it was due to this small trade link that numerous Indians including Kashmiris had been visiting Central Asian trading marts and that several Central Asian traders were attracted to the markets in Leh and Srinagar. This mutual intercourse played a key role in the strengthening of social ties between the peoples of the two regions. Numerous Indians, some of them from Srinagar, Chitral and Hunza had taken up their residence in Central Asia for carrying on their business activities[152]. However, due to the disturbed and unsettled conditions in Soviet Central Asia in the post-Bolshevik period and also the British restrictions on Indian exports to that quarter, the flow of goods between the two regions was adversely affected. With the State takeover of trade in the Soviet Union there was little scope for the continuation of the overland trade between India and Central Asia, as it was solely conducted through the medium of private traders.

152. See G.L. Dmitriev, *Iz istorii Sredneziatsko-Indiskikh Otnoshenii vtoroi poloviny XIX-nachala -XX veka*. Tashkent, 1965.

3

Cultural Intercourse

Notwithstanding the great mountain barriers of Karakoram and Hindu Kush ranges there existed since remote times close socio-economic and cultural ties between the peoples of Central Asia and northern India including the present-day Jammu and Kashmir State. This is amply borne out by numerous investigations of ancient ruins excavated in this area by the Soviet and the Indian archaeologists. Neolithic finds in Burzahom and Gufkral in Kashmir such as stone and bone tools including axes, chisels, harpoons, needles etc. bear close resemblance to those found at Tesma and Tashkent in Central Asia. The discovery of lotus flower motifs and the Brahami inscriptions in a Buddhist cave monastery excavated at Kara Tepe[1] is a clear pointer to the Indian influence over Central Asian culture in ancient times. Coming down to the Kushan period when Central Asia and north-western India were integrated into a single kingdom, one finds that various cities like Khotan, Kashgar, Balkh and Bamiyan had developed into important centres of Buddhism[2]. The discovery of terracota tiles in Harwan near Srinagar depicting figures in the Central Asian ethnic type and dress style and also containing Kharoshthi numerals of about 300

---

1. G.M. Bongard Levin, "India and Central Asia : historical-cultural contacts in ancient times.". In *Central Asia*. Edited by Amalendu Guha. New Delhi, 1970. p.101.
2. K. A. Nizami, "India's cultural relations with Central Asia during the medieval period". In *Ibid*. p.158.

A.D.[3], testifies to the Central Asian imprint over Kashmir's society and culture. In the post-Kushan period the direct linkage between the two regions is witnessed during Lalitaditya's reign(eighth century A.D.). After his victory over the Tukhars, then settled in Tukharistan which has been identified by Stein as the area comprising Badakshan and the upper reaches of the Oxus river[4], Lalitaditya is reported to have inducted a Turkish Chief Minister, Cankuna by name, into his court. Kalhana attributes several meritorious works including the building of *Stupas* and *Viharas* to Cankuna[5]. After the consolidation of Islam in Central Asia contacts with the Hindu Kingdom of Kashmir developed further. Both the Central Asian mercenaries and artisans had free access to the courts of Hindu rulers in Kashmir. Kalhana's reference to the hospitality provided by king Kalasa(1063-89 AD) to one *Turuska* artist[6] and also to the grant of favours upon hundreds of *Turuska* captains by king Harsa[7] (1089-1101 AD) is an indication of the influence enjoyed by Central Asian Turks in Kashmir during the eleventh century. The presence of Turks in the armies of Hindu Kings of Kashmir and also the regular influx of Central Asian traders and adventurers were partly responsible for the percolation of some Muslim practices in the valley.

The fourteenth century saw the establishment of Islam in Kashmir at the hands of one Syed Sharaf-u-Din (popularly known as Bulbul Shah) of Turkestan[8] and Shah Mir who is also believed to have been of Turkish origin[9]. Bulbul Shah continues to be revered by the Kashmiri Muslims even to this day. Recently, a big stone mosque has been constructed near his grave in Bulbul Lankar (situated near the fifth bridge in Srinagar) which draws its name from a free kitchen (*langar*) established by Rinchan Shah (1320-23 AD) in memory of his spiritual master. The

3. R.S. Sharma: "Central Asia and early Indian cavalry (c 200 B.C.-1200 AD)". In *Central Asia*. p. 179.
4. M.A. Stein, *Tr, Kalhana's Rajatarangini*. London, 1900. Vol.1. p. 90.
According to Alberuni, Kashmiris celebrated an annual festival in commemoration of the victory which their king had won over the Turks. See his *India*. Edited by E.C. Sachau. Delhi, 1964. (Reprint). Vol.2 p.178.
5. Stein, *Rajatarangini*. Vol.1. pp. 143-44.
6. *Ibid.* Vol.1. p 311.
7. *Ibid.*, Vol.1. p. 357.
8. A.Q. Rafiqi, *Sufism in Kashmir*. p. 17.
Mohibbul Hasan, *Kashmir under the Sultans*. Calcutta, 1959. p. 39.
9. *Ibid.* p.43.
Shah Mir ruled in Kashmir as Sultan Shams-ud-Din from 1339 to 1342 AD. His dynasty remained in power up to 1561 AD.

subsequent development of Islam in the valley owes a lot to the activities of hundreds of syeds and sufis who travelled over long distances to reach Kashmir as a result of Timur's atrocities in their homeland. Consequently numerous sufi orders were carried from their place of origin at Suhraward, Gilan, Yasi, Bukhara and Samarkand to Kashmir and other parts of India [10]. Whereas Central Asian missionaries like Syed Ali Hamadani, Muhammad Hamadani, Syed Hilal, Syed Habibullah Kasani, Qazi Habibullah, Jamal-ud-din Bukhari, Sheikh Baba Ali Wali, Khwaja Ahmad Yasavi Nakshbandi[11] propagated their doctrine in Kashmir, numerous Kashmiri scholars and saints like Srikanth alias Sheikh Sulaiman [12], Mulla Mohsin Fani[13], Sheikh Baha-ud-din popularly known as Ganjbuksh, Sheikh Yakub Sarfi[14] travelled to Samarkand, Bukhara and Khorezm to learn more about Islamic theology and also to have religious discourses with their spiritual guides. After his return to Kashmir, Yakub Sarfi composed among other works *Muqamat-i-Murshad* in which he describes the life and miracles of his *pir* Sheikh Hussain of Khorezm (Khiva).

The horizon of socio-economic and cultural ties with Central Asia expanded particularly during the benevolent rule of Sultan Zain-ul-Abidin[15] (1420-70 AD). He not only maintained friendly relations with Shah Rukh, son of Timur, and Mirza Abu Said--the Timurid ruler of Trans-Oxiana[16], but also used the same for the material benefit of the Kashmiris. By providing all sorts of facilities to the master-craftsmen of Samarkand and Bukhara, who came to Kashmir during his reign, he helped in popularising their skills among the Kashmiris. He also sent some Kashmiris to Central Asia to get trained in the art of bookbinding and papier-machie[17], thus reviving those industries in Kashmir. Numerous other arts such as window-cutting, stone-cutting, silk, shawl and carpet-

---

10. K.A. Nizami, *op cit*. p. 161.
11. Rafiqi, *op cit*. pp. 31-33, 124.
12. *Ibid*, p. 93.
13. P.N.K. Bamzai, *Kashmir and Central Asia*. p. 217.
14. Rafiqi, *op cit* .pp. 114-17, 118.
15. The popular view that Shahi Khan (Zain-ul-Abidin) had visited the court of Timur as a young prince and stayed in Samarkand for seven long years, has been disputed both by Parmu and Mohibbul Hassan.
    For details see R.K. Parmu, *History of Muslim rule in Kashmir*. Delhi, 1969. p. 159. Mohibbul Hassan : *op cit*. p. 60
16. M.Hasan, *op cit*. pp. 72-73
17. *Ibid*., p. 92.

weaving flourished in the valley during his reign. Such cultural interaction received fresh impetus under Mirza Hyder Dughlat [18], who is reported to have introduced the Central Asian style of dress and diet in Kashmir. Being a man of letters and lover of music himself, Mirza Dughlat encouraged the development of music and fine arts and popularised the use of latticed window work and various musical instruments like lutes, dulcimers, harps and flutes in Kashmir [19]. During his stay in Kashmir Mirza Hyder Dughlat composed his *"Tarikh-i-Rashidi"* the contemporaneous history of Mughal Khans of Central Asia. The Mughal rulers of India who gained supremacy in Kashmir (1586-1753 AD) after Dughlat and the independent Kashmiri Chak rulers, contributed much to the enrichment of its natural beauty by laying out numerous gardens. Combining the indigenous features of beautiful landscape and the Central Asian garden traditions of flowing cascades, fountains and terraces, the Mughal gardens of Kashmir have remained a powerful attraction for both the local people and the visiting tourists.

The incorporation of Kashmir within the fold of Afghan kingdom under Ahmad Shah Abdali in 1753 AD [20] resulted in a more frequent intercourse with Central Asia via Srinagar-Baramulla-Muzaffarabad-Peshawar and Kabul route. Heavy demand for Kashmir shawls among the Central Asian nobility and the upper stratum of Russian society encouraged the Kashmiri shawl traders and manufacturers to settle in the Punjab and Afghanistan[21] wherefrom Central Asia was easily accessible. Two Russians, Filip Yefremov and Rafael Danibegov, and a Bukharan-Abdul Karim, all of whom made an overland journey from Central Asia to Kashmir in the last quarter of the eighteenth century, left an eye-witness account of the life and conditions prevailing in Kashmir under the Pathan governors. Unfortunately little notice has been taken of these accounts in writing the history of Kashmir under the Afghans. Yefremov was struck by the fineness and purity of

---

18. Mirza Hyder Dughlat was born at Tashkent in about 1490-1500 A.D. Drawing lineage from the Chagtai branch of the Mongols, Dughlat was related to Babar on Mother's side.
19. R.K. Parmu, *op cit.* p 226.
20. Kashmir remained under the Pathan rule up to 1819 A.D. when the Sikhs replaced it.
21. Migrations of Kashmiri weavers to Noorpur, Amritsar, Lahore and Peshawar were largely due to the oppressive taxation of shawl goods produced in Kashmir under the Afghan and Sikh rule. According to a nineteenth century estimate about hundred houses were occupied by Kashmiris in Kandhar alone out of a total of 8730 houses. See A.Hamilton, *Afghanistan*. London, 1906. p. 194.

Kashmir shawls [22]. He has described Kashmiris as "a very commercial people" [23] who went as far as Bukhara to trade their goods. A large number of Kashmiris had taken up their residence in Ladakh [24] so as to facilitate their trading with neighbouring Central Asia. From Yefremov's description of the modes of production in Kashmir and Ladakh it becomes clear that the people of both these areas met their dress and food requirements indigenously. The long and loose home made cotton garment worn by Kashmiris has been compared to Russian peasant's shirt [25]. Yefremov did not miss to note the conspicuous absence of cotton and mulberry plantation in Ladakh and the use of fire-pots by Kashmiris. Danibegov's account contains full details about the shawl industry in Kashmir and the taxes levied on it by the Afghan government. He was taken aback on seeing the "most evil system"[26] of polyandry in Ladakh, which has survived till date. Kashmiris have been described as being poor and ill-conditioned,[27] who however did not miss their Friday appointment of getting themselves entertained by boating in Dal Lake[28]. Use of boats and *doongas* (mini house-boats) for visiting Dal Lake and the Mughal gardens around it, has continued to be a favourite pastime with the people of Srinagar even today. Use of Russian-made silks was popular amongst the Ladakhis in Danibegov's time[29]. Similarly Abdul Karim who claims to have visited Kashmir thrice using both the Kabul-Muzaffarabad-Srinagar and Bukhara-Semipalan tinsk-Ili-Aksu-Kashgar-Leh routes [30] found himself at home in the valley. He was so fascinated by its atmosphere that he compared it to the scent of perfumed musk [31]. Near the Dal Lake Abdul Karim found female dancers performing with the approval of the authorities [32]. During the first quarter of the nineteenth century another traveller from Russia, Agha Mehdi Rafailov visited Kashmir at least twice. He lavished praises on the "beautiful, green and fertile land" of Kashmir "abounding in horticulture" and he described its people as "healthy, beautiful, cunning and practical but

22. P.M. Kemp, *Ed* and *Tr, Russian travellers to India and Persia (1624 - 1798)*. p. 69
23. *Ibid.*, p. 83.
24. *Ibid.*, p. 79.
25. *Ibid.*, p. 81.
26. *Ibid.*, p. 121.
27. *Ibid.*, p. 119.
28. P.M. Kemp: *op cit*. p. 120.
29. *Ibid.*, p. 121.
30. C. Schefer, *Histoire de L' Asie Centrale par Mir Abdoul Kerim Boukhary*. p. 236.
31. *Ibid.*, p. 241.
32. *Ibid.*, p. 242.

extremely hospitable" [33]. The circulation of such accounts in Russia not only gave an idea of the people of Kashmir to the Russian peoples but also paved the way for future bilateral intercourse by identifying the routes of communication between the two regions.

A Kashmiri born in the post-eighteenth century era inherited a composite culture that had sprung out of a synthesis of the indigenous and the Central Asian traditions over a period of time. With the introduction of the Islamic mode of government and the Persian as court language in Kashmir under the Sultanate a large number of Persian and Turki words got assimilated into the Kashmiri language. The patronage extended by Zain-ul-Abidin to men of art and letters not only encouraged the people towards creative activity but also helped in the diffusion of diverse literatures. Existence of a number of illustrated manuscripts of Kashmiri origin in numerous museums and libraries throughout the world speaks about the flourishing state of art of calligraphy in Kashmir in the past. The fame acquired by Kashmiri artisans in their art of wood-craving, door and window panel-making *(panjras), Khatam bandi* (ornamented ceilings), papiermachie like kalamdans (pen cases), flower vases etc, brick and tile works, namdah, carpet and shawl-making is partly due to their adoption of Central Asian patterns. Even today the Kashmiri carpet manufacturers find it more convenient to introduce their goods in the market as Bukhara, Samarkand and Ferghana carpets. Numerous such sign-boards are displayed in Srinagar by the Kashmiri artisans. The polished tiles used in the tomb of Madin Sahib near Srinagar, painted ceilings, carved doorways and latticed windows that are still visible in various mosques in Kashmir, have their parallels in the tombs and buildings of Samarkand, Bukhara and Khiva. Though shawl making was not unknown to ancient Kashmir, such innovations as the weaving of colour pattern on the loom itself and needle embroidery are commonly attributed to the immigrant Central Asians. Seeing that a loom could produce only one patterned shawl in about a year's time, one Armenian merchant Khwaja Yusuf is reported to have introduced a low cost process of needle embroidery with the help of a Kashmiri, Ali Baba, in the early nineteenth century [34]. This resulted in a large scale production of shawls. Occupying an admirable place in the Central

---

33. *AVPR.F. Spb. Glav. Arkhiv*(USSR). 11-26, 1811. d.4.L.11-12; 11-3, 1811, d.5, L-12. Cited in D.Kaushik, *India and Central Asia* p. 83.
34. John Irwin, *Shawls : A study in Indo-European influences*. London, 1955. p. 3

Asian and Russian nobility, Kashmir shawls formed an essential ingredient in the tray of presents exchanged between the ruling classes on various occasions. While announcing his capture of Khojend, General Cherniaev included two such shawls in his basket of presents that were sent along with a letter to Khudayar Khan, the ruler of Kokand [35]. Similarly when the Amir of Bukhara was invited to attend the coronation ceremony of the Tsar Emperor at St. Petersburgh, he deputed his heir-apparent with costly presents including shawls [36]. That the Bukhara ruler had sent jwellery and Kashmir shawls for use of the Tsarina[37] indicates the .prestigious position held by Kashmir shawls in Russia at that time. Even as late as on April 16, 1920 the Beg of Baisun is reported to have sent twenty pieces of Kashmir shawls as a part of his annual tribute to the Amir of Bukhara[38]. That shawls in different sizes and ornamented patterns were commonly used in Bukhara, Kokand, Turkestan and Russia as turbans, handkerchiefs, stockings and leggings, door and window curtains, waist belts, quilt covers, shrouds for tombs, etc., that is in every walk of life, becomes clear from Moorcroft's account of shawl manufactures of Kashmir[39]. The Central Asian merchants of Kokandi and Andijani origin, who thronged the markets of Ladakh and Kashmir even upto later years of the nineteenth century, made it a point to purchase small quantities of shawls for their use as turbans.

The discovery of certain manuscripts of Kashmiri origin in various libraries of Leningrad, Uzbekistan and Tadjikistan throws fresh light on the developed state of calligraphic and miniature painting art in Kashmir which found a receptive market in Central Asia. On the examination of these manuscripts certain Soviet scholars have concluded that the art of book illustration had reached a developed stage in the eighteenth and early nineteenth century [40]. Handmade and illustrated manuscripts made in Kashmir found their way to Central Asia through the medium of travelling merchants and Haj pilgrims. The abundance of illustrations related to the text and the lavish use of floral ornamentation on binding covers made such manuscripts more popular with the Central Asian nobility, who acquired the same for their personal libraries. A Kashmiri

35. Sodhi, Hukm Singh, *History of Khokand*. Lahore, 1876. p.25.
36. *Foreign. Secret E*. July 1883. 40-41.
37. *Ibid*.
38. Gustav Krist, *Alone through the forbidden land*. London, 1939. p. 176.
39. J.Irwin, *op cit*. Appendix. pp. 37-45.
40. A.Adamova and T.Greck, *Miniatures from Kashmiri paintings*. Leningrad, 1976. p.61.

copy of *Mahbub-ul-Qutab* (Heart's darling : a collection of moral tales and anecdotes) authored by one Barkhurdari *ibn* Mahmud Turkman Farahi, was in the possession of the Amir of Bukhara [41]. An inscription recorded on its first folio reveals that it was transcribed in Kashmir in Rabi II and 1112 AH (September-October 1700 AD) [42]. Similarly the last folio of another manuscript namely *Matla As-sadain wa Majma al bahrain* indicates that it had been purchased by one Nazar Mohammad Farghani in Kashmir[43]. It is important to note here that this work which was devoted to the reign of Timur and Timurids and authored by a Central Asian-Abdur Razak Samarkandi, in 1482 AD should have been reproduced in Kashmir. That this exchange of literary and other religious books continued even as late as the nineteenth century becomes clear from the narrative of Wolff's travels in Central Asia. Wolff has recorded that when he wrote a life-sketch of the Prophet Muhammad at the request of the Amir of Bukhara, it was copied in large numbers in Bukhara and several copies of the same were sent by a Kashmiri merchant, then in Bukhara, to his home [44]. Numerous other manuscripts like *Diwan* of Hafiz, Saddi's *Bostan*, Jami's *Yusuf and Zulaikha* which are preserved in the Academy of Sciences at Leningrad and Uzbekistan, also originated from Kashmir between late eighteenth and mid-nineteenth century . This not only testifies to the popularity of Persian literary works in the pre-modern Kashmir but also to their production by Kashmiri calligraphists and artist for consumption in Central Asian markets. *Kalami Kitabs* (hand made manuscripts) and calligraphed copies of Quran, that were produced in Kashmiri homes, formed an important item of export to Central Asia even in the late nineteenth century[45]. A manuscript of Rumi's *mathnavi* which was copied by one Muhammad Kashmiri, is still preserved in the library of the Institute of Oriental Studies, Tajik Academy of Sciences, Dushanbe[46]. The library also possesses a MS entitled *Ansabe-e-Salah,* which is a collection of the writings of Syed Mir Ali Hamdani including his letter written to Sultan Qutub-ud-Din of Kashmir[47]. The Firdausi library in Dushanbe, the capital of Tadjikistan, too possess some manuscripts of Kashmiri origin. These are *Diwan* of

41. *Ibid.*, p. 71.
42. *Ibid.*, p. 70.
43. *Ibid.*, p. 73.
44. J.Wolff, *Narrative of a mission to Bukhara*. London,1846. p. 278.
45. J.E.T. Aitchison: *Handbook of trade products of Leh*. p. 140.
46. Pandit, K.N *My Tajik friends; a travelogue of Soviet Central Asia*. New Delhi, 1985. p. 32.
47. *Ibid.*

Ghani Kashmiri, *Diwan* of one Ismail Kashmiri which was copied by Mulla Muhammad Rajab *ibn* Mulla Abdul Walli of Herat in 1826 AD, a MS of Quran with a Persian commentary on its margin and a MS entitled *Zakhirat-ul-mulk* authored by Syed Mir Ali Hamadani, which was copied by Kashmiri calligraphist in 877 AH, that is 1472 AD.[48] That the Soviet academicians are evincing keen interest in the study of such literary works produced in Kashmir, becomes clear from the publication of the *Diwan* of Ghani Kashmiri, a famous Kashmiri poet, in Tajik script. Legendary themes of *Shirin and Farhad, Yusuf and Zulaikha, Laila and Majnun, Sohrab and Rustam, Shahnama* of Firdaus which were commonly narrated and sung in the towns and villages of Kashmir became more popular after their adaptations and translations by Kashmiri poets in the local language became freely available by the end of the last century.

The incorporation of Central Asia and Kashmir into the Russian and British empires respectively did not, however, prevent the peoples of these regions from sharing common habits of dress, food and amusements. Gold or silver embroidered skull cap popularly known as *Kallapush* in Kashmir and used both by Hindu and Muslim ladies, was akin to the *Kallapush* (skull cap) used by Uzbek men[49]. Though its use in Kashmir is presently limited to being the head-dress of elderly ladies, *Kallapush* still forms an essential ingredient of the bridal dress of Kashmiri Pandit ladies. Similarly the head-gear of Tajik woman called *Qasaba* is Typical of the village woman in Kashmir, where too it is known by the same name, viz; *Qasaba*. To quote a modern Kashmiri writer : " The *chapan* of a Central Asian, the *choga* of a Gilgiti, the long goatskin overall of a Ladakhi and the loose long *phiran* of a Kashmiri belong to the same parent stock''[50]. A twentieth century traveller in Central Asia found the use of *manqal* (a copper basin holding burning charcoal) universal amongst the Turkomans, sarts and Kirghizs living in Turkmania, Uzbekistan and the Pamirs respectively[51]. The same practice is still prevalent among the Kashmiris who use *manqals* (earthern braziers containing burning coals) to warm up their bodies. There is every possibility of the modern

48. *Ibid.*, pp. 46, 59.
49. According to Col. L.F. Kostenko *Kallapushes* (Tubeteikas) are caps that just cover the surface of the shaven head, being made of Russian chintz or locally made silks. These are lined with silk embroidery. With turbans wrapped around it, the *Kallapushes* constituted a head-dress of pride and luxury for all the Muslims of Central Asia. See his Turkestan Region. 1880. Vol. 3. p. 27.
50. P.N.K. Bamzai, *Kashmir and Central Asia*. p. 10.
51. Gustav Krist, *op cit*. p. 33.

Kashmiri *kangri* (an earthern firepot covered with willow work) having been adapted from the original *manqal* which is still used but mainly by the lower rungs of Kashmiri society. Both the Central Asians and Kashmiris drink the same hot tea in the same type of *piala* (a big porcelain cup) and relish the same *pillau* (stuffed rice with meat). The people in both the regions are rice-eaters and non-vegetarian. Their utensils are remarkably similar. The *Samovar* which stands for a tea-urn in both the Russian and Kashmiri languages, continues to be a popular institution among the people of this whole region. Indian tea, spices and other manufactured goods like muslin, shawls and brocades were so popular among the Central Asians that the Tsarist preventive measures to restrict the import of these articles from British India did not meet with total success. The people used to frequent *chai-khanas* (tea houses) for gossip and fun. Male *batchas* (dancing boys) were a common source of amusement. A British traveller, A. Hardinge, while passing through Central Asia in 1888 witnessed some of the performances of *batchas* in Charjui which were enjoyed much by the natives. According to him, *batcha*-boys continued to be a recognised institution in Bukhara and were even tolerated within Russian Turkestan[52]. The popularity of *batcha* dance in Central Asia had a parallel in the Kashmiri folk dance where male dancers still amuse the audience. The musical instruments used in Kashmir like santoor, pipe*(surnai)*, rabab, *sarangi* and *tumbaknari* (the single membrane drum) were virtually the same as those used in Central Asia. The use of tobacco either by smoking *chillim* (hubble-bubble) or by chewing *nas* (fine *powdered* tobacco) was common among the people in both the regions. The hubble-bubbles are practically the same even today. Both in Kashmir and Central Asia houses were covered with mud roofs which were often used as the ground for planting poppy and lily flowers. It was a delightful experience to see the house tops full of flowers in different colours during the spring season. The abundance of apples, grapes, walnuts, mulberries, apricots and other delicious fruits in Russian Central Asia finds its parallel in the luxuriant and variegated horticultural produce of Kashmir. Similarly, chinar the famous shady tree is peculiar only to this region.

Apart from such common sociological and ecological traits which act as the binding links between the two peoples, the present day Kashmiri society has assimilated its Central Asian connection in other

---

52. *Foreign. Secret F.* January 1889. 233 -235.

forms too. A large number of families bearing such surnames as Qadiri, *Pirzada, Akhun, Beg, Kashgari, Turki, Bukhari, Nakshbandi, Mughal, Gani, Mirza, Qazilbash, Baba, Jilani, Hamadani* etc. are a living example of the cultural assimilation that took place as result of immigration of Central Asians into Kashmir in medieval times. Whereas *Akhuns* are descendants of those who acted as religious teachers in early times, *Bukharis* like those of *Qadiris, Andrabis* and *Mantiqis* draw their lineage from those syeds who migrated to Kashmir from Bukhara and Turkestan during the Timurid rule. The Jammu and Kashmir Census Report for 1911 records the population of *Turks, Begs, Bukharis, Mirzas, Qazilbashes, Akhuns, Babas, Nakashbandis* and *Qadiris* then living in this state as 2407, 6831,9237,1336,48,17436,11267,35 and 262 respectively[53]. Those Kashmiris who used to trade with Kashgar(in Chinese Turkestan) or acted as accountants to the Turki merchants in Kashmir, received the suffixes of *Kashgari (s)* and *Turki (s)* respectively[54]. Several Kashmiri Pandit families bear these surnames even today.

The conspicuous role played by the *Nakshbandi* family in Kashmir during the period of this study deserves special mention. They not only maintained close contact with their *murids* (followers) in Central Asia but also remained quite active in the socio-political life in Kashmir. They were ahead of their fellow Kashmiris in intellect and thrift which factor facilitated their recognition as an aristocratic and a respectful family. Commanding a large following in Russian Turkestan they proved of much service to the British at a time when their sources of intelligence in Kashmir and Central Asia were quite negligible. *Nakshbandis* were the direct descendents of one Khoja Abdul Rahim of Tashkent who had withdrawn to Kashmir following the dispossession of his patrimonial rule in Tashkent[55]. By dint of his high learning and Khoja lineage Abdul Rahim soon came to be accepted as a respected Pir in Kashmir. He is also reported to have introduced Kashgarian fine wool into Kashmir[56]. On one of his usual jaunts to the valley Abdul Rahim brought some woollen ropes and felts from Yarkand which were later found to be made of such

---

53. Matin-uz-Zaman Khan, *Census of India, 1911; Kashmir*. Part I: Report. Lucknow,1912. p. 233. Part II:Tables. Lukhnow, 1912. pp. 126-132. Total population of Muslims in J&K State in 1911 was 23, 98, 320.
54. Muhammad Din Fauq, *Tarikh-i-aqwami Kashmir*. Lahore, 1934. pp. 25, 37.
55. Moorcroft to Metcalfe dated 12 May 1821. *Foreign. Political*. 10 October 1823. 21.
56. See Moorcroft's note on Shawl wool trade. 1821. *Foreign Political*. 10 October 1823. 27.

fine wool as was suited for the making of Kashmir shawl[57]. With this discovery Kashmiri traders started importing shawl wool from Yarkand in large quantities[58] to supplement their supplies that were received from Changthang and Lhassa. The Pathan Governors of Kashmir granted extensive jagirs of land which fetched an annual income of about ten thousand rupees in favour of Abdul Rahim Nakshbandi[59]. On his death his son, Shah Niyaz, inherited these jagirs. He earned more fame by using the income from these lands for such benevolent acts as the founding of Khanqah-i-Nakshband (in 1212 A.H)[60], and several other mosques as also the digging of canal named *Daulat-i-Kul* probably on account of the high expenditure involved in it[61]. But soon after the occupation of Kashmir by Ranjit Singh in 1819 A.D., Shah Niyaz retreated to Ladakh following the confiscation of his jagirs by the Sikhs[62]. There he found himself treated with much respect by the local people and also the visiting Central Asian traders and pilgrims. Shah Niyaz's stay in Ladakh facilitated the renewal of his contacts with Central Asia--his original home. It was at Leh that Moorcroft came into contact with Shah Niyaz and used his influence for neutralising the opposition offered by the Kashmiri traders and Ladakh administration to his commercial and political ventures. Well-versed in Turki dressed in elegant Central Asian robes and wearing Russian leather boots Shah Niyaz came handy to the willy Moorcroft for extending British influence over the Central Asian trade and politics. That Shah Niyaz's word carried weight in Ferghana is indicated by the despatch of his disciple Peerzada to the court of Omar Khan, the ruler of Kokand Khanate(via Leh-Yarkand route) with the object of facilitating a favourable reception of Moorcroft's party there.[63] On his part Moorcroft reciprocated by interceding with Maharaja Ranjit

---

57. *Ibid.*
58. *Ibid.*
    Shawl wool of Yarkand and Turfan continued to be imported into Kashmir from Chinese Turkestan as late as till 1940s
59. Moorcroft to Metcalfe 12 May 1821. *op. cit.*
60. Muhammad Din Fauq, *op cit* . p. 152.
61. *Ibid.*
62. Moorcroft, *Travels*. Vol.1. p. 242.
63. Moorcroft to Metcalfe 12 May 1821. *op cit.*

Singh for the restoration of Shah Niyaz's jagirs in Kashmir, which request was later granted.[64]

The Nakshband mosque situated near Srinagar holds a prestigious position as one of the important Muslim shrines in Kashmir. The martyrs of Kashmir freedom struggle (1931-47) too stand buried within its compound. After Shah Niyaz his sons, Muhammad Shah and Ahmad Shah, acted as hospitable hosts to important European visitors coming to the valley. Besides, the British authorities in India were regularly posted by them with all local news of importance. However, they did not let their British connection come in the way of their dealings with the Dogra rulers of Kashmir. By dint of their wit, wisdom and drive the Nakshbandi family has continued to enjoy privileged position in Kashmir as late as the present century. A Christian missionary, Joseph Wolff who visited Kashmir in 1832, has described Muhammad Shah Nakshbandi as "the greatest murshid of Turkestan"[65] and the "Chief mullah"[66] of Kashmir. Of the descendants of Khoja Muhammad Shah two held the posts of Tehsildars under the Dogras. Khoja Salam Shah made a name as Assistant Governor of Kashmir under Maharaja Hari Singh (1925-47) by his vigorous anti-hoarding and black-marketing compaign in Srinagar. A Kashmiri proverb "*Salam Shahun Swach*" coined by the local people to describe a situation of relief from scarcity and high prices, stands out as a mark of remembrance for the measures introduced by Salam Shah to relieve the people from misery of scarcity, famine and price rise. Similarly Khoja Hassan Shah Nakshbandi, the grandson of Ahmad Shah, was one of the few enlightened Muslims who dared to petition the then

---

64. Muhammad-ud-din Fauq, *op cit*. pp. 153-54.
    According to W.M. Young, the Secretary to Punjab Government, Majaraja Ranjit Singh sanctioned a jagir valuing five thousand rupees per annum in favour of Khoja Shah Niaz. Out of which sum one thousand rupees were set apart for the family shrine (Nakshband mosque).
    See W.M. Young to C.Grant, Secretary, Foreign Department, GOI, 28 Sept. 1882. *Foreign. A. Pol. E.* Oct. 1882. 28-31
    According to Charles Ellison Bates the village of Bryn situated along the banks of Dal Lake near Srinagar belonged to the family of Muhammad Shah Nakshbandi as their Jagir.
    See his *Gazetteer of Kashmir*. London, 1873. p. 372.
65. J. Wolff, *Narrative of a mission to Bukhara*. London, 1846. p.222.
66. *Ibid*. p 15.

Vicerory Lord Reading during his visit to Kashmir in 1924 seeking the upliftment of the oppressed masses in Kashmir.[6] Enjoying numerous privileges and holding an important place as a jagirdar and also as a member of the State Rice Board constituted by the Maharaja in 1921[68], Hasan Shah Nakshbandi's bold action in publicly airing the grievances of his fellow countrymen was bound to evoke a sharp reaction from the Kashmir ruler. Hassan Shah's jagir valuing four thousand rupees a year was confiscated and his son Noor Shah (Tehsildar) was dismissed from the State services.[69] However these privileges were restored to Nakshbandis by Maharaja Hari Singh but only after securing apologies from them. According to an eye-witness account Hassan Shah Nakshbandi attended the royal Durbar on August 25, 1927 and offered *nazrana* (tribute) and written apology to the Maharaja after which he took his seat among the jagirdars.[70]

During the nineteenth century the Nakshbandis constituted a close cultural and emotional link between Kashmir and Central Asia. The British missions enroute to Central Asia would make it a point to secure the letters of recommendation from Nakshbandi brothers for their numerous disciples in Turkestan so as to facilitate their travels and adventures in that forbidden land. Similarly the Central Asian pilgrims during their transit journey to Srinagar enroute to Mecca or back home would not miss their appointment with their Nakshbandi *pirs* in Kashmir and would often stay with them. One of the sons of Muhammad Shah Nakshbandi was married to a Turkestani bride while others had taken Kashmiri wives. Syed Yakub Khan Tora, the official envoy of the ruler

---

67. The memorandum listing about seventeen demands was signed by the leading Muslims of Kashmir and presented to the Viceroy during his official visit to valley in October 1924. Other signatories to the memorandum were Khwaja Saad-ud-Din Shawl, Mirwaiz Kashmir, Maulavi Ahmadullah, Mirwaiz Hamadani, Agha Syed Hussain Shah Jalali, Mufti sharif-ud-Din, Khwaja Hassan Shah Mahandi.
See M,Y. Saraf, *Kashmiris fight for freedom*, Lahore,1978. Vol. 1. pp. 336-338.
68. G.H Khan, *Freedom movement in Kashmir* 1931-40. New Delhi, 1980. pp. 80-109.
69. *Ibid*. p. 95.
This action of the State Government was strongly condemned by the Muslims whether residing in or outside Kashmir valley. According to M.Y. Saraf, Noor Shah Nakshabandi was compelled to proceed on forced leave and his written protest against this unilateral action was treated as a resignation. After this he was retired from service. See his *Kashmiris fight for freedom*. p. 339.
70. Personal diary of Hafiz Mohammad Ismail(1907-1950) dated 25 August 1927(MS) cited in G.H.Khan, *Ibid*. p. 98.

of Kashgaria, during his visits to Kashmir in 1872 and 1875 stayed at Gafur Shah Nakshbandi's house. When the Chinese reoccupied Kashgaria in 1878, Ghulam shah Nakshbandi promptly informed the British Officer on Special Duty in Kashmir, F.Henvey, about the flight of Beg Kuli Beg, the last independent ruler of Kashgaria, to Tashkent.[71] While in Kashmir the Nakshbandis closely kept themselves abreast of the political developments in Central Asia--their place of origin. They used their position to their full advantage by acting as the confidants of the British Indian authorities and the agents of the Dogra rulers of Kashmir at the same time. By playing such a dual role and without arousing the suspicions of the British or Dogra masters, the Nakshbandis exhibited their political acumen and the art of conducting diplomatic assignment.

Among the numerous Kashmiri visitors to Central Asia during the nineteenth century, names of Mohan Lal, Ahmad Shah Nakashbandi and Mehta Sher Singh deserve special mention, because all of them have recorded their impressions about the political and socio-economic conditions then prevailing in that area.[72] Whereas Mohan Lal and Ahmad Shah were employed for their journeys in Central Asia by Alexander Burnes (in 1831-33) and Major Mac Gregor (in 1852) respectively for promoting the general British cause in that region, Mehta Sher Singh was deputed by Maharaja Ranbir Singh of Kashmir on a secret fact-finding mission to Russian Central Asia. Both Mohan Lal and Burnes came across a number of Kashmiri merchants at Meshed[73] and Bukhara[74] respectively. According to Burnes the Kashmiri rafugars(shawl dorners) travelled long distances to reach Russia where they used to alter the designs of their shawl goods in accordance with tastes and demands of their Russian and Central Asian customers.[75]

---

71. *Foreign. Political A.* January 1880. 1.
72. For further details see Mohan Lal, *Travels in the Punjab, Afghanistan and Turkestan.* London, 1846(Reprinted at Calcutta,1977).
(Mohan Lal belonged to a Kashmiri Pandit family that had settled in Delhi during the Mughal rule). Ahmad Shah Nakshbandi, "Narrative of travels through Yarkand, Kokan, Bokhara and Kabul". *Journal of Asiatic Society of Bengal*. 1856, pp. 344-357. Mehta Sher Singh, *Safar nama*(Urdu MS, JKA)
73. Mohan Lal, *Travels*. p.111.
74. A. Burnes, *Travels into Bokhara*. Oxford Unigversity Press, 1973(Reprint). Vol. 1. p.298.
75. *Ibid.*Vol. 2. p. 435.

The incidence of slave trade between Chitral and Central Asia during the nineteenth century lent yet another dimension to the social intercourse between the two regions. The existence of a custom with the Chief of Chitral to present slaves belonging to his territory and the adjoining principalitities of Gilgit, Yasin and Hunza to the Mir of Badakhshan has been reported both by Burnes[76] and Faiz Buksh.[77] The Badakshi ruler in turn sold these slaves in the markets of Balkh, Kabul and Bukhara and made large profits from this transaction. Being hardy and industrious such slaves were usually employed by their lazy Uzbek and Turki masters as labour for cultivating lands, herding of cattle and livestock and in other day-to-day manual work. That this feudal practice of slavery vanished in the Central Asian Khanates after the establishment of Tsarist administration in Russian Turkestan[78], is further substantiated by the report of a contemporary Indian traveller. During his visit to Kokand in 1879 Shah Khushwakt[79] saw many former slaves of Chitral, Yasin and Gilgit living a free life there. They were found to be cultivating lands and owing shops.[80] It is not, however, clear as to whether Chitrali female slaves who were employed in the *harems* of the Central Asian feudal lords, were also freed from bondage or not.

In short, the movement of men and materials like pilgrims, slaves, books, shawls, gold tillas, Russian textiles, Kokandi silk, Bukharan rumals (silk handkerchiefs) and coral formed an essential ingredient of the socio-economic intercourse between Central Asia and Kashmir. Such Russian items as copper coin (Kopek), stripped *atlas* and drill cloth were popularly known in Kashmir as *Bugh-i-Russki, latha Rus-ka, Shaitan Tari* respectively. The import of Bukharan or Kokandi *tillas* (gold coins) and Russian gold rubles into Kashmir via Yarkand-Leh route[81] in sufficiently large quantities ensured a regular supply of bullion

76. *Ibid*. p. 209.
77. Faiz Buksh, *Confidential report on Badakshan, Balkh and Bokhara*, Lahore, 1871. p. 27.
78. Slave trading was abolished by general Kaufmann in Russian Turkestan in 1868.
79. *Foreign. Secret*. November 1879. 152-191. Shah Khushwakt had been deputed by Biddulph, the British Officer on Special Duty in Gilgit, in May 1878 on a spying mission to Hunza, Kabul, Bukhara, Samarkand and Kokand.
80. *Ibid*.
81. Indo-Central Asian traders used to import Russian gold currency and paper rubles to India in large quantities, as the same proved to be an easy medium of transferring their capital to India without any risk. In 1880s when Shikarpuri traders had to close down their business in Russian Central Asia, they retraced their steps to India via Kashgar-Leh route bringing alongwith them enough gold in coins and dust. *(For further details see Chapter 2)*.

to the jewellers in Kashmir. Though the poor and backward condition of the people in Kashmir did not permit them to use the gold ornaments, yet Russian gold coins later substituted by the English sovereigns were presented on auspicious occasions of marriage in Kashmir even in the recent past. Central Asian Haj pilgrims continued to flock to Kashmir enroute to Meccabraving all the hazards of strenuous journey over the mountain ranges, hot plains of India and fatigues of sea-travel to reach their destination. Though the development of rail and road transport facilities in Russian Turkestan resulted in a diversion of this traffic, yet such visitors could be found in Kashmir even in the early years of the twentieth century but in small numbers. The closure of Kashgar-Kokand road following political disturbances did not prevent a party of Kokandi Haj pilgrims from coming to Kashmir via a longer and circuituous route of Almati (Vernoe), Ili, Aksu, Yarkand, and Leh in 1869[82]. During 1894-95 an Andijani, Ahmad Khoja by name, lost as many as three members of his family out of a total of eight including himself, his wife and one daughter[83] in the course of such a journey via Kashmir and Ladakh. But such frightening experiences did not daunt other Central Asians from using this difficult route which can also be ascribed to their keen desire to see Kashmir. Being peaceful and devoid of robbers and free from political turmoil, which was not the case in Central Asian Khanates, the Kashmir route was preferred by the Central Asians intending to undertake a Haj pilgrimage. Obviously the overland Yarkand-Leh-Kashmir-India route was a safe passage for the Central Assian travellers who mostly belonged to the rich strata of society and carried with them large quantities of bullion and precious items, like carpets and silks to meet their travel expenses.

The religious institutions in Bukhara attracted the Kashmiri scholars who went there to acquire knowledge about Islamic theology. That Kashmiris used to travel as far as Central Asia in pursuit of knowledge even as late as the nineteenth century, is indicated by the account of Vambery who visited Central Asia in 1863.[84] Vambery also noticed some Kashmiri mendicants mixing freely with the Central Asian pilgrims at Meshed.[85] An English missionary-cum traveller, Arthur Neve, found during his ride through Banihal in the late nineteenth century a Muslim

82. *Foreign Pol. A*. Sept.1869. 232-234.
83. *Foreign. Secret F*. November 1895. 669-74.
84. A.Vambery, *Travels in Central Asia*. London, 1864. P.365.
85. A.Vambery, *Sketches of Central Asia*. London, 1868. p.16.

mendicant wearing "a tall pointed Turkoman hat of black fur, a parti-coloured cloak and loose Afgan trousers".[86] There is every likelihood of this Muslim Sufi named Buland Shah, who had travelled widely in Bukhara and Turkestan,[87] being a Central Asian by Birth. He must have taken up his abode in Kashmir. Later, Kashmir's scenic beauty lured the famous Uzbek poet, Furqat (1858-1909) too in the late nineteenth century. Furqat after spending some time in Kashmir migrated to Yarkand to spend his last days there. One of his poems "In Kashmir" was published by the Tashkent paper *Turkistan Viloyatining Gazeti* during 1896-97.

With the establishment of the Khoja rule in Chinese Turkestan (1865-77) under Yakub Beg of Kokand, the visits of Andijani and Bukharan traders to the marketing centres of Leh, Srinagar and Amritsar from their trading marts at Yarkand and Kashgar, became more frequent. Besides, numerous Kokandi dignitaries, who had followed the fortunes of Yakub Beg to Kashgar, began to visit Kashmir occassionally. When Buzarg Khan Tora, who belonged to the ruling Khoja family of Kokand, was totally dispossessed of power by Yakub Beg in Kashgaria, he came to Ladakh in the autumn of 1868.[88] In fact Yakub Beg sought to exile his rival Khoja chief from his kingdom by sending him nominally on a pilgrimage to Mecca via Kashmir. But Buzarg Khan chose to return to his home in Kokand via Kashmir, Punjab and Bukhara [89] rather than go on Haj. That the Central Asian nobility and the affluent people preferred to travel through the safer Kashmir-Yarkand-Kokand route rather than the insecure Kabul-Bukhara route, is further proved by the way a Kokandi envoy in India made his return journey via Kashmir even though the Afghan chiefs had made arrangements for his passage through their territory. Similarly Beg Kuli Beg, the last Khoja ruler of Kashgaria when pursued by Chinese troops in early 1878 sent his treasure valuing more than one and a quarter Lakh rupees to India via the Karakoram pass through his trusted empolyees [90]. He was anxious to establish friendly relations with the Kashmir ruler, possibly to prepare the way for his permanent settlement in Kashmir. But when Beg Kuli Beg sent some

---

86. A Neve, *Thirty years in Kashmir*. London, 1913.pp.54-55.
87. *Ibid.*
88. *Foreign. Pol. A.* Sept.1868. 216-217.
89. Cayley to Thronton, 12 October 1869. *Foreign. SJ.* 1869. 350-361.
90. *Ladakh Diary* 15-28 February 1878. *Foreign. Pol. A.* May 1878. 256-275.

presents to Maharaja Ranbir Singh of Kashmir from Lahore, the latter returned the same treating the former ruler of Kashgaria as an exile and a mere traveller[91]. Following this the fugitive Khoja chief retreated to Kokand.

It was during one of his visits to Kashmir in 1875 that Syed Yakub Tora, the accredited envoy of Yakub Beg (ruler of Kashgaria) requested Maharaja Ranbir Singh to restore the Jagirs [92] which his ancestors had possessed in Kamraj (Baramulla district) but had since lapsed from his control. The Maharaja granted this request only after the British Indian government interceded on behalf of Yakub Khan Tora. In a bid to please his British masters, the Kashmir ruler ordered an annual cash payment of ten thousand rupees and grant of land yielding eleven thousand rupees annually, with effect from March 12, 1875.[93] Following this Yakub Khan Tora stationed his family and agents in the valley for collecting the payment and also to recover the revenues accruing from the sanctioned jagir. But once his political master, Yakub Beg was no more on the scene in Kashgaria, Yakub Khan Tora wanted to take up his abode in Kashmir. In 1878, he tried heard to secure British permission to settle permanently in Kashmir[94]. His offer to serve the British interests in Balkh, Badakshan, Bukhara, Afghanistan, Kashgar and Russian Turkestan did not produce the desired result. However, in view of his past services in promoting the British cause in Kashgaria, the British Indian authorities sanctioned in 1882 an annual allowance of ten thousand rupees in favour of Yakub Khan Tora simultaneously forfeiting all his claims on the Kashmir government[95].

The case of two Central Asian princes, each belonging to the ruling family of Bukhara and Kokand, who in the year 1880 were granted political asylum by the British Indian government, makes an interesting reading. Whereas Syed Abdul Malik Tora, the eldest son of Amir of Bukhara had rebelled against his father, Abdul Karim Khan was related to Khudayar Khan--the ex-ruler of Kokand Khanate. Both of them were

---

91. *Foreign. Political A.* June 1882. 355-388.
92. *Foreign. Secret.* May 1875. 118-124.
93. *Foreign. A. Polittical E.* October 1882. 7-25. Syed Yakub Khan Tora received twenty one thousand rupees annually from 12 March 1875 till 31 August 1882, from the Kashmir Durbar.
94. *Foreign. Secret.* June 1878. 35-44.
95. *Foreign. A Political E.* October 1882. 7-25.

not only allowed to settle in Peshawar but also provided with a fat amount of annual subsidy to meet their personal expenses. From the year 1880 when the Bukharan prince migrated to Punjab[96], till his death in 1909, hardly a year passed when he did not come to Kashmir to spend the summer months there. In doing so he had to seek annual permission from the British authorities who did not let him settle permanently in Kashmir. The extent of his emotional attachment with Kashmir can be gauged from the fact that he took up his residence at Abbotabad, which though outside the borders of Kashmir was still nearer to the place of his longing. Each summer Abdul Malik Tora visited Kashmir alongwith his large family. Similarly his Kokandi companion, Abdul Karim Khan , developed intimate relations with Amanul Mulk, the Mehtar of Chitral, soon after his settlement in Peshawar. Both of them used to exchange presents frequently[97]. Karim Khan even laid his covetous eye upon the daughter of Aman-ul-Mulk and he often sent Abdul Gaffar Beg, the ex-Dewan Begi of Uratippa, to Chitral for negotiating this marriage[98]. Though Karim Khan did not succeed in securing the hand of Aman-ul-Mulk's daughter, he was given a girl belonging to the Mehtar of Chitral's family in marriage[99]. The establishment of such matrimonial ties between the ruling families of Kokand and Chitral spoke of the existing social bonds between the two regions. Certain Muslim priests (pirs) in Chitral such as Shahzada Lais had their followers *(murids)* in Ferghana and there existed a regular inter-course between them.

The Anglo-Russian rivalry over Central Asia lent new dimensions to such social intercourse. Though the restrictive policies of the Russian and British governments inhibited the traditional movement of people between the two regions, yet the imperialist expansion in this area also provided an impetus to the local chiefs and princes to forge new friendships. Fearful of Russian invasion the Central Asian rulers sent their emissaries to India with the object of securing British aid. From the Indian side Maharaja Ranbir Singh of Kashmir and Safdar Ali, the Chief of Hunza despatched several envoys to meet the Russians in Turkestan and to develop friendship with them in a bid to check the British thrust. On their part both the Tsarist and the British governments employed

96. *Foreign. Secret.* June 1880. 139-144.
97. *Foreign. Secret F.* April 1890. 32-33.
98. *Foreign. Secret E.* March 1884. 212-214.
99. *Foreign. Frontr. B.* April 1892. 107-111.

native traders and adventures for communication with their prospective allies (chiefs) in India and Central Asia. In such a power game the common Indians, Kashmiris and Central Asians were engaged in secret missions. The key to their success in collecting authentic and up-to-date information relevant to the strategic interests of their antagonistic employers lay only in the traditional mutual and harmonious relations that already existed between the peoples of India and Central Asia. One Mohammad Rahim of Bukhara proved of much use to Ney Elias, the British officer stationed at Ladakh during his stay there in 1882[100]. Similarly, one Sheikh Gulam Raza, a Persian by birth served the same purpose for the Russians. During his stay in Srinagar for a few months, Raza had frequent meetings with the Governor of Kashmir, Dewan Badri Nath and other local people[101]. The doubts cast by the then British officer on Special Duty in Kashmir, Oliver St. John, about Raza's political antecedents[102] received confirmation from the accounts of an Indian traveller, Aziz-ud-Din, who met Raza at Meshed in 1884. During their conversation Raza had spoken about his visit to India and Kashmir in the preceding year in connection with the business entrusted to him by the Russian Consul at Meshed[103]. Towards the end of the nineteenth century one Kabir Shah, a Kashmiri residing at Tashkent accompanied a Russian mission under Colonel Polotsov on their overland journey to India via Gilgit-Srinagar route. Being conversant with the local language and people, Kabir Shah came in handy to the Russians in their probing adventures in Kashmir and on its frontiers. Similarly in 1904, the British political Agent in Chitral, Captain R.L. Kennion, deputed two Chitrali servants of Pir Shahzada Lais to Kokand ostensibly to collect dues from his *murids* in Ferghana but actually to obtain intelligence about the Russian military activity in Central Asia[104].

On his part Maharja Ranbir Singh played a key role in promoting the cause of cultural exchange between Kashmir and Russian Central Asia. He was the first Dogra ruler to establish direct liaison with the Russians in Central Asia by sending trusted emissaries carrying messages of goodwill and friendship. He continued to maintain such relations throughout

100. *Foreign. A Political E.* October 1883. 62-65.
101. *Foreign. Secret E.* September 1883. 224
102. *Ibid.*
103. *L.M.'s report of travels in Central Asia, 1884-85*. Calcuta, 1886. L.M. (Lambert's man) *alias* Aziz-ud-Din was deputed by the British Indian authorities to Central Asia on an intelligence mission.
104. *Foreign. Secret F.*, May 1905. 242 - 295.

his lifetime by keeping a host of agents stationed in Russian Turkestan to keep him informed about the developments in that quarter and also to convey him the messages from Russians, if any. In 1866 Ranbir Singh deputed one of his trusted officers Mehta Sher Singh to undertake a journey to Russian Turkestan, the Khanates of Kokand and Bukhara[105]. After spending about a year in Central Asia, Mehta Sher Singh presented a detailed report about that country to Maharaja Ranbir Singh [106]. His tour diary contains an illustration depicting the contemporary court life in Bukhara which was then ruled by Muzaffar Khan [107]. Mehta Sher Singh found several inns occupied exclusively by Indian traders mostly Shikarpuri Hindus at all major trading centres in Central Asia such as Karshi, Mazar Baha-ud-Din, Bukhara, Samarkand, Tashkent and Kokand. According to him there was a Granth Sahib in one Hindu serai at Karshi, which was placed there by one Baba Bishan Singh of Dera Baba Nanak [108]. At another place then called as Mazar-i-Baha-ud-Din, not far from Bukhara proper, Mehta Sher Singh found a well in a *serai* (inn) wholly occupied by Hindus, which was reported to have been got dug by Baba Guru Nanak, the founder of the Sikh religion [109]. In the course of his travels in Central Asia, Mehta Sher Singh spent about twenty days in Bukhara Shariff, twelve days in Samarkand, about a month each in Tashkent (then a Russian territory) and in Andijan (then under Khuda Yar Khan). To gather news by employing and retaining trusted Kashmiris and Afghans in Kabul, Yarkand and Russian Central Asia in the guise of traders was a favourite pastime with Ranbir Singh. In this context, the activities of Lal Din, a resident of Kabul, Ahmad Daraz and Mohsin Shah, both Kashmiris, who used to shuttle between Kashmir and Central Asia via Peshawar-Kabul route rather than the Leh-Yarkand route as horse-dealers [110], are noteworthy. The settlement of certain Dogra Brahmans at Samarkand and Katta Kurghan during Ranbir Singh's time further enriched the cultural intercourse between the two sides. One Narain Das of Jammu is reported to have spent about five years in Katta Kurghan enjoying full hospitality of the local Russian administration. The frequent visits of Baba Karam Prakash and other Kashmiri emissaries to Central Asia have already been described. Several other agents such as

105. Mehta Sher Singh, *Safar nama*.
106. *Ibid*.
107. *Ibid*.
108. *Ibid*., folio 34.
109. *Ibid*., folio 38.
110. *Foreign. Secret*. March 1882.. 268. Leh-Yarkand route was avoided in order to escape detection by the British agent in Ladakh.

Ganga Ram, a Dogra of Dhanisal in Riasi district of Jammu division, lived in Samarkand for about four years and acquired proficiency in the Russian language [111]. On his return to Kashmir Ganga Ram was appointed as a Tehsildar. Another Dogra, Bhagwan Das, even owned a *serai* (inn) at Dawal, situated midway between Katta Kurghan and Samarkand [112]. Similarly, Mansukh is reported to have lived in Katta Kurghan for about eight years. He was running there a shop selling Russian goods, stationery etc [113]. He too knew Russian and Uzbek languages. By establishing a school for teaching Russian language in Kashmir, Maharaja Ranbir Singh sought to remove the language barriers in the course of his friendly communications with the Russians in Central Asia. According to a British report, the Maharaja actually engaged a *Maulavi* (Muslim teacher) who pretended to know Russian, to teach the young prince [114]. But the teacher proved to be an impostor who possessed no knowledge of that language [115]. Following the death of Ranbir Singh in 1885 the British moved fast in establishing firm control over the internal administration of the State, thus preventing the recurrence of such cultural exchanges between the Kashmir princes and the Russians in Central Asia.

Keen interest was evinced in Kashmir affairs in Russian Central Asia. A Russian officer, P.I. Pachino, as early as 1867 collected "Tales about Kashmir as told by Kashmiris" from numerous Kashmiris living in or visiting Tashkent and published the same in Russian language. Knowing several Eastern languages like Persian, Arabic and Turki, Pachino made several attempts to reach Kashmir. In the late years of the nineteenth century the Russian government made it compulsory for its officers to learn Hindustani language. Their task was facilitated by the presence of several Indians in Central Asia. A Kashmiri, Kabir Shah Mustafin, who lived in Tashkent was also employed for teaching Hindustani at the Russian Military School [116]. The documents relating to this course, that are preserved in the Central State Archives on military history of the USSR contain references to the fruitful services rendered by Mustafin in conducting this language course [117].

---

111. *Foreign. Secret F.* January 1884. 40-95.
112. *Ibid.*
113. *ForeignSecret.* August 1882. 349-359.
114. *Foreign. Secret.* December 1879. 829-830 A.
115. *Ibid.*
116. *Foreign. Secret F.* Nov. 1899. 47-50.
117. *Ts. GVIA SSR.* F. 1396, op. 2. d.1532.L 9-10. cited in D.Kaushik, *India and Central Asia.* p.60.

The frontier dependencies of Kashmir in Gilgit, Hunza and Chitral maintained relatively closer contacts with the adjoining territory of Russian Central Asia. The coterminity of borders between the two sides and the predominity of Ismaili sect of Muslims in this area facilitated the bilateral exchange. Russian Captain Grombchevsky's first visit to Hunza in 1888 brought the people of Hunza close to the Russians. Next year this officer travelled as far as the borders of Ladakh with the objecting of visiting this lamaland. But he was not allowed by the British to enter Ladakh forcing him to retrace his steps via the Russian Pamirs. The exchange of letters and courtesies the Russian officers and the Chief of Hunza, Safdar Ali, continued thereafter. In 1890 Safdar Ali deputed some of his men to Russian Turkestan to seek aid for meeting an imminent British attack. His men received a hospitable treatment in Turkestan. Safdar Ali continued to maintain intimate relations with the Russian authorities even from his exile in Chinese Turkestan following the British take-over of Hunza in 1891. The Hunza people continued to harbour an exaggerated view of the Russian power in Asia even after being subjected to British control. In the early twentieth century the Political Agent in Gilgit discovered that about one hundred families in Hunza were still following Safdar Ali [118], which meant that they continued to be pro-Russian. Russian made cotton prints and other piece goods were largely consumed in the markets of Hunza, Nagar and Chitral. As late as 1909, a visiting British traveller, P.T.Etherton, was surprised to find a large portrait of the Russian General Kuropatkin hanging alongside that of King Edward VII of England in the room of Mir Muhammad Nazim Khan of Hunza, a British tributary [119].

The Anglo-Russian rivalary over Central Asia had one important negative impact upon the bilateral relations between Kashmir and Central Asia. It was the imposition of stringent curbs upon the free movement of Central Asians in India and the Kashmiris in the Russian territory as part of their counter-espionage measures. Towards the end of 1903 one Abdul Aziz was turned out of Gilgit on the mere suspicion of being a Russian spy [120]. Similarly one Syed Mohammad Usman, whose brother resided in the village Gulab Dajji, Tehsil Nehalpora, Kashmir,

---

118. Major B.E.M. Gurdon to Macartney, 16 November 1904. *Foreign. Sec.F.* May 1905. 150-153.
119. P.T. Etherton, *Across the roof of the world*. London, 1911. p. 46.
120. *Kashgar Diary* 5-20 December 1903.

was imprisoned at Namangan for forty seven days on the charge of being a British spy [121]. He was therefore forced to retreat to Kashgar in July 1904 via Tashkent, Bukhara, Samarkand, Kokand, Andijan and Osh.[122] In the same year another Kashmiri named Ismail was reported to have been turned out of Samarkand and his letters were intercepted on the suspicion of his being a British spy [123]. Once the new Tashkent Railway was opened for traffic, the Kashmiri settlers in Yarkand and Kashgar were tempted to make a *Haj* pil grimage toMecca via Russian Turkestan. In the year 1904 a large number of such Kashmiris applied to the Russian Consulate at Kashgar for issue of passports to allow them travel through the Russian parts of Central Asia [124].But the Russian Consulate refused to treat these Kashmiris as British Indian subjects even though they were treated as such by the Chinese authorities in Sinkiang [125]. The Kashmiris got the required Russian passports only after thery were treated as Chinese subjects [126]. The big power rivalry was too bitter and blunt to take any note of the humanitarian problems that had arisen out of the restrictions imposed on the free movement of people between Kashmir and Central Asia. In 1903 one Mohy-ud-Din, a Bukharan by birth but settled in Kashmir since childhood, was not allowed by the Russian Consul at Kashgar to accompany his sister to her home in Bukhara via Kashmir-Yarkand-Kashgar route [127]. The mere possession of a "Certificate for travellers" which was issued to Mohy-ud-Din by British authorities in Gilgit as part of their routine exercise to check the entry of undesirable elements into Kashmir frontiers, was sufficient ground for the Russian Consul at Kashgar to refuse him the required permission [128]. This was done despite the fact that Mohy-ud-Din had earlier in 1902 come to Kashgar from Bukhara enroute to Kashmir alongwith his sister [129].

---

121. *Kashgar News Abstract* 21-31 July 1904. *Foreign.Frontr. B.*Dec. 1904.22. Syed Mohammad Usman had come to Kashmir in 1896-97 from Ceylon where his father had settled. After staying in Kashmir with his brother for about one year, Usman travelled through Leh, Yarkand, Aksu, Urmchi, Tashkent, Bukhara and Samarkand.
122. *Ibid.*
123. Lt.Col. H.A. Deane, Chief Commissioner, N.W.F.Province to E.H.S. Clarke, Assistant Secretary, Foreign Deptt. GOI, dated 10 September 1904. *Foreign Sec. F.* Oct. 1904. 42-109.
124. *Foreign. Frontr. B.* February 1904. 384.
125. *Ibid.*
126. *Ibid.*
127. *Ibid.*
128. *Ibid.*
129. *Ibid.*

The British Resident in Kashmir functioned as a watch-dog to keep a track of the movements of any Central Asian visitors to the State. On one occassion in early 1909, the Resident asked Raja Amar Singh, the Chief Minister, Jammu and Kashmir State, to put one Abdur Rahman of Bukhara, who was doing business in Russian glassware at Bombay, under surveillance as soon as he entered the State [130]. On receipt of the directive the Kashmir government alerted all its police outposts to keep a watch on any such Bukharan visitor [131]. As a follow-up action, the Superintendent of Police, Jammu reported the arrival of one Abdul Rahman of Bukhara on June 11, 1910, enroute his journey to Yarkand via Jammu-Banihal-Srinagar route [132]. That he had come from Ajmer.[133] shows the natural attachment of the Central Asian people with India and her places of pilgrimage. But this Bukharan traveller was quite different from Abdur Rahman who was a suspicious character in the British Residency records, and whose photograph had been supplied to the State administration [134]. Yet Maharaja Partap Singh took care to have a photograph of Abdul Rahman (who had come from Ajmer)sent to the British Resident in Kashmir [135], so that he remained free from future complications, if any. Thus the presence of a British Resident in Kashmir, who would goad the State administration into meeting the British imperial requirements in the region, acted as a deterrent to the free movement of Central Asians inside the territory of Jammu and Kashmir.

After the establishment of Soviet power in Central Asia the British became too sensitive to allow any influx of men or materials from that side into Kashmir and India. Not only was the import of Russian rubles via Ladakh prohibited but the Kashmir government was forced to confiscate all such currency from the local people. The British, however, allowed the erstwhile Russian officers who had occupied important positions in the Turkestan administration before the Bolsheviks came to power, to enter India via Chitral, Gilgit or Ladakh routes. First report about the arrival of Russian refugees inside the territory of Jammu and

---

130. *O E.R.* No. 243/N-73 of 1909. (JKA).
131. *Ibid.*
132. *Ibid.*
133. *Ibid.*
134. *Ibid.*
135. *Ibid.*

Kashmir, reached the state authorities in November 1918 form the *Wazir Wazarat* (Governor) of Gilgit [136]. He was prompt enough to report the appearance of about one hundred Russian soldiers and a colonel, who were accompanied by some women, in the Mastuj area of Chitral [137]. He also confirmed that these Russians were anti-Bolshevik refugees [138]. Another party of such refugees led by Colonel Timaviev arrived at Chitral in the year 1920[139]. Some other anti-Bolshevik officers like Kultchalk, Korolkov[140] etc. arrived at Gilgit in the autumn of 1919 alongwith their families. Even though the influx of such white Russian refugees into India was too small to present any problem in finding their means of livelihood, they sooner or later left India to settle permanently in Europe. However, during their stay in India they engaged themselves in various occupations. For instance, one Colonel V.V.Fenin, who was the Chief of the Pamirs detachment under the former Russian government and who alongwith his family had come to India via Chitral at the close of 1918, used to work in Peshawar as an agent of the Indo-Persian Trading Corporation, London, till he left India in January 1929 for good[141].

It was in 1920 that some prominent inhabitants of the Russian Pamirs addressed separate petitions to Mehtar Aman-ul-Mulk of Chitral and the British agent residing there seeking British protection [142] in the wake of Bolshevik attempts to establish their authority over that area. In doing so the people of this area seemed to have been influenced by two factors. Firstly, they being the followers of the Ismaili sect regarded it as their prime duty to heed the advice rendered by their spiritual master, Agha Khan of Bombay. It may be recalled that Agha Khan had sent letters to his followers in the Pamirs exhorting them to treat the British government as their friend and ally. In fact the petitioners, referred to the receipt of such advice from Agha Khan, due to which they decided to seek the British protection [143]. Secondly, the erstwhile Russian Officer in

136. *O.E.R.* No. 115/E-56 of 1918. (JKA).
137. *Ibid.*
138. *Ibid.*
139. *Foreign. Extl.B. Secret.* August 1920. 538-39.
140. *Foreign Frontr.B.* January 1920. 23-31. The British authorities in Gilgit and Srinagar spent an amount of 1480 rupees for repatriation of some of these refugees to Bombay. See *Foreign Pol. ExtlB.* August 1921. 441-556.
141. *Foreign. Political.* 68 - X(Secret). 1929.
142. *Foreign. Extl B.Secret.* August 1920. 538-39.
143. *Ibid.*

the Pamirs Detachment, Colonel Timaviev being an officer of the old regime brought these petitions to Chitral and presented the same to the British officer at Mastuj [144]. Apart from being influenced by his anti-Bolshevik Sentiments, Timaviev's action of openly propounding the British cause in the Pamirs must have been motivated by his desire to secure preferential treatment from the British Indian government. But the British Chief Commissioner in the North Western Frontier Province, Hamilton Grant, was not disposed to take any action on these petitions[145]. It is important to record here that no native resident of the Russian Pamirs accompanied Timaviev and his party of Russian refugees on their way to India via Chitral. The inhabitants of the Pamirs seemed to have soon adjusted themselves to the new conditions in Soviet Central Asia.

But such was not the case with the ruling classes there. Finding themselves insecure and unsafe, the Central Asian ruling elite tried to flee to safer places. The ex-ruler of Bukhara made several attempts to seek refugee in Kashmir via the Pamirs-Gilgit and Kashgar-Yarkand routes [146]. Before fleeing to Afghanistan, the ex-ruler of Bukhara entrusted a large consignment of Karakul skins to some of his trusted men. In fact a party of Amir's dependents headed by Toraqul Tuksabah arrived at Peshawar in July 1920 carrying with them these skins for sale.[147] On September 25, 1920 they sailed from Bombay towards England where Lord Curzon, the British Foreign Minister provided them numerous facilities including a recommendation to the French and American Ambassadors resident in London for facilitating the journey of these Bukharans from England to Paris and New York to sell their precious skins [148]. They sold these skins in Europe for about twenty lakh rupees out of which sum only fifteen lakh rupees were given to the ex-Amir [149]. Some other Bukharan refugees effected their passage to India via Kabul and pleaded with the British authorities in the North-West Frontier Province for assistance against the Bolsheviks [150]. One Haji Burhan-ud-Din, Private Secretary to the ex-Amir of Bukhara, took the

144. *Ibid.*
145. *Ibid.*
146. *Foreign & Pol.* 69-M(Secret). 1923.
147. *Foreign & Pol. Extl B.* January 1921. 529-569.
148. *Ibid.*
149. *Foreign Political* 354-X(Secret). 1931.
150. H.A.F. Metcalf, Secretary to Chief Commissioner, N.W.F. Province, 18 August 1921. *Foreign & Pol.* 69-M.Secret. 1923

Kokand-Kashgar route and met the British Consul at Kashgar. Burhan-ud-Din delivered two letters of the Amir to the British Consul General for onward transmission to the British Emperor and the Viceroy of India [151]. The fugitive ruler of Bukhara had in these letters sought British aid to enable him to fight the Bolsheviks. In early 1922 another emissary of the Bukharan ex-ruler named Hyder Khoja Mirbadalef travelled as far as Gangtok to meet his former acquaintance, F.M. Bailey, the Political Officer in Sikkim, with the hope of securing some assistance from him[152]. Mirbadalef requested Bailey to arrange British aid for the ex-Amir of Bukhara in his fight against the Bolsheviks [153]. He informed Bailey that the Bukharan ruler had fled to Khuzar wherefrom he desired to go to Gilgit but was prevented from doing so by a large Bolshevik force arriving from the Pamirs via Kharogh [154]. The ex-ruler of Bukhara could not seek refuge in Kashmir territory and had instead to content himself with migration to Afghanistan [155].

In quite contrast to the Russian refugees who had no racial affinity with the Indians, the Muslim refugees from Russian Central Asia including the erstwhile Khanates of Bukhara and Khiva found themselves at home in India. Most of them took their abode in Punjab and Delhi. Since such refugees belonged to the nobility and ruling classes in the erstwhile Bukhara Khanate, they faced no difficulty in obtaining means of sustenance as they possesed money and gold in abundance. For instance Turaqul Bai and Ismail Beg, ex-Dewan Begi of the ex-Amir of Bukhara, who in 1923 had been entrusted by the Amir a sum of five lakh rupees for the welfare of Bukhara, later invested this money in purchasing Karakul skins for sale in London [156]. Ironically enough, even the subscriptions raised by the "*Anjuman Saadat Bukhara Wa Turkestan*",

---

151. *Ibid.*

On 7 March 1921 the GOI instructed the British Consul General at Kashgar to convey the following reply of the Viceroy to the ex-Amir of Bukhara:

"I have received your letters and as requested have transmitted to the King-Emperor that addressed to His Majestry. His Majesty's government regret their inability to comply with your request".

152. *Ibid.*
153. *Ibid.*
154. *Ibid.*
155. *Ibid.*

The ex-Amir was reported to have been allowed twelve thousand rupees (Afghan) as monthly expenses by the Kabul government but all his correspondence was censored.

156. *Foreign. Political.* 354-X(Secret). 1931.

an association formed in 1929-30 in Peshawar to safeguard the interests of Muslim refugees from Central Asia, were found to have been misused by the office-bearers of this association for their personal requirements[157]. In short no large scale migration of indigenous peoples of Central Asia to India via Kashmir took place as a sequel to the socialist revolution there. This stands out as a sharp contrast to the influx of Russians and Muslims from Soviet Central Asia to India via Farghana-Kashgar-Leh, Pamirs-Gilgit, Afghanistan-Chitral routes during the height of the collectivization campaign in Soviet Union.

The success of the October revolution in Russia in 1917 heralded a new era for the oppressed peoples of the East. Although its impact on the masses in Kashmir was not felt immediately, some young Kashmiris who were settled in Lahore, appeared to have been attracted towards the Bolshevik ideas of equality of nations and freedom from oppression and exploitation. According to a Soviet scholar, M.A. Persits one Abdul Majid, a young man in his twenties who belonged to a Kashmiri trader's family and worked as a clerk, migrated alongwith a group of Indian revolutionary emigrees to Central Asia in 1920 [158]. The Kashmiri descent of Abdul Majid is proved conclusively by the British Indian police records, wherein he was stated to be the son of one Mir Faiz Buksh Kashmiri and resident of Dhal Mohalla, Lahore city [159]. On the examination of 84 questionnaires filled by Indian emigrees during their stay in Soviet Russia, Persits found that only three or four " revealed Communist sympathies" [160]. Abdul Majid was one of them and he had written in his replies that he "heartily agreed with the Communist programme"[161]. It was in October 1920 that he arrived in Tashkent where he joined the Tashkent Military school to receive training in arms [162]. After this school had been closed in 1921 as a sequel to the Anglo-Russian agreement,

157. *Ibid.*

158. M.A. Persists, *Revolutionaries of India in Soviet Russia.* Moscow, Progress, 1983. p.112. Persits, claims to have traced the Kashmiri descent of Abdul Majid from a questionnaire filled in by the latter during his stay in Soviet Russia.

159. Cited in Subodh Roy, *Communism in India with unpublished documents 1919-1924.* Calcutta, 1971. pp. 246-253. Subodh Roy, *Communism in India: unpublished documents* 1925-1934. Calcutta, 1972. pp.115-16.

160. M.A. Persits, *op cit.* p.112.

161. *Ibid.*

162. Rafiq Ahmad, one of the collagues of Abdul Majid in Tashkent, has confirmed that they learnt gunnery and machine gun operation at the school. See Muzaffar Ahmad: "The story of Rafiq Ahmad's travels". In *The Communist party of India and its formation abroad.* p.30.

Abdul Majid alongwith some other Indians went to Moscow to receive training in the Communist ideology at the Communist University of Toilers of the East[163]. It was in early 1922 that Abdul Majid accompanied a group of Soviet trained Indian revolutionaries on a long and arduous journey from Central Asia across the Pamirs to India to tell his compatriots about the achievements of the revolution in Central Asia and to spread Communism in India[164]. As soon as this group of revolutionaries reached Chitral in November 1922, all of them were arrested and charged under Section 121-A of Indian Penal Code of a conspiracy to deprive the British Emperor of the sovereignty over India. Abdul Majid was one among those who were convicted in the Peshawar conspiracy case, and he was sentenced to one year's rigorous, imprisonment in May 1923[165]. Soon after his release from jail in April 1924 Abdul Majid worked relentlessly for organizing Communist organisations and coordinating the trade union activity in Punjab. He was instrumental in the formation of Punjab Labour Board in March 1925. He was one of the Chief organisers of Nao Jawan Bharat Sabha (Young India Association) which was formed in the spring of 1926.[166] Braving all the hazards and miseries, Abdul Majid alongwith Sohan Singh Josh formed the Anti-Imperialist League with a view to secure Indian liberation from British imperialism[167]. He was one of the accused in Meerut conspiracy case (1929-33) and it was on September 18, 1929 that Abdul Majid along with some others threatened to go on hunger strike if they were not accorded the status of political prisoners and conditions in jail were not improved[168]. There was yet another Kashmiri resident of Lahore named Shams-ud-Din Hassan (son of Imam Din Kashmiri) who was also working for the cause of Communist movement in Punjab. Shams-ud-Din Hassan was not only the titular editor of *Inquilab*, but also the Provincial Secretary of All India Trade Union Congress. He played a key role in North Western railway strike of 1925 and also participated in the Indian Communist Conference held at Kanpur in December 1926.[169]

163. Muzaffar Ahmad, *Ibid.* p.77. M.A. Persits, *op cit.* p. 240.
164. Subodh Roy, *Communism in India with unpublished documents 1919-24*. pp. 246-253. Rafiq Ahmad has given a vivid account of this journey from Tashkent to Chitral over snowy mountain ranges in the Pamirs and Hindu Kush. See his "Story of Travels" in Muzzaffar Ahmad: *Communist Party of India and its formation abroad*. pp. 36-38.
165. For copy of the judgement of J.H.R.Fraser, Sessions Judge, Peshawar dated 18 May 1923 See Subodh Roy, *Communism in India with unpublished documents* 1919-1924. pp. 246-53.
166. *Ibid.* p. 374.
167. Subodh Roy, *Communism in India : unpublished documents 1925-1934*. p. 239.
168. *Ibid* pp.147-149.
169. Subodh Roy, *Communism in India with unpublished documents 1919-24*. p. 351.

From the above it is clear that Communist ideology had made a considerable impact on the educated Kashmiri youth who were then living in Lahore. Despite the numerous obstacles placed in the way of cultural intercourse between the peoples of Central Asia and Kashmir on account of imperialist rivalry between Britain and Tsarist Russia and the subsequent British hostility to the newly established Soviet power, the flow of men and ideas did not stop altogether.

4

Shadow of Anglo- Russian Rivalry Over Kashmir

By 1820 both Britain and Russia had emerged as the most powerful States in Eurasia. Exercising control over vast territorial empires in Asia, both these powers were separated from each other by weakand unstable Khanates of Central Asia. The Anglo - Russian rivalrywas a result of the convergence of their imperialist designs over Central Asia, from two opposite directions. Whereas Britain was scared of the unchecked growth of Russian power in Asia which would undermine the British power and prestige in India, Russia felt tempted to restrain the hostile British moves in Europe by playing up the Russian threat to India. So during the first half of the nineteenth century Britain was busy exploring the means to prevent the absorption of the intervening Central Asian Khanates into Russia. It also sought to extend commercial activities in the area with the hope of supplanting Russsian infuence there and creating a friendly buffer between the two expires. Both these powers viewed Central Asia as a land of promise which could assimilate their manufactured goods and supply in return raw materials like cotton,silk and wool. The activities of British officers like Moorcroft, Burnes, Connolly, Abbott and Shakespeare in Bukhara, Khiva and Kokand during the first half of the nineteenth century, instead of meeting the desired objective of creating a permanent influence in these Muslim Khanates only helped in activising the Russian forward policy towards Central Asia. Russia saw to it that the entry of British manufactured goods into Bukhara,Khiva,

Kokand and other Central Asian trading centres was blocked for ever. Even after the incorporation of the Central Asian Khanates in the Russian empire, the British continued to send experienced officers on reconnaissance and diplomatic missions to this area. In doing so their modus operandi was not disimilar to that adopted by Tsarist Russia. Thus Valikhanov and Robert Shaw went as traders to Eastern Turkestan to test its commercial and political climate. Ignatyev, Kuropatkin, Forsyth and Younghusband went on official diplomatic missions. Similarly Grombchevsky met his counterpart in the person of Younghusband in Hunza. Once Russia had gained total control over Western Turkestan, Britain geared up its machinery to carve out a friendly buffer in Chinese Turkestan. To put India-Sinkiang trade on a firm footing was the watchword of this policy. Since this trade passed through Kashmir and Ladakh, the Kashmir ruler was coaxed to concede the right to station a British officer in the frontier town of Leh, ostensibly to look after the interests of the Central Asian traders but actually to monitor the developments across the borders. Britain's fear of a possible Russian expansion towards Kashgaria led it to follow a policy of appeasement towards the Chinese authorities in Sinkiang. The reports about the overtures made by certain Indian chiefs to Russia and the psychological impact created by the Russian successes in Asia amongst the Indians at large, were additional factors in determining the British attitude towards Kashmir State. The 1873 agreement, by which Britain secured the Russian assurance to treat Afghanistan as outside its sphere of influence, could not keep the two-power rivalry in check. Only the centre of rivalry shifted from Hindu Kush to the Pamirs. Even the Pamir boundary agreement of 1895, by which the Pamirs were demarcated and the coterminity between the two empires was eliminated for ever, could not help in ending the bitterness between the two. The colonial rivalry found expression in the frequent exchange of verbal duels between Petrovsky and Macartney, the representatives of Russia and Britain in Kashgar, on various issues such as the petty property disputes of Ladakhi, Andijani and Kashgari traders, nationality cases of these traders, Hunza claim on Raskam lands etc. Even the trivial incident of the bird-shooting at Tashkurgan, where Russian and British Indian officers were stationed and who pressed opposing claims on the bird that fell to the unknown shooter, figured in these exchanges. The Anglo-Russian contest now shifted to the borders of Kashmir skirting Sinkiang and its effect was felt in the remote but strategically located Tashkurgan and Raskam lands. It is this two-power conflict of political and commercial interests in the vast expanse of Central Asia, that had a direct bearing on Kashmir. In such a competition on the international chess-board of Central Asia, Britain used Kashmir not only as a listening post to monitor the Russian activities beyond the Hindu Kush and Karakoram ranges but also as a base to secure control right up to the south of the Hindu Kush. This implied a greater degree of control over the State of Jammu and Kashmir by the British, which object was achieved in 1885 by appointing a full-fledged Resident in Kashmir. Maharaja Ranbir Singh who perceived his kingdom as a buffer between the British and Russian empires, had a premonition of the coming events. In the year 1876 he gave vent to his feelings in an informal meeting with a visiting Englishman, Edward E. Meakin. His words proved to be prophetic:

> It is like a button stuck on a sort of gigantic needle that runs through the train, and when the carriages are pushed at one end or the other you hear a 'houff, houff', and bang they go against the poor little button....... I am a buffer; on one side of me there is the big train of the British possessions and whenever they push northward they tilt up against me; then on the other side is the shaky concern Afghanistan, and on the other side of it is the ponderous train and engine called Roos. Every now and then there is a tilting of Roos towards Afghanistan, and simultaneously there is a tilting upwards of the great engine in Calcutta, and I am the poor little button between them. Some day, perhaps not far distant, there will be a tilting from the North, and Afghanistan will smash up. Then there will be a tremendous tilt from the south, and I shall be buried in the wreck and lost! It may not come in my time, but it is sure to come when that poor little button is on the pin-pointing to his son, the present Maharaja (Pratap Singh).[1]

---

1. Cited in Willian Digby, *Condemned unheard: the government of India and H.H. the Maharaja of Kashmir*. London, 1890. pp. 7-8.

(1) BRITISH POLICY TOWARDS CENTRAL ASIA (1800-1867)* : AN OVERVIEW

After having subjugated the interior of India and also having consolidated its foothold along the Indian sea-coast, the British power in India began to concentrate upon its land frontiers. By the beginning of the nineteenth century the British had established their undisputed ascendancy within India. In the words of Alfred Lyall it had "nothing to fear from Indian rivals"[2]. From now onwards the British focussed their attention on the riches of the Punjab and looked beyond at the formidable mountain barriers of the Hindu Kush for consolidating their position in India. They now engaged themselves into a larger diplomatic struggle with foreign powers with the object of ensuring permanent ascendancy over the Indian subcontinent. The first half of the nineteenth century was so eventful that it witnessed the subjugation of Mysore, Oudh, Marathas and Punjab by the English East India Company. Besides a vassal state of Jammu and Kashmir was carved in the extreme north under a friendly ally-Gulab singh.

In the beginning of the nineteenth century particularly after the settlement of the Franco-Russian differences at Tilsit (July 1807), British policy in Asia was hinged upon their sole objective of maintaining the strategic balance of power in Europe in their favour. In 1800 Minto took the initiative of despatching several official diplomatic missions to Middle East, Afghanistan and Punjab under John Malcolm, Elphinstone and Metcalfe, respectively with an object of forging British alliance with these independent kingdoms that intervened between British India and Russia [3]. The control of vast resources of India proved a boon to the British who used India only as a pawn to promote their interests in Europe. It was in 1819 that one William Moorcroft- a veterinary surgeon by profession-who joined as Superintendent of the East India

---

* It was in 1865 that the Russians occupied Tashkent. Two years later (in 1867) a separate Governorate General of Turkestan was formed with Gen. Kaufmann as its first Russian Governor General.

2. Alfred Lyall, *Rise and expansion of the British Dominion in India*. London, 1820. pp. 280-81.

3. For further details see M.E. Yapp, *Strategies of Britain, Iran and Afghanistan 1798-1850*. Oxford, Claredon Press, 1980.

Company's military stud at Bengal in 1808, went on a mission to Balkh and Bukhara, ostensibly to secure horses of Turkoman breed but actually he surveyed the lands lying beyond the Indian northern frontiers. Earlier in 1812 he had dispatched his intelligent and trusted Indian assistant, Mir Izzet Ullah, on a mission to Central Asia. Izzet Ullah who had travelled through Attock, Kashmir, Ladakh, Yarkand, Kashgar, Kokand, Samarkand, Bukhara returning to India via Balkh, Khulm, Bamian and Kabul in 1813 [4], was instrumental in introducing Central Asia to the British.

But it was Moorcroft who sowed the seeds of a future British policy towards Central Asia. During his mission to Bukhara (1819-25), Moorcroft threw open the internal political and economic conditions prevailing in the Central Asian Khanates to the British Indian authorities. Moorcroft's journey to Bukhara can hardly be characterised as private, since he left Calcutta in ending 1819 with the official consent of the British Indian government [5]. He was not only allowed to receive the salary due to him as Superintendent of Stud, but also authorised to take along with him a variety of British goods for creating a demand for them in the Central Asian markets [6]. But the British Indian government found it expedient not to vest in him any "accredited authority or political designation".[7] He actually indulged in such political activities as the reconnaissance of the territories then unknown to the British, establishment of friendly ties with the Chiefs of Ladakh and Bukhara and communication of up-to-date intelligence concerning the territories traversed by him in the context of the apprehended Russian advance towards Central Asia and Kashmir. When Moorcroft reached Lahore in May 1820, he entered into friendly negotiations with Maharaja Ranjit Singh and secured his permission to go to Ladakh through Mandi and Kullu [8]. He also obtained the freedom to travel through Kashmir in case he could not proceed to Bukhara via the Leh-Yarkand route. But Moorcroft's proposal to Ranjit Singh for establishing a "fixed scale of duties" for the admission of British merchandise into

4. W. Moorcroft, *Travels*. Vol. 1, p. xviii.
5. *Ibid.*, Vol. 1, p. xxiv.
6. Moorcroft had taken with him English piece goods such as cotton, broadcloth and hardware worth about 4000 pounds on behalf of M/S Palmer & Co. and Mackillop and Co. of Calcutta with a view to create demand for British goods in Central Asia. See *Ibid.*, pp. 2-3.
7. *Ibid.*, p. xxvi.
8. *Ibid.*, p. 103.

Punjab did not meet with a positive response [9]. Soon after his arrival at Leh in September 1820 Moorcroft tried in vain to obtain the permission of Yarkand authorities for passing through that city enroute to Kokand and Bukhara [10]. He had to extend his stay at Leh for two years. Moorcroft made full use of his presence in Ladakh for negotiating with the Ladakhi authorities an agreement to secure for the British "liberty to trade with Ladakh and through it to other countries, moderate duties and a permanent factory at Leh" [11]. He succeeded in concluding a Treaty with Ladakh which in his own words was "calculated to throw open to the enterprise of the British merchants and thorough them to the manufactures of Great Britain the whole of Central Asia from China to the Caspian Sea" [12]. Alarmed by the dispatch of mission to Ladakh under Agha Mehdi, Moorcroft became alive to the need of extending British influence over Ladakh which would prove a "strong outwork" [13] against the Russian expansion on the north, besides being centre of trade between Central Asia and India. Favoured by the circumstance of heavy demand of tribute by Ranjit Singh upon the ruler of Ladakh, Moorcroft secured the willing allegiance of Ladakh to the British government. He not only forwarded this letter of allegiance to his government at Calcutta but also communicated with Ranjit Singh on the subject[14]. However, the British Indian government thought it advisable not to accept this offer keeping in view the importance of maintaining friendly relations with Ranjit Singh at that time [15]. Thus Moorcroft was reprimanded for his action and the ruler of Punjab was accordingly informed about the "unauthorized" action of Moorcroft [16]. By this time the British had begun to lay their covetous eyes on Punjab and Sind, both of which were considered to be the key to the development of British commercial dealings with the neighbouring territories including Central Asia. Hence their reaction to Moorcroft's action in Ladakh was calculated to appease the Punjab ruler. A closer scrutiny of Moorcroft's activities in Lahore, Ladakh and Bukhara vis-a-vis British official

9. *Ibid.*
10. Kashmiri traders resident in Yarkand and Ladakh made repeated attempts to influence the authorities at those places for denying trading facilities to the British merchants, fearing erosion of their monopoly over the shawl-wool trade. Their machinations in Yarkand succeeded in preventing Moorcroft's entry to that place.
11. *Ibid.*, p. 255
12. *Ibid.*, p. 257.
13. *Ibid.*, p. 420.
14. *Ibid.* p. 421
15. *Ibid.*
16. *Ibid.*

attitude leads us to assume that the British priorities in the first quarter of the nineteenth century lay in Sind and Punjab rather than beyond the Himalayan mountains. But they were alive to the importance of possessing an up-to-date information about the countries in Central Asia. Alexander Burnes' mission to Sind and Punjab in 1830s to probe the navigational possibilities of the river Indus and also its possible role in the future commercial intercourse with Central Asia, further strengthens our view.

The year 1830 marked the beginning of the British forward policy in Central Asia. Though the British did not anticipate any direct invasion of India by Russia yet the Russian presence in Central Asia was thought to provoke "unrest in India and so compel Britain to adopt expensive military postures in order to preserve internal security and to provide for external defence" [17]. This alleged Russian threat to India was also viewed to operate as a check upon the free course of British policy in Europe [18]. To prevent anysuch possibility, the British government began to think in terms of extending its political influence in Central Asian Khanates by means of commerce. And to achieve that end possession of a direct control over the Indus and Punjab was a must. This policy was clearly spelt out by the Secret Committee of the Court of Directors in its dispatch dated January 12, 1830 addressed to the then Governor General of India, Lord William Bentinck. The Secret Committee stressed the need for obtaining "every possible information regarding countries situated between Caspian Sea and the Indus" [19]. The Committee was not worried so much by the actual Russian invasion of India as by the moral effect likely to be produced amongst the British subjects in India and also " the financial embarrassments due to necessity of military preparations" [20]. Bentinck was thus prompted to dispatch Burnes and Connolly to Sind, Punjab and Central Asia with a double object of gathering all possible information about these unknown tracts and to explore the possibility of opening the Indus for navigation. The importance of Indus as an easy route for transporting British goods into Central Asia via Kabul came into sharp focus. The British wanted to send their materials and not men to Central Asia in the first instance [21]. By

17. M.E. Yapp, *op.cit.* p. 202.
18. *Ibid.*
19. *Foreign Secret.* 25 Nov. 1831. 1-3.
20. *Ibid.*
21. Bentinck had even received the green signal from the Home Government to make an advance of up to an amount of 5000 pounds to some native merchants for selling goods in the Central Asian markets.
    See dispatch of Secret Committee dated 17 Feb. 1830.

underlining the advantages of Indus for promoting trade between India and Central Asia, both Burnes and Connolly prepared the ground for the future British policy towards Sind and Punjab. The signing of a commercial treaty with Ranjit Singh and a convention with the Amirs of Sind for opening the river Indus to the British commerce were in fact the preliminary steps towards future British activity in Central Asia.

The need to safeguard British interests in Kashmir, Ladakh and adjoining territories was highlighted both by Moorcroft and Burnes. If Moorcroft wanted Ladakh to be placed directly under the British, Burnes desired his government to forestall the Russians by helping the divided Uzbeks to form "one grand confederacy which would be an effectual barrier to the progress of Russian and Persian ambitions" in Central Asia [22]. Burnes saw in the development of commercial intercourse between Russia and Kokand Khanate the possibility of extension of Russian commerce and political influence to Chinese Turkestan and therefrom to Kashmir and Ladakh [23]. By pointing out the easy means of communication available between Kokand and Russia on the one hand and Kashgar, Yarkand and Ladakh on the other, Burnes only hinted at the possible direction of Russian threat [24]. He therefore advocated the establishment of a mart on the Indus for extending British commercial influence in Central Asia.

The British received considerable amount of intelligence from their Political Agent posted at Ludhiana named Captain L. M. Wade. Wade's source of information was one Abdul Rahim of Bukhara [25] who used to feed him with information about events in Kokand, Eastern Turkestan and Kashmir. During the second quarter of the nineteenth century, the main thrust of the British policy was to carve a useful influence in the Central Asian Khanates in order to thwart Russians there. In spite of the geographical barriers the British went ahead with

22. A. Burnes to W.H.Mc Naughten, Secretary to the Governor-General of India, dated Kabul, 15 March 1838. *Foreign P.C.* 18 July 1838. 59-60.
23. Burnes to Mc Naughten 1 Feb. 1838.
24. *Ibid. Foreign Secret.* 1 Aug. 1838. 14-15.
25. One can say for sure that this Bukharan worked for the East India Company through Wade during the years 1835-37, because the Ludhiana Agent refers to him in his secret despatches only during that period. The Austrian traveller B.C. Hugel also mentions Abdul Rahim as an agent of the East India Company in his diary dated 17 Oct.1835 written near Srinagar.
See Hugel, *Kashmir and Punjab*. pp. 97-98.

despatching experienced officers to these Muslim Khanates for forging friendly ties with them. When Stoddart went to meet the Amir of Bukhara in 1838 under orders of the British Ambassador in Persia,[26] he used the occasion for pressing the Bukharan ruler to release Russian slaves and prisoners with a view to removing the genuine grounds for Russian hostilities against that Khanate. During the year 1840 several officers like Abbott, Shakespear, and Connolly operated in Khiva. Form there Connolly extended his operations to Kokand wherefrom he went to the court of Nasrullah at Bukhara in a bid to persuade him to rise against Russia[27]. But the despotic ruler of Bukhara made both Stoddart and Connolly to suffer inhuman torture. The British debacles in Afghanistan also acted as a factor in influencing Nasrullah's decision to execute these British officers[28]. Thus the British efforts to establish friendly rapport with the Central Asian rulers and the dream of creating a confederacy of Central Asian Khanates as a buffer against the Russian expansion met a crushing blow. Not only that, the fate of Stoddart and Connolly proved to be a big deterrent to the despatch of British officers to Central Asia for a long time to come. In view of this debacle, the onus of collecting up-to-date intelligence about Russian movements in Central Asia fell on native Indian agents commissioned on numerous missions[29]. Their task was supplemented to a considerable extent by the British Ambassadors posted at St.Petersburgh and Persia.

The British policy towards these Muslim Khanates in Central Asia was put to a critical test when the rulers of Kokand and Bukhara sought British assistance in repelling the forward thrust of Russia. In the eyes of Central Asian rulers, the British authorities in India were powerful enough to thwart the Russian designs on their Khanates. So, fearful of the Russian advance and desirous of securing their realms, these rulers made several attempts to establish cordial relations with the British in India. Kokand was the first Khanate to make such overtures, soon after it had lost Ak Musjid to Russia. It was in 1854 that the Khan of Kokand despatched an envoy to Punjab to meet the British authroities for

26. H.Lansdell, *Russian Central Asia*. London 1893. Vol. II, p.74.
27. *Ibid.*,p.76.
28. Connolly and Stoddart were executed on June 24, 1842.
29. The Punjab Government used to send numerous Indians on such missions. One Allahdad Khan while making enquiries about Lt. Wyburd lost his life in Badakshan. He had been of much help to Colonel Stoddart at Bukhara and R.Shakespear at Oorgunj.
See *Foreign. Political*. 29 Sept. 1854. 147-49.

seeking the services of some European officers who could drill troops in that Khanate thus making them capable of withstanding any future Russian aggression [30].

The arrival of this accredited envoy created a lot of commotion in the British Indian ruling circles. Though there existed a consensus as to the need for using the occasion as a means of developing direct relations with the Central Asian rulers and also of acquiring reliable information about the developments there, differences existed regarding the course to be followed in meeting the demands of the Kokand ruler. H.B. Edwardes, the Superintendent and Commissioner of Peshawar Division pleaded for rendering "any assistance to Kokand which might save it from becoming a Russian province" but short of direct involvement in any military operations [31]. Since the tragic fate of Connolly and Stoddart still loomed large over the British official mind, Edwardes thought it advisable to lend native drill instructors drawn from Cavalry of Sind crops and Gorkha Infantry Regiments rather than any British military officers to Kokand [32]. John Lawrence, the Chief Commissioner of Punjab, took a more cautious view and proposed to dismiss the Kokand envoy with just a "friendly letter for the King of Kokand" and "a moderate sum" besides allowing him to "enlist a given number of native officers," who would volunteer themselves for their own safety [33]. But Lord Dalhousie, the then Governor General of India, attached great importance to this event as it provided reliable intelligence about the Russian activity in Central Asia [34]. He instructed the Punjab government to assist the Kokand envoy in obtaining the services of native officers who would like to volunteer for service in Kokand [35].

Since the British rulers of India were not prepared to allow themselves to be militarily involved in the Central Asian affairs, the Kokand mission to India failed in its object. It could neither secure the

---

30. *Foreign S.C.* 24 Nov. 1854. 1-5.
31. *Ibid.*
32. *Ibid.*
33. *Ibid.*
34. *Ibid.*
35. *Ibid.* In opposition to Lawrence's contention, Dalhousie ordered that these native officers would receive half pay up to a period of five years in India over and above their allowances in Kokand.

services of Birtish officers, [36] nor did any of the native officers from Punjab volunteer to go to such a distant place. The British Indian government limited its role only to provide utmost hospitality to the Kokand envoy and gifting arms for use of the Kokand army against any possible Russian aggression [37]. This opportunity was also used for sending a native surveyor namely Baboo Shuja alongwith the embassy on its return to Kokand. The said surveyor who was to assess the position of Russians on the Kokand border, could not, however, proceed beyond the territories of Jammu and Kashmir [38]. By expressing the sentiments of sympathy with the Khan of Kokand, the British wished to keep him favourably disposed towards them as against the Russians.

The year 1866 saw the arrival of an envoy from the Amir of Bukhara in India, in the person of Khoja Mahomed Parsa who was the Chief Mufti in Bukhara. Apart from bringing alongwith him friendly letters and presents both for the Queen of England and the Viceroy of India, [39] the Bukharan envoy sought British support against Russia which had lately placed a Bukhara agent in captivity. Though this mission was well received, the Viceroy while regretting the Russian proceedings against Bukhara expressed his inability to render "any effective aid either by advice or in any other form" [40]. Few years later, in 1872 when the ruler of Bukhara had expressed his desire to have an accredited British agent resident there [41], the British Indian government spurned the offer considering the "interests of British subjects at Bukhara not of sufficient importance" as to warrant representation through an accredited agent [42].

Obviously the British did not want to incur any trouble for themselves by getting involved in any military conflict between the

---

36. *Foreign.S.C.* 30 Nov. 1855. 27.
Two British officers Lt. Hodson and G.O. Mayes who had offered their services to the Kokand envoy, were not permitted by the government to go there.
37. *Ibid.* The envoy was also provided with ten thousand rupees as expenses of his journey other than daily allowances and presents for the Khan of Kokand.
38. See *Foreign. Secret.* 27 March 1857. 21-22
39. *Foreign. Political* A. Jan 1867. 171-180.
40. These sentiments were repeated in the Viceroy's letter dated 24 Jan. 1867 sent to the Amir of Bukhara through this envoy.
41. *Foreign. Secret.* Sept. 1872. 186-192.
The Bukhara ruler had conveyed his desire to the British Ambassador at Constantinople on 5 July 1872, through his envoy there.
42 *Ibid.*

Central Asian Khanates and Tsarist Russia. As regards the posting of accredited British officers in Kokand and Bukhara, the British Indian government did not avail of the opportunities provided by the voluntary offers from the rulers of these Khanates due to the barbarism and fanaticism rampant in those areas which would endanger the security of British officers. But they continued to obtain up-to-date information regarding Russian movements in Central Asia-political, commerical or military-by pressing into service native agents often disguised as merchants or mendicants. One Khwaja Ahmad Shah Nakshbandi of Kashmir who commanded good respect among the people of Kokand and Kashgaria, was sent on a mission to Central Asia by Major Mac Gregor and Col. Mackeson in 1852 to find out the whereabouts of Lt. Wyburd. On his return Nakshbandi submitted details of the routes besides throwing ample light on the general socio-political conditions in the territories traversed by him. In 1854 Major Coke, the then Deputy Commissioner of Kohat, deputed two parties of Syeds one via Swat and Badakhshan and the other through Kabul to Bukhara and Kokand for collecting intelligence of events there[43]. One of these Syeds, Mohammad Kasim succeeded in reaching as far as Ak Musjid wherefrom he reported about its occupation by the Russian force. This Syed had also met Khuda Yar Khan, the then ruler of Kokand, who used the occasion to send a letter to John Lawrence, the Chief Commissioner of Punjab, soliciting British assistance for meeting Russian threat[44]. Similarly Ghulam Rabbani was deputed by Pundit Munphool, an officer in the Punjab government, to Central Asia. Leaving Kabul in disguise on October 4, 1865, Rabbani travelled through Bamian, Khorrum, Haibak, Tashkurgan, Mazar Sharif, Balkh, Karshi, Khoja Mubarak and reached Bukhara in February 1866[45]. Therefrom he visited Tashkent, Samarkand and Katta Kurgan. He even watched the movements of General Cherniaev by following him upto the Chirchik river in the suburbs of Tashkent[46]. Rabbani returned to India in the Company of an envoy from Bukhara to the Indian government[47]. Soon after in 1869

43. *Foreign-Secret*. 23 Feb. 1855. 21-24.
44. *Foreign Secret*. 23 Feb. 1855. 21-24.
Mohammad Kasim's report about the exchange of friendly emissaries between Bukhara and Russia received confirmation from a local agent working for the Punjab government at Shaibarghan (in Balkh) who reported about the capture of Samarkand by Russia and Bukhara.
See *Foreign. Political* A. Oct. 1868. 402-403.
45. *Foreign. Political A*. Nov. 1867. 91-92.
46. *Ibid.*
47. *Ibid.*

Ibrahim Khan was despatched on an intelligence mission to Bukhara by the British Commissioner of Peshawar Division [48].

The British, it is evident, did their best to stall the Russian advance towards Central Asia employing all means at their command but short of a direct military involvement in any conflict between the Central Asian Muslim Khanates and Tsarist Russia. Sensing the danger to the lives of English officers in these States ruled by barbaric despots, the British put into service the native Indian agents. They feigned friendly to these Central Asian rulers, but when asked to render military aid in times of distress did not even lend the services of military officers. In doing so, their gestures were quite similar to the Russian response to overtures of the friendship from certain Indian princes. The circumstances of Russian advance in Central Asia were fully utilised for consolidating British control over Kashmir and its frontier tributaries and also for extending its influence right up to the Hindu Kush passes. Unsuccessful in extending their influence beyond the Hindu Kush watershed, the British directed their energies to Chinese Turkestan across the Karakoram and Kuen Lun ranges.

The post-1867 era saw Russians firmly established in Central Asia which, however, did not daunt the British from sending secret intelligence missions to that area. Elaborate arrangements were now made to keep track of the movements of Russian troops, strength of their garrisons, extension of railway communications and also about the Russian contacts with Afghanistan and other hill states. C.M. Mac Gregor, the Quarter Master General of India was mainly instrumental in laying a spying network for monitoring developments in Russian Turkestan and Trans-Caspia [49]. Even as late as 1889, Brigadier C.S.Maclean when posted in Khorasan, employed secret news-writers at Ashkabad, Kuchan, Bunjnurd, Deargz, Sarakhs, Panjdeh, Yulatan, Merv, Charjui, Kerki, Bukhara, Samarkand, Kulab, Kelat, Turbat-i-Sheikh Jam, Paskamer

48. *Foreign. Political B.* Nov. 1871. 31.
Ibrahim Khan left Peshawar on 30 Aug. 1869 for Bukhara via Kabul and Tashkurghan. On his return he gave a detailed account of the commercial and other activities of Bukhara

49. Mac Gregor recommended the collection of Central Asian intelligence through (i) British military attaches posted in Berlin, Vienna and St. Petersburgh, (ii) office employees in Russia, Turkey and Persia, (iii) secret native agents at various Central Asian towns and also at Kabul, Herat and Kandhar.
See *Foreign. Sec. F.* March 1889. 303-313.

and Uzunada [50]. Since such native agents could neither furnish totally authentic news nor comprehend the scope of diplomatic and military maneouvres, the British attached importance to stationing of experienced officers in frontier outposts. This task was rendered easy by their paramount position in Kashmir, which proved to be a fruitful base for carrying out these operations. So in the 1890s, the British agents were operating from the frontier stations in Ladakh, Gilgit, Chitral and Kashgar--all working under the direction of the Resident in Kashmir who was now directly answerable to the Foreign Department.

(2) TIGHTENING OF BRITISH CONTROL OVER KASHMIR

The political relations between the British Indian government and Kashmir stood defined under the Treaty of Amritsar which transferred and made over to Gulab Singh the independent possession of the territories of Jammu and Kashmir State. Though this treaty bound the Kashmir ruler, neither to alter his territories nor to decide any disputes with the Sikhs without the prior British approval, it did not provide for the imposition of any British officer at Gulab Singh's court or restrain him from engaging in any independent diplomacy. In deciding to treat the Kashmir State unlike other Indian states the British seem to have been guided by considerations of political expediency. In spite of his personal dislike for Gulab Singh [51], Lord Hardinge cultivated him as a useful ally keeping in view the hostility of the Sikhs and Afghans towards the British. On their part the Dogra rulers of Kashmir accepted the British supremacy. Their adherence to the stipulated annual present of shawl goats and Kashmir shawls symbolised such a subservient relationship. Gulab Singh and his heirs were retained as guardians of the northern-most bastion of the British Indian empire against threat by any possible rival. By handing over to the Dogra ruler the independent possession of Kashmir, the British only extricated themselves from

50. *Foreign. Sec F.* Sept. 1889. 256-264.
51. Hardinge in one of his private letters described the Dogra chief as the "greatest rascal of Asia". Lord Hardinge to his wife, Camp Lahore 2 March 1846. Cited in Bikram Jit Hasrat, *Punjab Papers*. p. 104.

heavy expenditure on the security of such a vast strategic territory while simultaneously ensuring their influence over the area. But once the Sikhs were finally subjugated and their territories annexed, the British went ahead in extending their effective political control over Kashmir[52].

Posting of British Officer in Kashmir

Soon after handing over Kashmir to Gulab Singh, the British started meddling in the State administration. In an indirect reference to the misrule of a ruling prince vis-a-vis the British obligations towards the oppressed subjects, Lord Hardinge made it known to Gulab Singh in early 1848 that the British government would in no case "be the blind instruments of a ruler's injustice towards his people" [53]. He, in effect, forewarned the Kashmir ruler that the British could resort "to a system of direct interference" [54]. Gulab Singh clearly understood Hardinge's hint at the possibility of appointing a British officer in the State and retorted back saying that there existed no such provision in the Amirtsar treaty[55]. But he could not withstand the pressure to have a British officer on Special Duty in Kashmir during the summer seasons for supervising the conduct of European visitors to the valley [56]. From 1852 onwards the practice of deputing a British officer to reside in Srinagar during the summer season continued uninterrupted until he was replaced by a full-fledged British Resident in the State soon after the death of Maharaja Ranbir Singh. Since the activities of the Officer on Special Duty were confined to Kashmir only and that too for six months, he had no apparent role to play in the internal administration of the State. But officers like Girdlestone, Wynne and Henvey who were astute observers, used to file important reports on the political and economic situation in Kashmir to their government. In view of the stubborn resistance offered by Ranbir Singh to attempts to erode his authority within his jurisdiction, the British government was obliged to resort to a process of gradual but cautious interference in Kashmir. When the Kashmir ruler pointed to an unusual increase in the number of British

---

52. M.K. Teng, R.K.Kaul Bhat and Kaul, *Kashmir constitutional History and documents*. New Delhi, 1977. p. 17.
53. Governor General to Gulab Singh 7 Jan. 1848, cited in M. K. Teng etc., *op cit*. p.228
54. *Ibid.*
55. K.M. Panniker, *Gulab Singh*. p.132.
56. John Lawrence to Dewan Jwala Sahai 14 Jan. 1852. cited in M. K. Teng, *op cit*.p.228. Major Mac Gregor was the first Officer on Special Duty so appointed.

officers particularly in the military service visiting Kashmir, which meant an additional burden on the State in terms of food and carriage supplies, the Government of India decided to impose a limit of two hundred per year in the case of military officers visiting the valley[57]. However, in view of changing imperial priorities vis-a-vis the Russian advance in Central Asia, the British sought to impose their effective control over the internal and external affairs of the State by appointing experienced officers in the frontier outposts of Ladakh, Gilgit, Chitral etc. for monitoring the developments in Central Asia.

British Officer Stationed at Ladakh

It was William Moorcroft who had as early as in 1820s advocated the British take-over of Ladakh to exercise a dominating influence over the commerce and politics of Eastern Turkestan and other Central Asian Khanates. But the British preoccupation with the affairs in Sind, Afghanistan and Punjab had practically put Moorcroft's proposals into cold storage. The importance of Kashmir for the extension of British Indian influence in Central Asia once again came to the fore in 1847 when the British officers sent to demarcate the boundaries between the territories of Jammu and Kashmir and Chinese Turkestan witnessed the multi-national trading operations in Ladakh. British policy towards Kashmir was first directed at breaking the monopoly of this State over the import of shawlwool from Tibet and Chinese Turkestan so as to let the British Indian territory in Koonawar and Bushehr benefit from this trade. But once they were convinced that Ladakh enjoyed the advantageous position of being an established emporium of trade between India and Central Asia, political pressure on Gulab Singh for reducing the customs duties levied on this trade began to be mounted. Certain Yarkandi merchants who travelled down from Leh to Simla in 1848 to place before the Superintendent of Hill States their complaints of undue exactions by Basti Ram, Gulab Singh's officer in Ladakh, turned out to be the wilful instrument of British in browbeating the Kashmir ruler. A perusal of the papers relating to the arrival of these Yarkandi traders in Simla reveals that they were encouraged by Strachey at Leh to petition the British Indian Government for seeking protection through the appointment of a British officer in Ladakh. On

---

57. Secetary, Foreign Department, GOI to Secretary, Punjab Government 12 May 1865. *Foreign. Political A.* May 1865. 127-128.

the basis of these complaints Edwardes made a strong plea for the posting of a British officer at Ladakh to "protect our commercial interests"[58]. To Dalhousie this provided sufficient material for seeking an explanation from Gulab Singh. The Punjab Government, which was directed to take up the matter with the Kashmir ruler "in courteous but very decided language" [59], accordingly sought the dismissal of Basti Ram from State services [60].

The developments in this affair which involved the summoning of Basti Ram to Lahore in early 1850 for cross-examination followed by a personal visit to Ladakh by H.Lawrence to examine the extent of trading operations there and also the stand taken by Dalhousie, are a pointer to the way the British humiliated Gulab Singh's administration just to appease the Central Asian traders with a view to bolstering their image across the Karakoram mountains. Dalhousie did not agree with Lawrence who during his on-the spot enquiry had come to the conclusion that the cause for diminishing the Indo-Central Asian trade lay in "the difficulties of the route and competition from the Russian market more than the imposts on the road." [61] The Russian advance towards Kokand, the details of which were personally conveyed by an envoy from that Khanate to the British Indian authorities in 1854, gave another dimension to the British attitude towards Kashmir. While Dalhousie was convinced that any invasion of India from that side was "next to impossible", he at the same time thought that the extension of Russian influence into the Central Asian Khanates would be "infinite evil to the British Power in the east" [62].

The enthusiasm of British officers like Davies and Forsyth proved to be of vital importance in the formulation of an active policy towards Jammu and Kashmir State. By stressing its importance for the development of Indian trade with Central Asia both these officers urged their government to build up pressure on the Kashmir ruler for getting the

---

58. Edwardes to GOI 17 August 1848. *Foreign. Secret.* 27 Oct. 1849.27-46.
59. Governor General's minute, 24 August 1848. *Ibid.*
60. H.M. Lawrence, President of Board of Administration for Punjab to Maharaja Gulab Singh, Lahore 17 Sept. 1849. *Ibid.* Basti Ram was later absolved of these charges by Lawrence.
61. Minute by H.M. Lawrence 1 Nov. 1851; Governor General's minute 16 Feb. 1852. *Foregin F.C.* 20 Feb. 1852. 99-104.
62. *Foreign. S.C.*24 Nov. 1854. 1-25.

customs duties on foreign trade reduced. First important breakthrough in this direction was achieved in 1864 when R.Montogomery, Lt. Governor of Punjab, acting on the basis of Davies' proposals made Maharaja Ranbir Singh agree to limit transit duties on goods bound for Central Asia to 5 per cent *ad valorem.* But Forsyth described this reduction of duties as "little more than a sham" and pleaded for the posting of a British Agent at Leh "to protect the interests of British merchants"[63]. Finally in early 1867 a unilateral decision to appoint Dr. Cayley as the British officer at Ladakh was taken in utter disregard of the wishes of Maharaja Ranbir Singh. The duties assigned to this officer were ostensibly to "maintain the tariff fixed by the Maharaja of Kashmir in 1864" but actually to enquire "into the State of trade between India and Central Asia" and also to "collect and sift political information regarding the progress of events in Chinese Turkestan"[64]. While conveying its sanction to the deputation of a British officer to Ladakh every season, the Secretary of State made it clear to the Government of India that the said officer would "abstain from any pre-emptory acts and dictatorial language calculated to give offence to the Maharaja"[65]. Both the then Governor General of India and the Home government were of the same opinion that there should be no undue interference in the internal affairs of the Maharaja. Naturally such an arrangement was bound to be irksome and inconvenient to the Maharaja, since the arrival of a British officer at Ladakh and his direct dealings with both Indian and Central Asian traders meant a sharp erosion of the authority and prestige wielded by the Kashmir ruler both inside Ladakh territory and the neighbouring Central Asian Khanates. The Maharaja now came up with a reasonable proposal of removing all duties hitherto levied on merchandise conveyed by traders to and from British India via Ladakh and also allowing the British Officer on Special Duty in Kashmir to visit Ladakh for a month to see if traders had any grounds for complaint[66]. In return for these concessions Maharaja Ranbir requested the British Indian government that the appointment of the British officer to Ladakh should not be renewed next year[67]. Though the Governor General was

63. T.D. Forsyth, Commissioner, Jullunder Division to Punjab Govt. 18 July 1866. *Foreign. Political A*. Sept. 1866. 50-53.
64. *Foreign. Political A*. Nov. 1868. 82.
65. Secretary of State to GOI 15 Feb. 1868. *Foreign. Political A*. March 1864. 144.
66. In October 1868 the Maharaja of Kashmir had sent these proposals to the Governor General through his confidential Minister Jawalla Sahai. *Foreign. Political A*. Nov. 1868. 82.
67. *Ibid.*

inclined to accept Ranbir Singh's proposal, his hands were forced by the Punjab government which pressed to continue this arrangement. Lawrence, however, wrote to the Home government that the arrangement should be reviewed periodically[68]. There at Leh, Cayley proved himself quite indispensable to the British government by making startling disclosures about the frequent exchange of envoys between the Kashmir Durbar and Yakub Beg, the ruler of Kashgaria His reports about the commercial intercourse with Central Asia via Ladakh were extensive and authentic. His presence at Leh proved of extreme use for monitoring the developments in Central Asia particularly the state of affairs in Kokand, Kashgaria and the diplomatic exchanges between Russia and Yakub Beg.

The importance of Ladakh as a frontier listening outpost for tracking the Russian movements in adjacent Khanates of Kokand and Eastern Turkestan was fully realized by Mayo. What was originally intended by Lawrence to be a seasonal and temporary measure, was thus turned into a permanent Leh Agency by his successor. By virtue of a treaty concluded with Maharaja Ranbir Singh in April 1870 the British government bound the Kashmir ruler to treat the suitable trade route as a "free highway in perpetuity and at all times for all travellers and traders", and also to the appointment of two Joint Commissioners one each representing the Kashmir Durbar and the British government for supervising the trade route and settling disputes[69]. Thus came into existence British agency in Ladakh represented by the British Joint Commissioner at Leh. The opposite stand taken by Lawrence and his successor Mayo in respect of British policy towards Kashmir vis-a-vis Central Asia leads us to believe that Lawrence sought to maintain the friendly alliance with the Kashmir ruler by giving him the least cause for offence. He did not want to run the risk of political complications for the sake of cumbersome trade relations with Central Asia. On the other hand, Mayo set upon himself the task of promoting even such a modest connection for gaining political influence in Eastern Turkestan in a bid to outwit Russia. The reported hostilities between the Russians and Yakub Beg's men at the Russo-Kashgar frontier on Naryn river[70]

68. *Foreign. Political A.* Jan. 1870. 136.
69. C.U. Aitchison, *A collection of treaties*...Vol.12, pp.26-29.
70. H.Cayley to GOI 20 Sept. 1869. *Foreign. S.I.* Sept. 1869. 184-188. But these rumours were discounted by Robert Shaw, according to whom Russian and Yakub Beg's forces were separated by three days' journey across snowy range and not merely by the Naryn river.

further alerted Mayo to the possibility of a Russian threat to Kashgaria. His main concern remained to extend the British influence in Eastern Turkestan which was easily accessible from Ladakh. One is inclined to disagree with G.J.Alder's view that Mayo had a "much more positive conception of Central Asian policy" [71] than his hesitant predecessor on two counts. Firstly, Mayo could not prevent the conclusion of a friendly trade treaty between Yakub Beg and Russia [72], nor could his successor Northbrook secure the necessary ratification of a treaty concluded by Forsyth with the Kashgarian ruler, Yakub Beg on February 2, 1874. Secondly, the British failed to take due cognizance of the Chinese locus standi in Eastern Turkestan which was re-occupied by Chinese forces led by General Tso-Tsung Tang in 1877-78.

However, so far as the immediate results of British Agency at Leh are concerned, it did help in promoting the development of Indo-Central Asian trade resulting in the overall prosperity of both the Kashmiri and Punjabi traders. But the Agency played a vital role in eroding the influence of Kashmir ruler not only over the Central Asian trading and official class but even over his own subjects in Ladakh. Henceforth the frequent bilateral exchanges between the rulers of Kashgaria and Kashmir could not be kept secret from the ever-vigilant British officer. By directing the Kashgarian missions to Punjab, the said officer helped in the establishment of a direct political intercourse between his government and that of Yakub Beg. He played a vital role in monitoring the developments across the Karakoram mountains.

Towards Permanent Residency in Kashmir

Even though their officers had started functioning in Srinagar and Leh right from 1852 and 1867 respectively, the British were anxious to widen the limited sphere of activity of these officers. Every action of Mayo and his successors was directed at further tightening of British control over Kashmir. Their policy towards this norhternmost area had ceased to be "one of avowed conciliation and scrupulous forbearance"[73],

71. G.J.Alder, *British India's northern frontier, 1865-95*. p. 38.
72. This treaty, which was negotiated by General Kaulbars bore the seals of General Kaufmann dated Tashkent, 9 April 1872 as also of Yakub Beg dated Yangi Shahr, 8 June 1872. It provided the Russian merchants the freedom to trade and travel within the territories of Kashgaria.
73. Cited in Alder, *op cit*. p. 28.

as under Lawrence. The very idea of a British officer staying in Kashmir for summer months only and that too functioning under a local government in Punjab was ill-suited to the ambitious British policy in Central Asia. While pursuing a gradual but consistent policy of active interference in Kashmir, the British authorities conveniently ignored its proven fidelity during the second Anglo-Sikh war and also the 1857 uprising. First step towards improving the position of the British Officer on Special Duty in Kashmir was taken in 1871 when the Punjab government's control over this appointment was withdrawn and vested directly in the Foreign Department. This was soon followed in 1872 by removal of all restrictions placed on European travellers and offices for staying in Kashmir during winter [74]. This time neither the Maharaja was taken into confidence nor an official communication made to him announcing such a significant change. The new measure was important in more than one way. Not only did it flout the written assurance given by the British Indian government in early 1852 to Gulab Singh, on the basis of which the latter had agreed to the posting of British officer in Kashmir, but it was found to cause repercussions on the socio-economic conditions of Kashmiri peasants and labour. The revised copy of rules governing the visit of Europeans to Kashmir that was sent in routine to Kashmir Durbar in 1872 did not attract any notice there until after Robert Shaw was detected as staying in Srinagar during the winter of 1875-76 [75]. When the Kashmir ruler brought the matter to the notice of the imperial government, he was simply informed about the revised arrangements made in 1872. Ranbir Singh's vehement protests and appeals against this unilateral alteration, on grounds of both precedent and propriety, did not move the British authorities. Retorting back to Northbrook's argument that "as to why an Englishman should not go to Kashmir in the winter as freely as Maharaja's subjects can enter British India" [76], the Maharaja not only drew a sharp line of distinction between the two but also pointed to the miseries suffered by the people of Kashmir while carrying loads of Europeans. He wrote:

> The comparison does not hold good, as the Maharaja's subjects including the highest officials impress not a single British subject into service.

74. *Foreign. Political A.* May 1876. 62-64
75. *Ibid.*
76. *Foreign. Secret.* Autust 1877. 73-75.

> Whereas it is incumbent upon Maharaja's officials to force coolies to labour for every English traveller.
>
> It is true that the coolies are paid four annas each day when they actually carry the loads. But this heartless oppression is felt and dreaded so much that the helpless cultivator often betakes as his last recourse to the demoralizing trick of buying off the unrelenting coolie-fetcher or of persuading a hardier neighbour to go for him by paying from his own pockets four or five times the expected hire for a day .[77]

Even such a moving appeal by Ranbir Singh did not produce any effect on the British government, which described the revival of any such restrictions on Europeans' stay in Kashmir territory as prejudicial to the "present external relations of the empire"[78]. The British did not show any concern for the local people, who by being forced to act as coolies were exposed to the risk of not only losing fingers and toes from frostbite but also their lives. By making a promise of British assistance to Ranbir Singh for extending " a controlling and protective influence over the States lying beyond the borders of Kashmir" [79], the Viceroy tried to assuage his wounded sentiments. He even authorised the Maharaja to bring Chitral and its dependencies under his protection so that these frontier areas were brought within the sphere of British influence.

The reports about Russian overtures to the Kashmir ruler as communicated by the Maharaja himself, came in handy to the British for forcing upon Kashmir a permanent British Political Resident. This was in spite of their opinion that the "reported correspondence of Kashmir with Russia is prima facie improbable"[80] Even in anticipation of the required approval from the Home government, Northbrook decided to have a permanent British Resident in Kashmir. In a bid to implement his scheme, he informed the Punjab government that H.L. Wynne, then OSD at Kashmir and R. Shaw, then Joint Commissioner

---

77. See Letter from Maharaja Ranbir Singh to the Viceroy 27 Nov. 1876. *Ibid.*
78. Viceroy to Ranbir Singh 5 Jan. 1877. *Ibid.*
79. *Ibid.*
80. *Foreign. Secret.* March 1875. 19-29

at Leh should remain at their respective posts for the whole year [81], instead of usual six months. However, the said British officer in Kashmir was to continue the conduct of political relations of the Government of India with the Kashmir ruler through the Punjab administration [82], as heretofore. The new measure was supposed to have become necessary in view of the "important position of Maharaja's territories on the N.W. Frontier, the increasing importance attached to political affairs in Central Asia, the necessity of obtaining early and reliable information of all that takes place in the Himalayan passes and the closer relations being established with Yarkand" [83]. It was only due to the serious differences of opinion in the India office, London, which refused to approve Northbrook's proposals, that the question of appointing a permanent British Resident in Kashmir was deferred [84]. On a closer examination of Northbrook's stand on this issue, it becomes apparent that in spite of Secretary of State's clearcut directive that London did not want to "interfere with any temporary arrangements already communicated to Maharaja"[85], the Lt. Governor of Punjab, R.H. Davies, was allowed to go ahead with the plans to persuade the Maharaja to accept the new arrangements [86]. Ranbir Singh's offer to keep one of his sons as a hostage with the British instead of having a British Resident in Kashmir speaks volumes about his resistance to the increasing British interference [87]. The stiff stand taken by the British Indian authorities forced the Maharaja to offer an alternative which provided for the stay of the British Joint Commissioner at Leh for full year and the Officer on Special Duty in Kashmir for eight months [88]. He was, however, firm in his opposition to the appointment of a British Resident in Kashmir and also to the proposed alteration in the system of his communication with the Punjab government through his agent (*Moutemad*) attendant on the Lt. Governor [89]. These concessions were "sufficient for the present" [90] to Northbrook who already had received London's disapproval to any alteration in the existing arrangements.

---

81. Secretary, Foreign Department, GOI to Secretary, Punjab Government 12 Sept. 1873. *Ibid.*
82. *Ibid.*
83. *Ibid*
84. Secretary of State's telegram to the Viceroy of India, 12 Nov. 1873. *Ibid.*
85. Secretary of State's telegram to Vireroy of India, 27 Nov. 1873 *Ibid*
86. Davies met the Maharaja at Jammu on 5 and 6 Dec. 1873 in this connection.
87. Davies to Northbrook, 7 Dec. 1873. *Ibid.*
88. *Ibid.*
89. *Ibid.*
90. Northbrook to Davies, 25 March 1874. *Ibid.*

In allowing the Lt. Governor of Punjab to use his discretion for communication with the Kashmir ruler either directly or through the Maharaja's agent at Lahore or through the Officer on Special Duty in Kashmir, Northbrook had actually desired that the said British Officer be kept posted with all things in each case [91]. Such a vague position of the Officer on Special Duty was bound to cause some friction, since the Maharaja continued to treat him as a mere supervisor of European travellers' conduct in Kashmir. The Punjab government too was of the same opinion as it never considered this officer as a Political Agent. In the Punjab Government's opinion the Officer on Special Duty was to gather intelligence about matters in Central Asia and beyond the Kashmir frontier [92] rather than to act as a channel of communication with the Kashmir ruler . The confusion over the status of the Officer on Special Duty precipitated during Henderson's tenure at this post. Though belonging to the Imperial Foreign Service Cadre and designated as Resident (3rd class) with permission to wear political uniform, Henderson was practically ignored in the internal matters of Kashmir both by the Maharaja and the Punjab administration [93]. When Henderson was not invited to a reception given by the Kashmir ruler at Jammu on 5,6 and 7 March 1877 to celebrate the assumption of Imperial title by the Queen he took it as an insult both to his person and to the British government [94]. Henderson's official position was rendered weaker by Davies' refusal to allow him any locus standi in the mutual correspondence exchanged between the Kashmir Durbar and the Punjab government. In doing so, the Lt. Governor of Punjab was only following the "existing arrangements" in letter and spirit--though not in tune with the imperial government's desire. Finally the matter was referred to the Viceroy for clearcut instructions as to whether or not the Officer on Special Duty was to be treated as a Political Agent directly responsible to the Government of India[95]. The Punjab government underlined the need to make an "unreserved communication of the intention" to the

91. *Ibid.*

92. L. Griffin,, Secretary, Punjab Govt. to T.H. Thornton, Secretary, Foreign Department. GOI 2 April, 1877. *Foreign. Pol. A.* May 1877. 269-274.

93. In his letter to the Secretary, Punjab Govt. dated 15 Jan. 1877, Henderson cited the instance of correspondence exchanged between the Maharaja and the Punjab administration over the Madhopore canal question and Jhelum drift wood, about which he was totally unaware. *Ibid.*

94. P.D. Henderson to Punjab Government 5 March 1877. *Ibid.*

95. L.Griffin to Thornton, 2 April 1877. *Ibid.*

Maharaja[96]. Lytton, who like his predecessors viewed the Officer on Special Duty as a British political agent in everything but in name, thought it prudent to end the ambiguity once and for all. In view of Kashmir's importance in a wider imperial sense the British Indian government decided to place the Officer on Special Duty under the control of the Foreign Department with which he was to correspond directly on all imperial matters of Kashmir including its external relations[97]. However, the Punjab government was allowed the concession to deal with Kashmir in such matters of local interest as development of trade, extradition of criminals etc. with a rider that the Officer on Special Duty be kept informed about it simultaneously[98]. When the Joint Commissioner at Leh was also subordinated to the control of the Officer on Special Duty in Kashmir[99], the latter's position stood definitely elevated both in technical and practical terms to that of a Political Agent. Lytton's assurance to the Maharaja that this change did not amount to any addition to the functions or any change in the position of the Officer on Special Duty[100] did not convince Ranbir Singh who now found no difference between the said officer and a Political Agent. But the Kashmir ruler continued to ignore the Officer on Special Duty[101] quite successfully as he now conducted his communications with the Viceroy through his representative stationed at Fort William[102]. Henvey's weak position in Kashmir can be gauged from the fact that he did not even know about the presence of Bahadur Khan, an envoy from Chitral in Srinagar until after he met him at Jammu accidentally[103]. On the eve of his departure from Kashmir in 1882, Henvey recounted his experiences of five years as the Officer on Special Duty and expressed satisfaction over his office having risen to be a medium of communication between the Kashmir Durbar and the Government of India on all

---

96. *Ibid.*
97. Secretary Foreign Department, GOI to Punjab Government 14 May 1877. *Ibid.*
98. *Ibid.*
99. *Ibid.*
100. Lytton to Maharaja Ranbir Singh 14 May 1877. *Ibid.* The fact of Henderson being designated as Resident (third class) and paid monthly salary of two thousand rupees was deliberately concealed from the Kashmir ruler.
101. *Foreign Political A.* August 1878. 275-83.
102. Lytton had offered in May 1877 to the Maharaja to have a representative stationed at the headquarters of the Imperial Government. This concession was later withdrawn by Dufferin in 1886.
103. F. Henvey to A.C. Lyall, Secretary, Foreign Department, GOI, 9 June 1879. *Foreign. Secret.* Oct. 1879. 320-338.

matters pertaining to the external relations of the State [104]. He, however, desired the Punjab government to treat the Officer on Special Duty as the recognised advisor of British government in Kashmir affairs whether internal or external[105]. But he was not in favour of altering the designation of the Officer on Special Duty or for his retention in Kashmir for full year [106] since during the winter months the said officer used to operate from Sialkot, hardly twenty seven miles away from Jammu--the winter capital of State.

The British could not, however, establish a total paramountcy over the State till Ranbir Singh was there on the scene. During his lifetime the Maharaja had treated the Officer on Special Duty simply as a Police Magistrate to keep order among the European visitors in Kashmir. In opposition to the British desire, Ranbir Singh continued to communicate with the Lt. Governor of Punjab and the Viceroy through his representatives residing at their courts, rather than through the British Officer in Kashmir who was not even allowed to fly his flag. But Ranbir Singh's protracted illness came in handy to the British for reviving the move to replace the Officer on Special Duty by a full-fledged Resident with powers to supervise the State government. This time Oliver St. John [107] happened to be the main instrument in such a change. In his opinion, the deteriorating condition of the State's administration and economy had necessitated the establishment of a regular Residency in Kashmir, which he supposed would be welcomed by a majority of the Council Members of Ranbir Singh's Durbar[108]. Ripon also was in favour of taking a more decisive course of action so as to bring the State at par with other feudatories of the British in India. But he desired to postpone his operation till a suitable moment after Ranbir Singh's death with which "certain obligations and unwritten bonds would pass away" [109]. Before Ripon had officially taken up the case of the appointment of a British Resident in Kashmir with the India Office on April 7, 1884, he had obtained Kimberley's consent privately to the proposed measure [110].

---

104. Henvey to S.Grant, Secretary, Foreign Department, GOI, 9 Dec. 1882. *Foreign. Secret E.* Jan. 1883. 239-240.
105. *Ibid.*
106. *Ibid.*
107. Oliver St. John took over as Officer on Special Duty in Kashmir from F. Henvey on 1 Jan. 1883.
108. *Foreign. Sec. E.* May 1884. 354-57.
109. D.K.Ghosh, *Kashmir in transition.* p. 21.
110. *Ibid.* p. 22

Once again, the need to watch events beyond the north-western frontier of Kashmir and also to maintain the connection between Kashmir and its dependent chiefships, figured in Government of India's officical despatch to Kimberley as a justification of the proposal [111]. London now felt that circumstances had greatly changed since 1873 when a similar request from Northbrook was turned down[112]. Considering this measure "not only desirable but necessary" [113], the Home government now (1884) authorised Ripon to have a Resident appointed in the State at any time after the death of Ranbir Singh. Thus while Ranbir Singh was lying on his death-bed [114] the British were poised to forge a major breakthrough in imposing their total paramountcy over the State. Ripon's departure from India did not result in any deviation from the intended course of action, since the new Viceroy chose to follow his predecessor's policy in letter and spirit. With the death of Ranbir Singh on September 12, 1885 and the simultaneous accession of Pratap Singh to the Kashmir throne the British India government lost no time in announcing to the new Maharaja their decision to replace the Officer on Special Duty by a full-fledged Resident [115]. Once Oliver St. John asumed his new function as the Resident in Kashmir, he moved quickly to place the British imperial interests on a firm footing there. What came as another rude shock to Pratap Singh was the demand for establishing a British cantonment within his territories, which was supposed to have become necessary "owing to the inflammable situation beyond the north-west frontier and strategic considerations"[116]. The young Maharaja was so alarmed at this proposal that he hastened to Calcutta to plead with Lord Dufferin for maintaining the status quo in his relations with the British Indian government [117]. In spite of Pratap Singh's protests the Viceroy did not

111. *Foreign. Sec. E.* May 1884. 354-357.

112. Secretary of State to the Government of India 23 May 1884. *Foreign. Sec.E.* Dec. 1885. 192-245.

113. *Ibid.*

114. Hardly a week before his death, Ranbir Singh had written to Lord Dufferin expressing the hope that his descendants would be allowed to enjoy full rights created by the treaties without any interference in the internal administration of the State.

115. St. John met Pratap Singh in his Durbar on 15 Sept. 1885, that is while the mourning of his father's death was still on to announce this change in the status of the Officer on Special Duty.

116. Durand had asked St. John to inform the Maharaja about the probable need to station British forces in Kashmir in view of the events happening beyond the north-western frontier. See H. M. Durand to Resident in Kashmir 19 Oct. 1885. *Foreign. Sec. E.* Dec. 1885. 192-245.

117. Pratap Singh had a private interview with Lord Dufferin at Calcutta on 14 January 1886.

change his stand on the issue of allowing British traders to buy lands in Kashmir, and of discontinuing the practice of stationing a Kashmir Vakil at the Viceregal Court, as initiated under Lytton's regime in 1877. The cantonment question was, however, set aside for the time being, more due to the revised opinion of F. Roberts, the Commander-in-Chief, regarding its feasibility rather than the appeals of Pratap Singh [118]. But the British did succeed in exacting from the new Maharaja a voluntary offer to improve the Murree-Srinagar road and also to build a railway link with Punjab.

Every successive Resident did his best towards consolidating and further extending the British gains in the State. If St. John became the medium for establishing the Residency, his successor, Plowden, exerted this authority to the extreme. Apart from getting certain British Officers appointed to vital posts in the State, he also got the composition of the Kashmir Ministry changed to suit his designs. However, it fell to Plowden's successor, Col. Parry Nisbet [119] to deal with the situation arising from the discovery of 34 letters alleged to be in Maharaja's own hand-writing. Some of these letters disclosed Pratap Singh's intrigues with Russia and Dalip Singh and also hinted at the promises of large reward held out by the Maharaja to certain persons for transmitting letters across Gilgit into Russian Turkestan [120]. Though Lansdowne did not attach any importance to the discovery of these letters yet he used this circumstance as a pretext for a direct intervention in the State. The decision to vest full powers of the State government in a Council, which was to work under the umbrella of the Resident [121] now placed the State directly under the British authority without having recourse to outright annexation. This was but a first step towards implementing their active policy at the northern frontier which included the re-establishment of the Gilgit Agency. Now such projects as the construction

118. For details See D.K. Ghosh *op cit*. pp. 33-34.

119. Col.P.Nisbet joined as Resident on 13 Nov. 1888.

120. Nisbet to H. Durand, Secretary, Foreign Department, GOI, 27 Feb. 1889. *Foreign. Sec. E.* April 1889. 80-98.

121. Though Lansdowne cited Maharaja's voluntary offer of renunciation from office on 8 March 1889 as the basis of this decision, the British Resident in Kashmir had been urging forthe removal of Partap Singh from office and for the constitution of a fresh Council to act under himself.
See Nisbet to H. M. Durand 5 March 1889. *Ibid.*
Nisbet's private meetings with Pratap Singh at Jammu on 7 and 8 March 1889 are sufficient proof of the bullying tactics employed by the British Resident in forcing the Maharaja to issue an edict of abdication on 8 March 1889.

of Jhelum Valley cart-road, Jammu-Sialkot Railway and military road connecting Gilgit with Srinagar could be completed more expeditiously under the direct instructions of the British Resident. Similarly by placing the State army under seasoned English officers, the efficacy of newly-created Imperial Service Corps and the Gilgit Force for defending turbulent frontiers was much improved. Though the establishment of the Residency in Kashmir almost coincided with the Panjdeh crisis of 1885,[122] which nearly precipitated a war between Britain and Russia, it was not a sequel to the new development on the Russo-Afghan borders.

Right from 1846 when the Jammu and Kashmir State was carved, sustained effort was made by every succeeding Viceroy to increase the degree of British authority over Kashmir. The process which had been initiated during Harding's time by imposing a British Officer on Special Duty in Kashmir, completed its cycle during Dufferin's Viceroyalty when the said officer was finally turned into a full-fledged Resident with powers to supervise the State administration. Lansdowne went a step ahead by depriving the recognised ruler of powers to govern. The whole story reads like that of a camel and bedouin in the Arabian Nights. Naturally the British action in deposing the hereditary ruler of Jammu and Kashmir from power evoked strong reaction both in India and abroad. Indian press, particularly the *Amrita Bazar Patrika* took pains to expose the reason behind this move and described the British intention to secure control over the strategic Gilgit as the real motive behind this action[123]. Another Indian writer went to the extent of comparing it to the Russian occupation of Khiva though giving the credit of non-invasion and absense of bloodshed to the British method[124]. Even the liberal Irish Members of British Parliament like J.Bradlaugh and Lord Herschell by raising the issue in the House of Commons and House of Lords respectively, caused considerable anxiety to the British government both at home and in India[125]. The Russians too took a serious view of

122. It was on 30 March 1885 that Russian forces advanced upon Panjdeh on the border of Afghanistan. On account of the war scare created by this incident, Gladstone as Prime Minister of Britain obtained a vote of credit for one million Pounds sterling for Indian defence. But the war averted and negotiations for demarcation of Afghan frontiers started between Britain and Russia.

123. See *Amirta Bazar Patrika* 30 Oct. 1889.

124. See *Kashmir Conspiracy: a truth of Maharaja's case*. Lahore, 1890. Chap XXI.

125. William Digby, another Liberal M.P. lays thread-bare the whole story behind the British action in depriving Pratap Singh of powers in his book "*Condemned unheard: the Government of India and the Maharaja of Kashmir*" published from London in July 1890.

Lansdowne's action in deposing the Kashmir ruler. Describing it as the annexation of Kashmir, the Russians now apprehended serious threat to their interests in Central Asia[126]. The tightening of British control over Kashmir, which was an organic part of the British policy of establishing paramountcy over all the Indian princely States, assumed a special significance in the context of the Russian advance in Central Asia and also the reported exchanges between Kashmir ruler and the Russians. In opposition to the Russian moves across the Oxus, Britain was poised to secure its firm control up to the Hindu Kush watershed. Because of its strategic location, Kashmir assumed importance in this big power game as it could be used as a convenient outpost for extending British control over the tribal territories of Hunza, Nagar, Chitral and Yasin.

---

126. For translation of an article "Russian apprehensions about Kashmir" in Novoe Vremya, See *Pioneer* 2 Oct. 1889.

5

'Great Game' on Kashmir Frontiers

The Anglo-Russian agreement of 1873, whereby the British and Russian spheres of influence in Central Asia and Afghanistan were mutually agreed upon, instead of ushering in a new era of cordial relations between the two rival powers added new dimensions to the 'great game'. Whereas this agreement in effect gave the two sides freedom and a sort of legitimacy to their advance within their respective zones[1], at the same time it brought to surface the new problem of the actual delimitation of Afghan, Chinese and Russian frontiers in the upper Oxus region of the Pamirs. British attention to the complexity of this question was drawn by British officers like Gordon, Trotter and Biddulph who in 1874 explored the Wakhan and Pamirs area. They discovered that the Afghan territory in the eastern extremity lay on both sides of the river Oxus, which under the 1873 agreement was declared to be the dividing line between Afghanistan and Russia. This discovery disputed the very foundation of this accord. On examination of the Hindu Kush passes, the British explorers found them easy to cross, thus making India vulnerable to a attack from across the Hindu Kush. Both these discoveries were important from the strategical point of view and the British modified

1. Russia occupied Kokand in 1876 and Britain went on another war with Afghanistan in 1878.

their frontier policy accordingly. The deputation of Biddulph in 1876 to survey the Hindu Kush passes which was followed by the establishment of a British agency in Gilgit under the same officer in 1877, reflected the new British strategy to meet the challenge posed by the Russian approach to the Pamirs.

C.M. Mac Gregor, the Quarter Master General of Indian army (1880-85) also contributed a lot to mould the British Policy in the cast of Russophobia. In his book entitled "Defence of India" which was published in 1884, Mac Gregor openly aired his anti-Russian sentiments and recommended a number of measures designed to achieve the fragmentation of the Russian empire. He apprehended a Russian attack on India from the direction of Kabul, Herat, Chitral and Gilgit. Mac Gregor wanted the British government (a) to play the game of diplomacy with Russia, (b) to destroy Russian trade, (c) to make coalition with Austria, Germany and Turkey, (d) despatch commissions for demarcation of northern and north-western frontiers of Afghanistan, (e) to transfer Herat province to the British, (f) to transfer to the British the regions of Wakhan, Chitral and Yasin, (g) to attract Persia to British side, (h) to come closer to China, (i) to improve means of acquiring information about the Russian movements, (j) to despatch emissaries for instigating disorder in the Khanates of Central Asia and among the Turkmens and (k) to fragment the Russian empire[2]. When his book, though a classified publication, fell into the hands of the Russian Military Attache at the Russian Embassy in London, a serious view was taken of the British plans to fragment the Russian empire.[3] Mac Gregor's proposals aroused Russian suspicions about the British intentions and became a subject of diplomatic exchanges between the Russian and British governments.[4]

Meanwhile in 1885-86, Ney Elias was deputed by the British Indian government to reconnoiter the frontier areas of Sinkiang, Wakhan, Badakhshan and the Oxus head-waters. On his return Elias came up with a startling information. He pointed out that the two extreme ends of the Afghan and the Chinese frontier in the Pamirs area could be stretched and joined together to form a neutral buffer thus preventing any direct contact between India and Russia in the Hindu Kush and Dardistan

2. Cited in N. A. Khalfin, *op cit.* p. 220.
3. *Ibid*
4. *Ibid.* p. 221.

region. Elias's discovery was to become later "a cardinal feature of British policy towards the Pamirs".[5] The Wakhan corridor stands there even today as a testimony to Elias's strategum. The British forward policy in the area lying south of the Hindu Kush was also activised due to reports of direct dealings between the Hunza Chief, Safdar Ali and the Russian officer, Grombchevsky. To meet any possible Russian threat the British adopted a two-pronged strategy. They started inducing the Chinese to occupy as much area in the Pamirs as could be possible in order to keep the Russians away at a safe distance. To achieve this end Younghusband was deputed in June 1890 to the Pamirs to see as to "Where the Afghan and Chinese boundaries should be made to meet"[6]. Younghusband did succeed in persuading the Chinese authorities in Sinkiang to send a force to occupy Somatash, but he found himself outmanoeuvred by the Russians who had already occupied Somatash, thanks to a good liaison maintained by the Russian Consul in Kashgar with the Chinese *Taotai* there. Timely hint from *Taotai* had enabled Petrovsky to forewarn Grombchevsky, the Russian frontier officer at Marghilan, about the British ambitions. In fact Younghusband's mission to Chinese Turkestan "activised the Tsarist government which for some time had been following a policy of "wait and see" towards the Pamirs which resulted in the visit of the Governor General of Turkestan, A.Vrevsky, to the Alai Pamirs[7]. When Younghusband was making a return journey to India via the Pamirs in August 1891, he was forcibly expelled by a party of Russian Cossacks led by Colonel Ivanov near Bozai Gumbaz which was declared to be Russian territory. This fresh development sparked off a crisis in the Anglo-Russian relations and conflict was averted by the Russians adopting a low profile. But this incident made the British occupation of the Dardic territory lying below the Hindu Kush an urgent necessity.

By now the strategic importance of the Pamir had become clear to both the British and the Russians. Pamir was the meeting point of the Kashmir frontiers in Gilgit, Hunza and Chitral, the Afghan provinces of Badakhshan and Wakhan, the Russian territory of Kokand and the Sarikol area of Chinese Turkestan. It was a potential gateway to India. The British strategy geared itself to the task of creating a barrier between Russian and British empires right on the Pamirs, simultaneously extending

5. John Keay, *The Gilgit game*. London. p. 160.
6. *Ibid.* pp 208-209.
7. D.Kaushik, *Central Asia in modern times*. p. 59.

their effective control over the frontier areas in Gilgit, Hunza, Chitral and Yasin through the Maharaja of Kashmir. Several factors contributed to the shifting of British interest to Kashmir frontiers which from late 1870s onwards became the focal point of the 'great game'. Firstly, by occupying Kokand, Russia had acquired a legitimate claim over the Pamirs which were the summer pastures of Kirghiz subjects of the erstwhile Khanate of Kokand. Secondly, Chinese Turkestan came now within the effective range of Russia from their newly acquired territory in Kokand. The Chinese authority in Sinkiang being weak at that time, the British feared that the Russians would next occupy Sinkiang which would then prove to be an important supply base in the event of any further Russian attack on India via the Kashgar-Karakoram route. Thirdly, the reports of Gordon, Trotter and Biddulph had underlined the strategic importance of the Hindu Kush passes which were now considered to be easily accessible, thereby making India vulnerable to any outside attack from across the Hindu Kush and the Pamirs. Fourthly, neither the Chinese nor Afghans possessed any effective control over the Pamirs, leaving the area open for Russian penetration. Lastly the reports of Russian officers having explored the Pamirs and the Hindu Kush region further strengthened the British apprehensions.

Confronted with these strategic considerations, the British encouraged the Maharaja of Kashmir in his adventurist propensities to bring the warlike and unruly Dardic tribal chiefs inhabiting the obscure mountainous valleys of the Hindu Kush and Karakoram under his effective control. The Maharaja was given the freedom to choose any means from conciliation to military expeditions or both and was provided with the necessary arms and ammunition too. However, soon it was found that the Maharaja could not check Dardistan from drifting into a state of turmoil and unstability. This fluid situation was the result of frequent internecine wars between the tribal chiefs and also due to their occasional attacks on the Kashmir troops which often resulted in the lapse of Kashmir's control over these frontier dependencies. The wavering loyalty of these Muslim frontier chiefs towards the Hindu ruler of Kashmir and through him to the British India, the exalted image of Tsarist Russia in this region, the display of active Russian interest in this frontier belt and the open defiance of British power by Safdar Ali, the Chief of Hunza, who claimed both the Russian and Chinese support, forced the British to resort to direct action. The idea behind several military expeditions carried out jointly by the Kashmir forces and the British officers against Hunza,

Nagar, Chitral and Yasin was to put the defence of north and north-western frontiers on a firm footing. Once these unruly tribes were coerced into subjugation to Kashmir, a strong military garrison was established at Gilgit, thus making it the nucleus of the whole defence arrangements. Besides, a new force was raised from amongst the local tribes, which served a two-fold purpose. First it channelised the energies of warlike and turbulent Dardic tribals usefully and they now became an inalienable part of the defence of the north western frontier. Secondly, it reduced the actual expenditure of the British Indian government which was already spending lakhs of rupees for maintaining a garrison at Gilgit.

British diplomacy achieved the second objective of creating a buffer in the Pamirs between British and Russian empires by concluding the Pamirs Boundary Agreement in 1895. Although the 'great game' appeared to be over now, the focus of the two-power rivalry shifted to Sarikol and Taghdumbash Pamirs where Chinese possessions in Sinkiang and the British Indian territory of Hunza converged. Russian interest in this area emanated from their fears about possibility of the British extending their control over the Taghdumbash Pamirs where Chinese authority was nominal. The British and Russian official representatives kept themselves engaged in a war of nerves, each trying to outwit the other to have closer access to the Chinese authorities in Sinkiang. The British support to certain Hunza claims on Raskam lands and Taghdumbash Pamirs attracted strong Russian reaction. On their part the British considered the establishment of Russian post in Tashkurghan with the consent of the Chinese as new move to threaten Hunza and Gilgit and therefrom Kashmir and India. So far as the area around Kashmir frontiers is concerned, the Anglo-Russian convention of 1907 did not end their mutual suspicions in this region. This is borne out by the fact that a number of Russian military officers came to explore this frontier even after 1907. It was only during the World War I period that the two sides actually acted in unison to meet the common threat from Germany. The close cooperation between the British and Russian consuls at Kashgar during this phase in hounding out the suspected German agents from the Pamirs was natural in these circumstances. In the following pages, we shall discuss various strands of the 'great game' which concerned the north and north-western frontiers of Kashmir before the occurrence of October revolution in Soviet Russia.

(1) EXTENDING BRITISH CONTROL UPTO KASHMIR FRONTIERS

Mayo's viceroyalty was marked by a distinct shift from the policy of non-interference in the affairs of Kashmir as laid down by his predecessor in 1868. He initiated a process of enforcing British influence over all the external diplomatic proceedings of the Kashmir ruler. Though Mayo or his Foreign Department did not question Kashmir's jurisdiction over Gilgit, they sought to curb the Maharaja's propensities for further expansion in that direction, particularly when they learnt about the exchange of correspondence between the Maharaja of Kashmir and Mir of Badakhshan on the subject of Kashmir's tutelage over Punyal and Yasin[8]. The British were not totally unaware about the state of affairs in Gilgit and adjacent chiefships within Dardistan, thanks to the extensive work by Frederick Drew and Leitner in that area during 1860s. But their studies did not provide any insight into the strategical details of this area in the context of Russian approach to the Pamirs. Even Pandit Munphool, a native political agent despatched on a probing mission to the region in 1865 could not bring in all the desired information. It was Mayo who sought to fill the existing gaps in his stock of strategic information about Dardistan and adjacent area, by deputing a team of trained native explorers in the train of Forsyth's first mission to Kashgar in 1870. By this time another British explorer Hayward had started exploring the region under the patronage of the Royal Geographical Society, London and with the knowledge of the Indian Government. By mid-1870, Hayward had completed his two visits to Gilgit and Yasin and during these jaunts he did not keep secret of his political proclivities against the Kashmir ruler. However, he kept the Government of India posted about what he heard and saw and also about what transpired during his meetings with the local tribal chiefs. Partly influenced by Hayward's description of alleged atrocities by Kashmir troops in Yasin and partly motivated by a desire to put a stop to Maharaja Ranbir Singh's forward policy, Mayo decided to restrain the Kashmir ruler from extending his authority any further[9]. At a meeting in Sialkot he asked the Maharaja to "communicate with British government on matters of importance more

8. See *Foreign. Sec. I.* 1870. pp. 192-200.
9. See Memo of private interview between Lord Mayo and Maharaja Ranbir Singh at Sialkot on 3 May 1870.

frequently than heretofore''[10]. On his part Ranbir Singh stuck to his stand that the frontier territories in Ladakh, Baltistan, Gilgit, Yasin, Punyal, Hunza and Nagar formed a part of Gulab Singh's territory much before the Amritsar treaty was signed in 1846[11]. However, the British policy enunciated at Sialkot was not destined to stand the test of the time. The circumstances of Hayward's murder at the hands of the Mir of Yasin in July 1870 must have made the British alive to the dangers implicit in any direct dealings with the turbulent chiefs in Dardistan. Besides, the imperial requirements that demanded the extension of British influence upto the Hindu Kush watershed for offsetting any future Russian advance from their frontier outpost at Osh could not be met by Mayo's policy of restricting Kashmir ruler's forward movements. In 1874-75, the British Indian government received valuable survey reports on Wakhan, Pamirs and Sarikol region from Colonel Gordon, Biddulph and Trotter, who had been purposefully sent to Kashgar in the company of Forsyth's second mission of 1873. Gordon's disclosures about the existence of a practicable road from the Russian military post of Osh across the Alai to Sarikol brought into sharp focus the strategic importance of this area. When Gordon pointed at the vulnerability of India from the direction of Wakhan via Ishkoman and Baroghil passes, the need to strengthen British position in the tribal territories of Gilgit, Yasin and Chitral assumed high proportion. The discoveries made by Biddulph during his exploration in the Wakhan area during 1874 and at the passes lying south of Hindu Kush during 1876, only reinforced Gordon's viewpoint. By 1876, the British Indian government appeared to have been convinced about the necessity of extending Kashmir's control over Chitral and Yasin right up to the south of Ishkoman and Baroghil passes. The incorporation of Kokand by Russia, which pushed the Russian frontier beyond Osh, only helped incatalysing British counter moves in Dardistan and Kashmir. It is against background that Mayo's Sialkot stand of 1870 was replaced by Lytton's policy enunciated at Madhopor in 1876.

Stationing of British Agent in Gilgit, 1877.

The importance of Gilgit as convenient base for extending the British influence upto the territories lying south of the Hindu Kush had now been fully realized. To quote Alder, it was a "natural choice" being situ-

10. *Ibid.*
11. This position was explained in much detail by Ranbir Singh in his memo dated 21 July 1870 discussing Kashmir's relations with Gilgit, etc.

ated at the "hub of routes leading off to all parts of Dardistan"[12]. Though Eastern Turkestan continued to be regarded as a rich supply base to support any Russian force coming from its western flanks, the defence of Hindu Kush watershed was of immediate concern to the British. Following the advice of his predecessor (Lord Northbrook), Lytton formulated his proposals about the future course of action to be taken in this frontier belt, which he finally conveyed to Maharaja Ranbir Singh personally at Madhopore on 17 and 18 November 1876. Lytton impressed upon the Kashmir ruler the need to strengthen Indian frontiers by assuming control over the territory that lay between the Hindu Kush and Kashmir frontier, in order to secure command of such passes as were thought to be practicable for passage of Russian forces[13]. To the British, it was now of vital importance that the states like Chitral and Yasin "should come under the control of a friend and ally" like Maharaja of Kashmir, "rather than be absorbed by powers inimical to Kashmir"[14]. But while encouraging Ranbir singh to obtain "an effective but peaceful control over the countries lying between those passes and Kashmir frontier namely Chitral, Mastuj, Yasin and their dependencies"[15], the British secured the right to station an Agent at Gilgit "to collect information regarding the frontier and the progress of events beyond it"[16]. The Kashmir ruler relented to this measure only after obtaining written assurance from Lytton that the Gilgit Agent would in no case interfere in his internal administration. The Maharaja also volunteered to connect Gilgit, Srinagar and Jammu with the British Indian telegraph system. After having obtained Kashmir's concurrence, the formal announcement for the appointment of Captain J.Biddulph as Officer on Special Duty in Gilgit was made on 22 September 1877. The tasks assigned to him were not limited to mere collection of information about the topography and resources of the territory beyond the Kashmir frontier, but also to the extension of British influence among the tribal people by cultivating friendship with them[17]. A medical officer, who joined Biddulph soon after was to help in popularising the British image among these people through the

12. G.J. Alder, *op cit.* p.11
13. See Memo of conversation held at Madhopore on 17 and 18 Nov. 1876 between the Viceroy and Maharaja of Kashmir. *Foreign. Secret.* July 1877. 34-60B.
14. *Ibid.*
15. Lytton to Salisbury(Secretary of State) 11 June 1877. cited in *Ibid.*
16. *Ibid.*
17. T.H Thornton, Secretary, Foreign Department, GOI, to J. Biddulph, 22 Sept. 1877. *Foreign. Pol.A.* Feb. 1878. pp. 117-137.

healing touch of a doctor. Though Biddulph was quite successful in keeping a watchful eye on the Russian movements in Badakhshan, Afghan Turkestan and Kokand, he could not win over the support of Kashmir officials. One cannot dismiss his accusations against the State officials of plundering his baggage and also of creating a wedge between the tribal chiefs and the British government as unfounded. Biddulph's suspicions were strengthened by the experience of Shah Khushwakt, a native agent sent by him in May 1878 to Hunza, Kabul, Bukhara and Kokand on a spying mission[18], who suffered imprisonment in Hunza during his return journey for being a British emissary. He believed that no other person than Babu Nilambar, one of Kashmir Ministers, had disclosed to Ghazan Khan of Hunza through his Vakil about the nature of Khushwakt's activities[19]. To Biddulph's surprise, five thousand rifles gifted by the Government of India to the Kashmir ruler, for strengthening his frontier defence, had not been sent to Gilgit[20]. And when Henvey, the Officer on Special Duty in Kashmir, raised this issue with the Kashmir Durbar, he was curtly told that no conditions had been attached to gift of these arms [21]. Obviously Kashmir disparaged the foisting of a British agent on its territorial jurisdiction. By getting the Kashmir Governor at Gilgit removed, Biddulph only added to his difficulties. The end-result was that the British did not achieve the desired object of creating direct influence among the tribal chiefs. Nor could they enforce their authority over Kashmir which continued to resist such interference [22].

The Gilgit Officer, however, pulled on alone in this remote end of the Indian northern frontier upto 1880. The matter came to head when the successful assault by Hunza and Yasin on Gakuch and Sher Kila on 28 October 1880 exposed the military weakness of Kashmir to hold this

---

18. Leaving Gilgit on 17 May 1878, Shah Khushwakt took his route via Darel, Tangir, Maidan, Kabul, Mazar-i-Sharif, Bukhara, Samarkand, Khojend, Kokand, Marghilan, Osh, Andijan, Namangan, Karategin, Kolab, Wakhan, Hunza, Chitral, Darel and back to Gilgit. See *Foreign. Secret.* Nov. 1879. pp. 152 - 191.
19. *Ibid.*
20. *Foreign Secret.* Jan 1879. pp. 24-33.
21. *Ibid*
22. Alder has apty summed up the situation in these words: "Amid a tangle of mountain tops higher than Mont Blonc and far from the reservoirs of British military strength, British influence at Gilgit was just not strong enough, either to impress Chiefs like Aman-ul-Mulk, or to control the dubious activities of the Kashmir officials". See Alder, *op cit.* p.133.

territory. The precarious situation on the Gilgit frontiers had even put the personal safety of the British agent at Gilgit in danger. The inaccessibility of Gilgit that was barely connected with Srinagar by a rough track running over high mountains for 230 miles and open to traffic for six months only had encouraged the frontier chiefs of Dardistan to be insolent. The frontier uprising of late 1880 proved to be the proverbial last straw for the Gilgit Agency. To Ripon who already considered the Gilgit appointment as "a mistake",[23] the advantages accruing from its continuation were disproportionate to the embarrassments and anxieties suffered by the British. Finally it was decided in July 1881 to withdraw the Gilgit Agent, which however did not mean the British non-involvement in this area. In fact, the Agency was only kept in abeyance till 1888. The British reserved their right to re-appoint the Officer at Gilgit when necessary. The Secretary of State while consenting to this measure gave vent to his reservations over the issue by underlining the point that the withdrawal of the Agent might practically close a valuable channel of information as to the course of events in the countries between Kashmir and Russian Turkestan [24].

Re-establishment of Gilgit Agency, 1889

The British policy of withdrawing the Gilgit Agency in 1881 was bound to change in face of intricate problems involved in the defence of northern frontiers. Their desire to have a firm control over the territories up to the Hindu Kush could not be met by being out of the spot. The Afghan pressures on Chitral, which had already been drawn close to the Indian empire through its allegiance to Kashmir in late 1876, assumed seriousness in 1882 when Kabul claimed this territory "as one of its protected States [25]". Though the Government of India was quick in rebutting such claims [26], the reported Russian intrigues in and around Chitral caused additional concern. The newly-established Resident in Kashmir could hardly extend effective control of the Durbar or even the

23. *Ibid* p.138.
24. Secretary of State to GOI 16 Sept. 1881. *Foreign. Sec.* Jan. 1882. 741-776c.
25. King of Afghanistan to his Agent, General Amir Ahmed Khan, 20 March 1882. *Foreign Secret* April 1882. 353-360.
26. In his reply to General Amir Ahmad dated 3 May 1882, the Secretary, Foreign Department GOI (C.Grant) made it explicitly clear that "Government of India is under a solemn engagement to acknowledge the suzerainty of the Maharaja of Kashmir over Chitral and to afford His Highness countenance and material aid, if necessary in defending and maintaining his rights over that country".

British Indian Government over the turbulent chiefships of Hunza and Nagar. The Panjdeh crisis of 1885 also helped in focussing the British military opinion on the need to make elaborate arrangements for the defence of the north-west frontier. So it was not a mere coincidence that the year 1885 was marked by the despatch of two exploratory missions, one under Col. Lockhart, the Deputy Quarter Master General of India, to survey the lands south of Hindu Kush via Gilgit and Chitral, and the other under Ney Elias to Chinese Turkestan and the Pamirs. Meanwhile the Defence Committee's recommendation for extending Srinagar-Rawalpindi cart-road to Gilgit and Chitral [27], had been approved by Dufferin. The new Commander-in-chief, F.Roberts, even suggested that "we should have political control over the country around Chitral and Gilgit in order to secure the approaches to the former by the Dora pass and to the latter through Wakhan"[28]. The purpose of Lockhart's mission was to establish friendly relations with Chitral and Kafiristan and also to obtain accurate information about the routes, passes and resources of the country lying below the Hindu Kush [29]. During 1885-86, he not only surveyed about twelve thousand square miles of territory of Gilgit, Chitral, Hunza, Taghdumbash Pamirs and all the important passes across the Hindu Kush [30], but also secured the Chitral ruler Aman-ul-Mulk's promise to allow the passage of British troops through his territory in the event of a Russian attack from that side[31].

Lockhart's recommendations, though not accepted at the time, did provide a basis for the future British policy towards this frontier belt. He wanted the British government to acquire Gilgit from the Kashmir Durbar and establish there a garrison of locally raised troops under a British commandant carrying out both the political and civil functions [32]. The importance of Gilgit "as the defensive nucleus of Dardistan"[33] was once again underlined by Lockhart in the following words:

> The acquisition of Gilgit would secure us the continued loyalty of Chitral, carrying with it our right of way through the Mehtar's

27. See D.K. Ghosh, *op cit*. p. 159.
28. Cited in *Ibid*. p. 160.
29. Government of India to the Secretary of State,
28. 28 August 1885. *Foreign Sec. F*. Dec. 1885. 118-124
30. G.J. Alder, *op cit*. p. 155.
31. *Foreign. Sec. F*. Jan 1888. 115-118.
32. *Ibid.*
33. D.K Ghosh, *op cit* . p. 161.

> dominions, and his active cooperation in time of need. In my opinion it would ensure the safety of Hindu Kush'.[34]

By May 1887, the Secretary in the Foreign Department (GOI) H.M Durand, too had reached almost the same conclusions. By recommending the re-establishment of the Gilgit Agency with a garrison of Kashmir troops and local levies, Durand wanted the British Indian government to adopt a more active policy towards this northern frontier so that in the event of any difficulties with Russia, Kashmir would not be "more or less shaky and inclined to hedge"[35]. It was in October 1887 that more clear directives reached the Resident in Kashmir regarding the revised policy of the Indian government about the frontier defence. He was informed:

> Time has come for establishing on the north-west frontier of Kashmir an effective political control, which will enable us to watch the passes of the Hindu Kush and the country beyond, and a military organization sufficient both to control the Chiefships over the border and also to check, in the event of war with Russia, any demonstration towards the passes not backed by a respectable force'[36].

Since the British wanted to execute their scheme with the cooperation of the Kashmir Durbar, the British Resident in Kashmir, Plowden, was asked to use his influence there to make it a smooth running [37]. In fact, Plowden was authorised to promise a military rank to the Maharaja's younger brother, for making the Gilgit scheme palatable to the Kashmir Durbar [38]. But Durand's guidelines to the Resident left little room for doubting the British intention to secure practical control of the frontier territory in Gilgit and up to Hindu Kush, though the Maharaja's Governor and his troops stationed in Gilgit were to be nominally left under the Kashmir Durbar[39].

The need to strengthen Kashmir's hold over its frontier tributaries assumed urgency in view of a joint attack by Hunza and Nagar on

34. *Foreign. Sec. F.* Jan. 1988. 115-118.
35. Cited in Ghosh, *op cit* p. 166.
36. H. M. Durand to the Resident in Kashmir, 18 October 1887. *Foreign Sec. F.* Jan. 1888. 115-118.
37. *Ibid.*
38. *Ibid.*
39. *Ibid.*

Kashmir posts at Chaprot and Chalt in early 1888. Besides, the Indian Government had in mind Ghazan Khan's refusal to permit Lockhart through his territories in April 1886 and also the Chinese links with Hunza. It was against this backdrop that Dufferin decided to depute Capt. A.G.A. Durand(younger brother of the Foreign Department Secretary, H.M.Durand) on a mission to Gilgit. He was required to:

> report on the military position at Gilgit with reference to the recent tribal disturbances and to future possible complications with Russia, and to work out a scheme for rendering Gilgit secure without the aid of British troops and for dominating from Gilgit, through the Kashmir forces, the country upto the Hindu Kush; thus rendering Kashmir territory thoroughly secure against attack and guarding against the possibility of a Russian force penetrating to Chitral and threatening our lines of communication between Kabul and Peshawar through the Kunar Valley .[40]

On his return in late 1888, Capt. Durand while reporting about the visit of a Russian officer(Grombchevsky) to Hunza in the autumn of that year, underlined the need to close the gap between the Chinese frontier post at Aktash and the Afghan frontier at Lake Victoria, which otherwise could give Russians access to Hunza[41]. Taking full note of the possible lines of Russian advance to Chitral and Hunza, Durand sought to seal them by proposing the re-establishment of a political agency at Gilgit and stationing of about 2000 Kashmir troops there to function under four British Officers[42]. He also recommended the improvement of Kashmir-Gilgit-Chitral road and the early completion of telegraph line to Gilgit [43]. The local chiefs of Chitral, Punyal, Hunza and Nagar were proposed to be encouraged in becoming an inseparable part of the Indian empire, by grant of increased subsidies to them[44]. Owing to Dufferin's departure from India, the task of implementing his active policy towards Gilgit fell upon his successor Lansdowne who readily accepted Durand's scheme.

---

40. H.M. Durand to Capt. A.G.A Durand 22 June 1888.
41. A.G.A Durand, ***Report on the present military situation in Gilgit***. Simla, 5 Dec. 1888. p.14.
42. *Ibid.* p. 45.
43. *Ibid.*p. 14
44. *Ibid.*

Lansdowne's task was rendered easier by the political changes in Kashmir in April 1889 when the State administration was brought under the direct control of the Indian government through the Resident. Accordingly Capt. Durand alongwith two British officers, Dr. Robertson and Lt. Manners-Smith, arrived in Kashmir in April 1889 to make preparation for their journey to Gilgit[45]. In fact, Durand left Srinagar for Gilgit in the middle of June 1889[46], that is few days before the Home government's approval to the re-establishment of Gilgit Agency had reached Lansdowne [47]. Durand's position was quite different from that of his predecessor Biddulph, who was not only handicapped by the absence of an armed escort but also had to face much obstruction from Kashmir officials. Now, the virtual administration of Dardistan [48] passed into the British hands through their Agent, though the Kashmir Governor at Gilgit continued to exercise civil authority over this territory.

(2) RUSSIAN STAND ON HUNZA CLAIMS OVER RASKAM LANDS

When in the spring of 1897 the Mir of Hunza sent some of his men to resume cultivation of some tracts in the Raskam valley, the simple affair snowballed into an international issue involving the three empires of the world-Britain, China and Russia. It was the action of the Chinese magistrate(Amban) at Yarkand in arresting the two Hunza men who had stayed at Raskam to look after their crops that actually sparked off the crisis. The matter was promptly taken up by the Mir of Hunza with the

45. A.G.A. Durand, *Making of a frontier*. p. 120.
46. *Ibid*. p.123. However, by virtue of a Notification issued by the Foreign Department, Government of India, on 6 August 1889 Capt. Durand was appointed as the British Agent at Gilgit with effect from 17 July 1889.
47. See Despatch from Secretary of State to GOI 28 June 1889. In their letter of 6 May 1889 to the Secretary of State, the Government of India had sought his approval to this proposal in view of the Russian advance "up to the frontiers of Afghanistan and great recent development her military power in Asia." *Foreign. Sec. F.* Oct. 1889. 104-132.
48. Capt. Durand identified the limits of Gilgit Agency with the Dardistan region, which comprised of Chitral, Yasin, Punyal, Gilgit valley, Hunza, Nagar, Astor Valley, Shin Republics of Gor, Chilas, Darel, Tangir and Kohistan.
See his *Making of a Frontier*. p. 198.

local Chinese authorities in the knowledge of full British support. The British interest in this affair was due to their suzerainty over Hunza which had been militarily enforced since 1891. They would have preferred to see this issue resolved locally through bilateral negotiations between the Hunza chief and the Chinese authorities in Sinkiang. But seeing that the Chinese had succumbed to the Russian pressure, the British extended their official support to the claims of Hunza. Russia viewed the Hunza move in exercising its rights in Raskam as part of a covert British design to extend their authority on this part of the Pamirs in their bid to outflank the Russian influence there. Russia saw to it that the Chinese did not give practical effect to their agreement whereby the Chief of Hunza had been allowed to cultivate this area. The two-power rivalry naturally came in handy for China which stood to gain by the postponement of the final settlement of this issue.

The rights of Hunza over Raskam and Taghdumbash are believed to have originated from the defeat suffered by the Kirghizs at these places at the hands of Salim Khan, the Chief of Hunza in around 1760 A.D.[49] This chief announced his victory and also the extension of his authority up to Dafdar through a message sent to this effect to the Chinese alongwith a trophy of Kirghiz heads [50]. China expressed its happiness over the defeat of their enemies - the Kirghizs by sending return gifts to Hunza. This gesture was duly acknowledged with a token present of gold dust by the Hunza chieftain [51]. Simultaneously Hunza received the concession of cultivation, grazing and taxation rights in Raskam and Taghdumbash Pamirs from China, which however could not be enforced during Yakub Beg's rule. While it continued to levy taxes from the Kirghiz settlers in Taghdumbash till early twentieth century, Hunza could not enforce its rights in Raskam after 1897 till 1914. The existence of Hunza forts in Azghar and the signs of cultivation at other places in this area indicated that hunza was in actual possession of Raskam for a considerable period.

Why the Raskam question cropped up only towards the end of the nineteenth century , can be explained by certain historical factors.

49. For further details see Capt. A.H. McMahon's (Political Agent in Gilgit) report to Resident in Kashmir dated 10 May 1898. *Foreign. Sec. F.* July 1898.327.

50. *Ibid.*

51. Thus came to be in vogue a custom of exchange of gold dust and return presents between Hunza and China which continued to be followed till early twentieth century except for the period when Yakub Beg ruled in Kashgaria.

Firstly, the Chinese authority in Sinkiang being generally weak, they could do nothing except silently watch Hunza exercise its jurisdiction over this area in the Pamirs. The local Chinese authorities did not run the risk of offending the successive chiefs of that principality who often sent foraying missions within the borders of Chinese Turkestan to enslave Kirghiz nomads and plunder their property. Secondly, the Chinese, derived satisfaction from the receipt of annual presents of gold dust deeming it to be a tribute from a loyal dependency, thus not bothering for Hunza rights in Raskam. On the other hand, Hunza adhered to this custom, mainly because it yielded substantial income in the shape of return Chinese presents, which valued about ten times more [52]. Besides, this occasion of sending emissaries to Chinese Turkestan was used to get certain outstanding matters cleared, mostly relating to Hunza rights in Raskam and Taghdumbash. Thirdly, the need to enforce its old cultivation rights in Raskam bacame more acute when the people of Hunza were faced with food shortage due to the loss of income from cessation of raiding and slave trading activities. The increase in population that followed the overall peace forced the Hunza chief to search for additional avenues of income and food[53], as there was no scope for bringing additional land under cultivation in his principality.

Now coming to the point of actual Russian involvement in what was a bilateral Hunza-China question concerning small tracts, it may be pointed out that Russia had not forgotten the extension of British authority in Hunza in 1891. The ex-chief of this principality, Safdar Ali, while in exile in Chinese Turkestan, continued to be in touch with Petrovsky the Russian Consul at Kashgar. Seeing that the Chinese *Taotai* at Kashgar had favourably disposed off the Hunza representation allowing the Kanjutis to cultivate some plots in Raskam valley, Petrovsky sent a letter to the next higher authority(*Futai*) the Lt. Governor of Sinkiang, advising him not to allow Kanjutis to settle down at that place as it lay on the frontier [54]. But the *Futai* too was in favour of granting this right to Hunza, though he sought to allay the Russian fears by proposing to levy an

52. As against his present of 15 miskalls of gold valuing about Rs. 120 at that time, the Hunza ruler used to receive return gifts of silk and cotton clothings, silver yamboo, tea bricks etc. amounting to about Rs 1100/-
53. While acknowledging such difficulties of the Hunza people, the Chinese Taotai in Kashgar granted them their right to cultivate lands in Raskam and also waived off the land tax earlier proposed to be levied on them.
    See Taotai's letter to Mir of Hunza 27 April 1898.
    Foreign Sec. F. July 1898. 342.
54. *Kashgar Diary* 15 April 1898. *Foreign Sec. F.* June 1898. 464-467

annual grain tax on such cultivators so that there remained no distinction between an ordinary Chinese subject and a Hunza cultivator at Raskam[55]. So when the actual possession of seven plots at Raskam was being handed over to the people of Hunza in early 1899 by the local Chinese authorities[56], Russia started pressurising China against such a course of action. The Russian representatives stationed at Peking and Kashgar warned the Chinese government hinting about the possible Russian occupation of Taghrama (in Sarikol) as a *quid pro quo* to the grant of Raskam lands to Hunza. Consequently the Tsungli Yamen stalled action on the promises given to Hunza chief and also took further steps to evict the recent Kanjuti cultivators from Raskam in a bid to save itself from the possible Russian inroads into the frontier district of Sarikol. On receipt of fresh directives from Peking, the local authorities in Sinkiang hastened to inform Mohammad Nazim Khan of Hunza about the revised Chinese decision not to allow any Kanjutis to settle in Raskam in view of the Russian objections[57]. The *Amban* (magistrate) at Yarkand also offered to compensate Hunza for the loss of grain that would result from the abandonment of Raskam lands by Kanjutis[58]. In order to placate his hurt sentiments, the *Amban* even sent two Begs of Sarikol to meet the Chief of Hunza personally and to explain the row caused between Russia and China over this issue[59]. Seeing that China had under Russian pressure gone back on its agreement of giving seven tracts in Raskam to Hunza, the British government decided to resist the action. Accordingly, the British Ambassadors at Peking and St. Petersburgh took up the matter with the Tsungli Yamen and the Russian Foreign Minister respectively. If Mouraviev's assurance given on 17 May 1899 to Scott, the British representative at St. Petersburgh, is any indication, then Russia was not inclined to use the grant of Raskam lands as a "pretext for acts of aggression on Kashgar".[60] But Kuropatkin's views coupled with Petrovsky's pleadings from Kashgar against allowing any further extension

55. *Ibid.*
Macartney the British Consul at Kashgar, learnt about this exchange of letters from his Chinese Munshi who had read the Futai's reply addressed to Petrovsky.
56. *Kashgar Diary* 15 Jan. 1899 *Foreign Sec F*. April 1899. 119-125.
See also *Foreign Sec. F*. May 1899. 84-87.
57. *Foreign Sec. F*. Aug. 1889. 168-201.
58. *Ibid.* The Amban had in his letter dated 7th of 3rd month of 25th year of Kuangshu 1316, even proposed to supply annually grain to such people to Hunza as would be sent to Yarkand for the purpose, taking due note of the food requirements of Hunza.
59. *Ibid.*
60. C. Scott to Salisbury. St. Petersburgh 17 May 1899. see *Foreign Sec. F*. August 1899. 183.

of the British influence in Sarikol appear to have hardened the Russian stand. This is evident from their action in seeking details about the extent and position of land in question from the British government [61] and also from the objections raised by Giers before the Tsungli Yamen in Peking[62]. Russian concern over the reported construction of a carriage road from the Indian frontier towards Sarikol was not only conveyed through the usual diplomatic channels in London [63], but also by General Kuropatkin in the course of his private conversation with a visiting British Military officer Col. Mac Swiney [64]. On both the occasions, the report was denied strongly. Russian War Minister's casual remarks made before Mac Swiney on 9 June 1899 that " if your Kanjutis go into Raskam, we shall be forced to take over Kashgar, Tashkurghan etc." [65], point to the seriousness attached by Russia to the Raskam affair. In such an atmosphere of mutual distrust and acrimony between the two imperial powers, China got encouraged to resist the British pressures by playing upon the Russian objections. When approached by the British representative at Peking, the Tsungli Yamen openly disclaimed the existence of any agreement between the Taotai of Kashgar and the Chief of Hunza over Raskam lands [66].

While Britain and Russia were engaged in thrashing out the issue both in Peking and London, there in St. Petersburgh Scott was labouring hard to allay the Russian apprehensions. It was only after receiving a written assurance that Britain sought only cultivation rather than territorial rights for Hunza in Raskam lands lying on the banks of the Yarkand river [67] (but not along the Taghdumbash Pamir as suspected by Kuropatkin), that the Russian government agreed to drop its objections to its lease to Hunza. When Giers wrote to the Tsungli Yamen in Peking informing about his government's withdrawal of the objections raised earlier, the Yamen gave its green signal to the local authorities in Sinkiang for carrying out the lease of Raskam lands to the people of Hunza [68]. But

61. Secretary of State to Viceroy. 1 July 1899. *Foreign Sec.F.* August 1899. 168-201.
62. *Foreign. Sec. F.* Sept. 1899. 210-240.
63. Secretary of State to the Viceroy 1 July 1899.
64. *Foreign. Sec. F.* Sept. 1899. 216.
65. *Ibid.*
66. Bax-Ironside(from Peking) to the Foreign Office, London. 20 May 1899.
67. *Foreign. Sec. F.* Sept. 1899. 210-240.
68. *Foreign. Sec. F.* Nov. 1899.25.
See also Telegram from the Governor of Sinkaing to G.Macartney, Kashgar, 8 Nov. 1899. But this time only five plots were decided to be leased to Hunza, exclusive of those at Azghar and Ursur.

Petrovsky was not going to let this happen. He continued to apply pressure on the Taotai of Kashgar by demanding the lease of Sarikol to the Russians. Even though both Giers and Mouraviev denied before the British Ambassadors at Peking and St. Petersburgh respectively from having instructed Petrovsky to stake a counter-claim for compensation in Sarikol[69], they did neither reprimand their representative at Kashgar for re-opening the issue nor assuage China's fear of fresh Russian demands in Sarikol as hinted at by Petrovsky. Instead, Petrovsky's views were openly appreciated as "reasonable"[70] by Giers in the course of his conversation with Mac Donald at Peking. Finding another chance to defer the lease of Raskam lands tc Hunza cultivators, the Chinese authorities now began to strengthen their position in and around Sarikol. They not only encouraged the settlement of Kirghiz and other Chinese subjects in Raskam, but also terminated any remaining traces of Hunza foothold in that valley by expelling the Kanjuti cultivators. When the British government, acting on Curzon's complaint lodged a protest note to China on 29 May 1901 against this action demanding the removal of Chinese settlers and also the reinstatement of Kanjutis in Raskam[71], it received vague, unsatisfactory and evasive replies from the Tsungli Yamen. Seeing renewed British pressure being applied on China, Russia "took steps to keep the Raskam pot mildly simmering"[72], thus forestalling any possible settlement of the issue in favour of Hunza. The Russian Ambassador at London, Baron Graevenitz addressed a note on 14 January 1903[73] to Lansdowne protesting against the terms claimed by Satow in his notes of May and November 1901 to the Chinese. Lansdowne's assurance that the proprietory rights claimed by Hunza in Raskam and supported by Britain were not political or territorial in character[74] appears to have answered the Russian purpose more so because the British did not pursue the matter any further.

The roots of Russian reaction in this whole affair lay in their apprehensions about the prospective British penetration into this area in order

---

69. *Foreign. Sec. F.* June 1900. 83-95.
70. *Ibid.*
71. E. Satow(British Ambassador, Peking) to the Chinese Plenipotentiaries, 29 May 1901. *Foreign Sec. F.* July 1902. 56.
72. Alastair Lamb, *The Sino-Indian border in Ladakh*. Canberra, 1973. p.59.
73. *Foreign. Sec. F.* Sept. 1903. 104-110.
74. *Ibid.*

to outflank the Russian position in the Pamirs [75]. Petrovsky must have also been worried about the growing British influence in the frontier area of Taghdumbash due to the presence of a British informer, Munshi sher Mohammad at Tashkurghan. The Chinese recognition of Hunza claims over Raskam and Taghdumbash Pamirs was important for the British because it could be utilised to their advantage in the event of any future Russian advance towards Kashgaria. Their fears assumed serious proportions in early 1901 when Russia secured Chinese permission to station a military post at Tashkent postal service but actually to checkmate any future British forward move in this area. Such a clash of imperialist interests in the Pamirs from two opposite directions was behind the whole Raskam issue which remained undecided even after the Tsarist and British rule was terminated in Russia and India respectively. The issue would have been decided in Hunza's favour in 1898 itself, but for the Russian pressure for not allowing the lease of Raskam lands to Hunza men, until in 1903 the British disclaimed any political or territorial (in other words sovereign) right for Hunza there, confining the same to cultivation and other proprietory rights.

When in mid-1899 the Chinese authorities in Kashgar informed the Hunza chief that the decision to disallow the use of Raskam lands by Kanjutis had been arrived at Peking after mutual discussions between the Tsungli Yamen and the British representative [76], they only made a half-hearted attempt to solve the issue on the basis of the British offer of 14 March 1899 [77]. China did not, however, make any official commitment in answer to these package proposals, which involved the actual delimitation of India-China border in this sector, thus precluding any agreed solution. After 1903, the settlement of the outstanding Raskam issue got relegated to secondary position because the British attached primary importance to the conclusion of the Anglo-Chinese convention on Tibet

75. Lamb has adroitly described the situation as: "Petrovsky saw the Hunza move into Raskam as the thin edge of a British wedge. He was in all probability, just as concerned at the prospect of the British turning the flank of the 1895 line in the Pamirs, as were the British at the prospect of the similar attempt by the Russians".
See *A. Lamb, op cit.* p. 40.

76. *Foreign. Sec. F.* August 1899. 168-201.
The Kashgar Taotai's letter of 2 July 1899 addressed to the Mir of Hunza is indicative of the Chinese official opinion about the Mac Donald proposals.

77. Calaude M.Mac Donald in his despatch dated 14 March 1399 to the Tsungli Yamen, Peking had offered to relinquish India's claim to "most of the Taghdumbash and Raskam districts" in exchange for the Chinese abandonment of "her shadowy claim to suzerainty over the State of Kanjut" (Hunza).

and also to securing of a Consular status for Macartney so as to bring him at par with his Russian counterpart in Kashgar. In spite of their desire to sever all connections of Hunza with China,[78] the British did not abandon Hunza claim in Raskam and Taghdumbash Pamirs. On his part the Mir of Hunza continued to levy annual grain taxes from the Kirghizs of Tashkurghan. It was only during the period 1899-1914 that Hunza refrained from enforcing its rights in Raskam. From 1914 onwards, when the Russian influence in Kashgaria was on the decline, Hunza adhered strictly to the practice of deputing its men to cultivate these lands, brushing aside the Chinese objections. In doing so, Hunza had received official concurrence from the British Indian government. The British fully understood the strategic importance of using Hunza rights in Raskam and Taghdumbash Pamirs to their advantage in the event of any future Russian incursions into Sinkiang. But due to their pre-occupation with other issues that were more relevant to their broader imperial interests, the British refrained from applying direct pressure upon China for solving this issue. With the result the India-China border in Hunza and Ladakh sectors skirting Sinkiang remained undelimited even after India beacame independent of the British rule in 1947.

(3) RUSSIAN ACTIVITY IN KASHMIR AND ITS FRONTIERS

With the British switching their active attention towards extending their control up to Hindu Kush, the Russians started evincing interest in the frontier tributaries of Kashmir like Gilgit, Hunza and Chitral. As already noted, Mayo's action in dissuading the Kashmir ruler from extending further his authority over the frontier principalities [79] was

78. In fact, Curzon was strongly in favour of implementing the Mac Donald proposals of 14 March 1899 so that connection between Hunza and China could be severed once and for all. In doing so, curzon was influenced by the fear of Russian domination of Chinese Turkestan which in turn would result in Russia staking claim over Hunza,and also by the possibility of Safdar Ai's settlement in Raskam oy the Chinese authorities in Kashgar, which would be real source of discomfiture to the new Mir of Hunza.

79. This was done by Lord Mayo in the course of his meeting with Ranbir Singh at Sialkot on 3 May 1870.

reversed some six years later by Lytton in 1876 in the wake of the Russian annexation of Kokand Khanate. It was Lytton who induced Maharaja Ranbir Singh to "obtain full control over the territories lying between them (passes south of the Hindu Kush) and the Kashmir frontier" [80], in order to secure command over such passes as were thought to be practicable for the passage of Russian forces. Thus the British gained political control over Chitral and Yasin through the Kashmir ruler and also secured the right to station an agent at Gilgit. Through the establishment of a regular agency at Gilgit under Capt. B. J. Biddulph in 1877, they monitored the Russian activities in Central Asia, Afghan Turkestan, Badakhshan and Kashmir frontiers. Such an increase in the British activity near the Oxus was bound to attract Russian notice. A Russian newspaper *Golos* in its issue dated 3 April 1878 covered fully the observations made by Biddulph on his exploration of the Hindu Kush passes in 1876. Similarly Kostenko in his work "*Turkestan Region*" published in 1880 took note of the discoveries made by Biddulph.

In 1883 news reached the British Indian government through no other person than Aman-ul-Mulk, Mehtar of Chitral, that Russian parties then exploring Shighnan and Roshan intended to enter Chitral too.

The Mehtar used this occasion as an opportunity to display his loyalty to the British by soliciting the advice of the Viceroy: "If I should kill them or make them prisoners and send them to your Excellency" [81]. Russia was thus taking steps to keep herself informed about the developments occurring to the south of Hindu Kush. Lockhart's mission to Chitral in 1885, followed by the re-establishment of the Gilgit Agency in 1889 and Capt. Durand's activities in Gilgit were not unknown to them. Russian Officer Grombchevsky's explorations in Hunza and Pamirs during 1888 and 1889 following on the heels of Lockhart have already been dealt with in detail. The despatch of several British expeditions to Pamirs and Chinese Turkestan during 1889-90 had their effect in arousing the Russian suspicions so much so that the Russian Consul at Kashgar, N.Petrovsky, reported to his Ministry of Foreign Affairs about the British desire to divide Pamirs between Afghanistan and China [82]. By now the

---

80. Lytton had detailed discussions with the Kashmir ruler on this issue at Madhopore on 17 and 18 November 1876. See *Foreign. Secret*. July 1871.34-60 B.
81. Mehtar of Chitral (Aman-Ul-Mulk) to Viceroy dated 22 Zilhaj1300 A.H. (22 Sept. 1883). *Foreign. Sec. E.* Jan. 1884. 124-151.
82. Khalfin, *op cit.*

Pamirs had turned into the center of Anglo-Russian rivalry. The instance of the physical expulsion of Younghusband by Col. Ivanov at Bozai Gumbaz in 1891 points to the seriousness attached by Russia to the British activities in and around the Pamirs.

After the British success in occupying Hunza in 1891, events changed fast in Chitral. Aman-ul-Mulk's death in 1892 caused uncertain conditions there and the mutual strife amongst his heirs facilitated the British intervention. Nizam-ul-Mulk's installation as Mehtar with British armed assistance paved the way for stationing a British officer within Chitral territory. No sooner had Robertson and Youngusband secured a place to operate in Mastuj, than they began to advocate stricter British control over Chitral. They soon found an ardent supporter of such an active forward policy in the person of George Curzon who himself visited Chitral in 1894. The year 1895 was so eventful for Chitral that it witnessed the murder of Nizam-ul-Mulk and the consequent siege of the British force which finally culminated in the total subjugation of Chitral by the British installing Shuja-ul-Mulk as its nominal head. All these developments were fully reported in the Russian press. Perhaps under the inspiration of the Russian foreign office, *Novoe Vremya* in its issue dated 27-29 December 1892 went to the extent of claiming that Russia too had "some interest" in the events taking place in Chitral, it being strategically important. However, the paper was fair in reporting about Kashmir ruler's rights over Gilgit, Yasin and Chitral. Another paper *St Petersburgh Herald* in its issue dated 13(25) Dec. 1892 while disputing the claims of Chinese and Afghan rights over the Alichur Pamirs claimed Russian rights over the whole of Pamir "upto the Hindu Kush, to the border of the independent states of Chitral, Yasin and Kanjut (Hunza)" as inherited form the Kokand Khanate's jurisdiction over these territories. The Russian official organ published from Tiflis, "*Kavakaz*" in its issues dated 2(14) December and 3(15) December 1892 even aniticipated a British threat to Chitral. Taking note of the British extension of telegraph line to Gilgit and the occupation of Hunza, the paper predicted a similar fate for Chitral. Referring to the strategic importance of Gilgit and the presence of a British agent there, the paper regarded it as the "base of a future English advance into Chitral". Explaining the physical obstacles on the way from the Russian frontier post at Osh to Little Pamir and onwards to Chitral, the Russian columnist described the British fear of a Russian invasion of India from this side as "absurd". However, expressing his concern at the possible British occupation of Chitral, he wanted the Russian government to pre-empt any such move by coming to an understanding with the Afghan ruler on the issue of Chitral. According to him "existence of Russian advanced posts in Shignan and on the Pamirs would place him(the Amir of Afghanistan) in a much more favourable position in his struggle for Chitral". Another paper "*Russian News*" published from Moscow in its issue dated 8(20) February 1893 expressed concern over the consolidation of British influence in Chitral. It felt that the British were "forestalling Russia", as England's position could be threatened only from the Hindu Kush through Chitral.

From 1890s onwards, one finds a sudden development of Russian interest in Kashmir frontiers particularly in Ladakh, Gilgit, Hunza and Chitral. The British refusal of permission to Grombchevsky for travelling down to Ladakh via Shahidullah and Karakoram in late 1889 did not daunt other Russian officers from attempting similar adventures. Since this strategic frontier territory was a sealed area even for the unauthorised British travellers,the Russians did sometimes succeed in overcoming this difficulty by securing the required permission directly from the British Foreign office much to the discomfiture of the British Indian government. More often, the Russians would placate London by allowing certain British officers to travel through their sensitive spots in Central Asia [83]. First Russian traveller to have succeeded in making an overland journey to Ladakh and Kashmir during this period was Prince Galitzin, who had been invited to visit Kashmir in August 1891 by the British Ambassador at St. Petersburgh (R. Morimer) [84].

Finding it impossible to disown Morimer's word,the British Indian government did allow Galitzin to enter Kashmir from Chinese Turkestan via Karakoram, Nubra valley and Leh [85]. But at the same time it took all precautions to ensure that the Russian would not set upon his inquisitive eyes on other routes towards Ladakh. Besides, a British officer Captain H.Picot was attached with the train of the Russian Prince on his proceedings. After spending the winter of 1891-92 in Kashmir,

83. The British Embassy at St. Petersburgh was officially informed by the Russian government on 9(22) January 1909 that foreigners were not allowed to enter Russian possessions in Central Asia.
84. Galitzin had probably won Morimer's heart by being hospitable to a Britisher named Beech at Ferghana in 1890.
See R.Morimer to Viceroy, 23 May 1891. *Foreign. See. F.* June 1891. 94-98.
85. In his reply dated 29 May 1891 to the British Ambassador at St. Petersburgh, the Viceroy wrote: "I wish he had not been invited".

Galitzin alongwith Picot left Leh on 1 June 1892 for Shahidullah (then the Chinese frontier post towards Ladakh) via Chang La, Marsemik and Chang Chenmo passes [86]. They proceeded towards Karghalik to Chinese Turkestan via Kilian pass. Thus the Russian visitor could have a chance to make an on-the-spot survey of two routes from Chinese Turkestan to Kashmir first via Karakoram-Nubra and Leh and then by Chang La, Marsemik, Chang Chenmo and Shahidullah. Similarly another Russian officer, Captain Novitsky of the General Staff travelled through Ladakh in July 1898 on his overland journey towards Yarkand, Kashgar and Russia [87].

The year 1899 witnessed organised trips by Russian military officers to the Kashmir frontier territories of Hunza and Gilgit. Captain Snesarev and Colonel Polotsov's overland journey to India via Hunza and Gilgit during this year deserve a special mention. While the former occupied the post of Military District Chief on the Pamirs with his headquarters at Kharog [88], the latter had led a reconnaissance trip up the Oxus in 1894. Besides they used the services of a Kashmiri, namely Kabir Ju (a Munshi employed at Tashkent for teaching Hindustani to Russian officers) for extracting some information from the officials employed in the British Agency at Gilgit [89]. This lends credence to Lt. Col. E.F.H.Mc Swiney's assertion that the mission of Polotsov was to reconnoiter Indian north-west frontier and that of Snesarev to study the organisation and administration of British Indian Army [90]. It was not a mere coincidence that the Russian government had permitted several British officers like Cobbold, Colonel Powell and Colonel Mc Swiney at about the same time to travel through Central Asia. In fact, this concession was later to be used as a *quid pro quo* for securing permission for more Russian officers to visit Indian borders. So when the Russian Ambassador at London sought British permission for four high-ranking military officers, Lt.Col.Shersky, Lt.Col.Kouznetsov, Count Mouraviev Amursky and Prince Curossov to travel to northern India from (i) Ishkashim via Dorah pass to Chitral, (ii)

86. *Foreign. Sec. F.* Jan. 1893. 296.
87. *Foreign. Sec. F.* Oct. 1898. 271-74.
In his book published by St. Petersburgh Military District Headquarters in 1899, V.F. Novitsky discussed the British military arrangements in the north-western frontier of India.
88. Kashgar Diary 16-31 Oct. 1902. *Foreign Frontier.* B. Aug. 1903. 288
89. *Foreign. Sec. F.* Nov. 1899. 47-50.
90. *Ibid.*
91. M.De Stall to Lord Salisbury (British Foreign Secretary) 18 Feb. 1899. *Foreign. Sec. F.* May 1899. 61-69.

Killa-i-Panja to Yasin (iii) lake Victoria to Yasin and (iv) Bozai Gumbaz to Hunza [91], the British Government was put in a quandry. Since Staal (Russian Ambassador in London) had cited the Russian Government's permission to British subjects to travel in Central Asia, Salisbury found it difficult to ignore his request for reciprocal treatment [92]. But the government of India stood firm in its objection to any Russian military expert examining the passes that constituted the "strategic defence of our northern frontier" [93]. The circumstance of Ishkashim, Kila-i-Panja and Bozai Gumbaz being within Afghan territory was used as an excuse by the Indian government to wriggle out of the complicated situation by pointing out the need to secure prior consent from the Afghan ruler [94]. However in deference to Salisbury's wishes they consented to the Russian party travelling down from Taghdumbash to Hunza and Gilgit via the Kilik pass [95]. But as a preautionary measure, British officers were detailed to accompany the Russian party from near the Kilik pass [96]. Though this Russian mission was officially described as aimed at making ethnographic, biological and meteorological enquiries under the auspices of the Russian Geographical Society [97], yet its composition and the routes chosen for exploration leave little doubt about the Russian desire to be thoroughly acquainted with the British frontier defence arrangements at the Hindu Kush watershed.

In April 1907 Captain Polotsov of the General Staff of Russian army appeared in Srinagar before the British Resident there asking for permission to travel back to Russia via Leh, Karakoram and Chinese Turkestan[98]. Although the Indian Intelligence Department feared that if allowed to proceed on this journey the Russian would use this opportunity for surveying the Mintaka and Kilik passes, Lord Minto as Viceroy overruled this objection, but attached a British Officer to accompany Polotsov on his overland journey to Russia [99]. No sooner, this officer had secured the necessary permission than another Russian M. Andriev presented himself before the British Resident in Kashmir requesting for being allowed to accompany Polotsov to his home in Russia [100]. After his

92. *Ibid.* Salisbury to Viceroy of India. 14 March 1899.
93. *Ibid.* Viceroy to Salisbury 17 March 1899.
94. *Ibid.*
95. *Ibid.*
96. *Ibid.* Salisbury to Viceroy, 15 April 1899.
97. *Ibid.* M.De stall to Salisbury 18 Feb. 1899.
98. *Foreign. Sec. F.* August 1907. 41-67 A.
99. *Ibid.*
100. *Ibid.*

request was refused, the Russian Consul General at Bombay brought pressure upon the Indian Government to allow Andriev to travel to his home in Tashkent via the Karakoram route as a special case. Accordingly the two Russians left Srinagar for Leh on 21 June 1907, accompanied by a British officer Major Fielding [101]. Soon after their arrival in Ladakh in mid-July, reports began to pour in about their objectionable activities. While Andriev, who knew and spoke Turki and Persian fluently was reported to have questioned traders at Leh about the extent of their trade with Tibet and Turkestan [102]. Polotsov was said to have made enquiries about routes form Shahidullah to Mustagh and thence to Taghdumbash[103]. Fielding complained that the two Russians had surveyed the whole frontier including the Kilik pass on the pretext of going to Taghdumbash[104]. These suspicions got further strengthened by reports coming from Kashgar and Gilgit. While the British informer at Yarkand, Buniad Ali, reported that the two Russians walked in that city disguised as Andijanis so as to avoid recognition [105], information reached Gilgit about their halt at Tashkurgan for four days to make enquiries about Chitral and Hunza routes [106]. Subsequently, when the Military Intelligence Department of the Indian Government came to know that both Polotsov and Andriev had landed at Bombay on one and the same day and that their mission in India was controlled by the Headquarters Department of the General Staff at St.Petersbugh, India office was informed about these proceedings of the Russian officers [107]. Though Whitehall was not disposed to press the matter with the Russian government, yet it cautioned the Indian government to be more careful while granting such permissions in future [108].

Hardly three years had elapsed when Captain Polotsov reappeared in Kashmir in April 1910, this time in the company of Prince Troubetzkoi of the Russian Civil Service, with the intention of making a return

101. *Ibid.* Resident in Kashmir to Secretary, Foreign Deptt. GOI, 21 June 1907.
102. *Ladakh Diary* 1 Aug. 1907. *Foreign Frontier. B.* Oct. 1907. 278-283.
103. Fielding to F. Younghusband, Resident in Kashmir from camp Togru Su river, 5 Aug. 1907. *Foreign. Sec. F.* Nov. 1907. 1-4.
104. *Ibid.*
105. *Kashgar news report* 1-10 Oct. 1907. *Foreign Sec. F.* Jan. 1908. 64-66.
106. *Gilgit Diary* 20-26 Oct. 1907. See *Ibid.*
107. L.W. Dane, Secretary, Foreign Department GOI, to Richmond Ritchie, Secretary, Political Department, India Office, London 9 Jan. 1908. *Foreign. Sec. F.* Jan 1908. 64-66.
108. R.Ritchie to L.W. Dane 21 Feb. 1908. *Foreign. Sec.F.* May 1908. 65.

overland journey to Russia via Kilik pass [109]. When the presence of Russian officers in Kashmir was reported by the British Resident to higher authorities at Simla, the British Indian Government was already seized of the matter, because the Russian Consul General in India, B.Arseniev, had made a personal call on the Foreign Department at Simla on 26 April 1910 to seek British permission for these two officers to return to Russia by the Gilgit route crossing either the Kilik or the Mintaka pass towards Tagndumbash Pamirs [110]. Though Polotsov had met Lord Minto during his previous visit to India in 1907 for seeking a similar permission which was then granted, this time he chose to avoid direct contact with the Viceroy. Instead he met the Commander-in Chief who not only obliged with an autograph letter of recommendation, but also gave official clearance to such a visit being allowed. But Minto, whose memory had not failed him, while recalling Polotsov's "unsatisfactory proceedings" in 1907 saw in his second visit the sole objective of obtaining military information [111]. He was refused the required permission and the Resident in Kashmir was accordingly asked not to allow the Russian "to proceed beyond the limits of ordinary travel for visitors" [112]. The two Russians appear to have stayed in Kashmir till early September 1910 when they were reported to have left Srinagar towards the Punjab [113]. Their renewed attempt to travel across Kashmir frontiers in Gilgit towards Russian Central Asia was thus thwarted.

Only a year later, the Russian Imperial Academy of Sciences started evincing interest in the collection of Zoological specimens from Western Kashmir, Ladakh, Karakoram, Quetta and Sikkim. The British government when formally approached by Russia with a request to allow a party of Russian entomologists to make such a journey in India[114] was put in a fix. While the India office being averse to allow the Russians any access to frontier regions in Sikkim, Ladakh, Karakoram and Quetta proposed to collect the required Zoological specimens through the agency of the Indian government, the Foreign office found it difficult to

---

109. Resident in Kashmir to Secretary, Foreign Deptt., GOI 30 April 1910. *Foreign. Sec. F.* June 1910. 3-5.
110. *Ibid.*
111. *Ibid.* See Lord Minto's minute dated 10 May 1910.
112. *Ibid.* See Secretary, Foreign Deptt. GOI, to Resident 12 May 1910.
113. Resident to Secretary, Foreign Deptt. GOI, 2 Sept. 1910. See *Foreign. Frontr. B.* Sept. 1910. 19.
114. Count Benckendorff to Sir Edward Grey, London 28 Nov. 1911. See *Foreign. Sec. F.* Sept. 1911. 1-44.

refuse such a permission[115]. However, the matter got resolved when the Indian government gave its clearance to. the said Russian expedition, if it travelled via Rawalpindi-Murreè-Baramulla-Srinagar-Sindh-Zojila-Dras-Kargil-Leh-Karakoram towards Kashgar [116]. The Russian party comprising Avinov (Gentleman-in-waiting to Tsar, Mamaev (Attache to Russian Ministry) and Jackolson (Member of Imperial Russian Geographical Society) spent the summer of 1912 in Kashmir and Ladakh wherefrom they travelled back to Russia via the Karakoram pass, Shahidulla and Kashgar [117]. The activities of this Russian expedition appear to have been restricted to that of catching butterflies in the upper reaches of Kashmir and Ladakh, on account of the "unobtrusive watch" being kept by the Resident in Kashmir over the party. But the inclusion of Quetta in the first Russian programme could serve no better purpose thanassessing the British strength at the Quetta, Rawalpindi and Attock. military stations.

Following the increased British activity in Gilgit, Hunza, Nagar, Chitral and North-Western Frontier Province, the Russians made sustained efforts to make an on-the-spot survey of the British military arrangements by despatching experienced officers of the Russian General Staff to that area. In 1897-98, one such officer Novitsky not only succeeded in examining the forts lying on this frontier, but also in returning to Russia overland by Leh-Yarkand-Kashgar route. In his semi-classified publication "Miltary sketches of India" brought out in 1899 (in Russian), he opined that this frontier belt was not fortified in a way to meet the much publicised Russian threat to India [118]. Taking due note of the weakness of most of such forts to stand the artillery attack of a modern European army [119], Novitsky concluded that the British cry of a Russian menace to India was meant to be used as a pretext for its own annexationist policy[120]. To support his point, he drew a comparison between the British expansion towards the Indian north-western frontier and that in Burma, Eastern China, Sudan and Fashoda [121]. Similar conclusions had also been drawn by Lt. Col. Kornilov after he visited

115. *Ibid.*
116. *Ibid.* See Viceroy's telegram to the Secretary of State 16 March 1912.
117. *Ibid.*
118. V.F.Novitsky, *Voenniye Ocherki Indii*. St.Petersburgh, 1899. Cited in Khalfin, *op cit*. pp. 209-210.
119. *Ibid.*
120. *Ibid.*
121. *Ibid.*

northern India in early twentieth century. According to him, Rawalpindi was the only really guarded place in this area[122]. It was Col. Polotsov who after his first visit to India during 1899 gave vent to his views in a book "North-Western Frontier of India". He wrote in favour of the Russian army crossing over Afghanistan and Indus river towards Punjab and Delhi, if war broke out between Britain and Russia elsewhere, a task which he believed was realizeable under certain international conditions [123]. Soviet Scholar N.A. Khalfin has quoted from a confidential note dated 8 December 1902 prepared at the Russian military headquarters to say, that Polotsov's proposals were dismissed as adventurist undesirable and impractiable by the highest military authorities including the Russian War Minister, General Kuropatkin [124]. Polotsov's opinions were of course based on his individual assessment of the British military strength, as he had not only conducted a survey of the Peshawar and Quetta district, [125] but also travelled via Gilgit during 1899. By repeating his visit to India in 1907 and again in 1910, with the sole purpose of making overland journey to Russia via Ladakh, Karakoram, Gilgit and Taghdumbash Pamirs, Polotsov obviously did so at the behest of the Russian General staff. During his stay in India, he used to report about the general political developments to Russian Foreign office [126]. So the British suspicions about his working under the directions of the Russian government, though too late to prevent his journey beyond Ladakh in 1907, were not unfounded. Accordingly in 1910, he was not allowed to go beyond Kashmir.

The routes and areas chosen by the Russian officers whether Novitsky, Kornilov, Polotsov, Avinov and others for their field trips in British India, present an invariable similarity. Their preference to traverse the frontier areas in and around Ishkashim, Chitral, Yasin, Hunza, Gilgit, Quetta, Peshawar and Rawalpindi was guided by the intelligence requirements of Russia.

---

122. See Kornilov. *Otchetei o poezdkev Indiyu* (Report of travels in India). Cited in Khalfin, *op. cit.* pp. 211-12.
123. *Ibid.* pp. 194.
124. Ibid. pp.194-97.
125. *Ibid.* p. 194.
126. In such report addressed to the Director, First Department of Ministry of External Affairs dated 4(17) April 1907, Polotsov communicated details about the proceedings at the 22nd session of the Indian National Congress held at Calcutta in Dec. 1906.
See *Central State Historical Archives. Uzbek SSR. Tashkent.* Fond 1 C/2, Opis 2, Dela 301 (Microfilm, in NAI).

Such reconnaissance missions were not a prelude to any Russian imperialist designs over northern India. It becomes clear on a preusal of Russian official opinions on such an adventure as are cited by Khalfin. In the eyes of the then Russian Foreign Minister, V. Lamzdorf, India was important for Russia as it represented a sensitive nerve of Great Britain, which when touched could force the British to shun its hostile stance [127]. Similarly General Kuropatkin, in contrast to the general British opinion of being an ardent supporter of Russian advance to India, is reported to have advocated alliance with Britain in order to achieve a peaceful agreement for partition of Asia between the two powers [128]. In fact during 1912, Russia made a categorical declaration to the British government to the effect that they had neither any desire to take over the administration of Chinese Turkestan, nor any wish to have any footing in Kashgar or the neighbourhood of Kashmir frontier [129]. What then had necessitated the despatch of such experienced military officers to British Indian frontiers? It appears that Tsarist Russia had not closed its option to pressurise Britain by a mere show of force at the India's north-western frontier, as and when such a necessity arose in order to relieve itself in Europe. And for judging the expediency of such a move they had but to be equipped with the up-to-date intelligence about the British military strength in this area more particularly after a series of British frontier campaigns in Hunza, Nagar, Chitral etc. In this context it is important to note that the Russian government had even started a special two-year course in Hindustani language for its military officers, who were requied to acquire field experience in India later [130]. The whole matter of Russian intelligence activities in India needs to be viewed in the context of the Anglo-Russian rivalry both in Asia and Europe. By stationing a military commandant with an armed escort at Tashkurghan, Russia only sought to counteract the influence created there by the native British informer. If this officer, in conjunction with the Russian Consul at Kashgar, used to employ native agents to obtain intelligence from Hunza, Gilgit and Chitral territories,[131] the practice was not known to the British who even used the services of the Agha Khan to extend their influence

127. Cited in Khalfin, *op cit.* p. 216.
128. *Ibid.* p. 219.
129. This assurance was given by the Russian Ambassador at London, M.Sazanoff to the British Secretary of State, Lord Crewe on 29 Sept. 1912. See *Foreign. Extl*.B.March 1913. 54-62.
130. *Turkestanski Gazetti* 9(22) Oct. 1903.
131. See *Foreign.Frontr.B.* May 1907. 262.
Foreign.Frontr.B. Nov. 1908. 98.
Foreign.Frontr.B. August 1908. 615.
Foreign.Frontr.B. Feb. 1907.272-274.

over the Ismaili residents in Wakhan and Sarikol.That the Russian officers commanding the Pamirs also indulged in such intelligence activities, was admitted by one such officer Lt. Kevekiss before a visiting British officer, Ralph P. Cobbold who travelled through Gilgit, Hunza, Pamirs and Chinese Turkestan in 1897[132]. According to Kevekiss, several Tajiks were employed by the Chief Political officer at Kharogh for collecting intelligence from Chitral and Gilgit[133]. Even the Prime Minister of the Mehtar of Yasin was reported to be supplying the Russians with information[134]. In this great game both powers were playing their role to the best of their ability employing all means within their power short of armed conflict. If the Russian officers got lured to travel overland from India to their country across the high snowy peaks of Karakoram ranges in Ladakh and Gilgit, the British too were eager to grab every opportunity to travel within Russian Central Asia. Both the powers sought to outwit each other by conceding stray permissions to such visits by their officers, just in the hope of receiving a reciprocal treatment from the other side. So the Russian consul at Calcutta, L.K. Reweliotty, was able to make an overland journey to his home via Gilgit, Kilik pass and Kashgar during the summer of 1913, only after two British officers had secured permission to travel in Russian Turkestan[135]. On one occasion, when the need to obtain military intellligence about the Russian strength at Kushak was felt, the British were prepared to allow the Russian military officers including those commanding the frontier pickets in Pamirs to make an overland trip to India via Gilgit and even permit them to see Malakand and Khyber[136]. The Anglo-Russian convention of 1907 which brought an aura of relaxed atmosphere could not totally eliminate the deep-rooted mistrust between the two erstwhile rivals. However, the World War I brought the two countries close together to meet the common threat. As a result, even the imperial agents posted in remote pickets like Tashkurghan and Kashgar (both in Chinese Turkestan) used to work in unison on several matters of common interest, quite contrary to their constant mutual strifes. But this brief period of mutual cooperation came to an end on the eve of the October Revolution in Russia. Now the British geared their imperial machinery not only to prevent the entry of Bolshevism into India but also to destablise the Soviet power in Russian Central Asia.

---

132. R.P.Cobbold, *Innermost Asia*. London, 1900. p. 269.
133. *Ibid.*
134. *Ibid.*
135. *Foreign. Frontier. B.* Feb. 1913. 38-40.
136. *Foreign Frontr. B.* June 1913. 47.

6

Kashmir and British Reaction to the Establishment of Soviet Power in Central Asia

Soon after the October revolution in Russia, the new Soviet government made significant announcements regarding the decree on peace, withdrawal from war, release of Austrian and German prisoners of war and repudiation of secret treaties. All such foreign policy moves and launching of propaganda crusade against the British colonialism in the East posed a serious challenge to the British colonial interests particularly in Persia, Afghanistan and India, where nationalist movements were gaining momentum. The British reaction to the Soviet moves was strong and spontaneous. Their immediate fear was that the success of the Bolshevik revolution in Central Asia would stir up "political disorder and ideological conflagration" in Persia, Afghanistan and India.[1] Consequently the quest for maintaining control over their Asian colonies and introducing political influence in Central Asia emerged as an important constituent in the formulation of the British policy towards Soviet Russia. The collapse of Russian authority in Transcaspia

---

1. F. Stanwood, *War, revolution and British imperialism in Central Asia*. London, 1983. p. 107.

and Central Asia encouraged the British to "exploit the anti-Bolshevik and pro-autonomous sentiments" amongst the Muslims there[2]. They planned to create and buttress "tiny independent states in the Caucasus, Transcaspia, Central Asia, Persia and Afghanistan, near the borders of India hostile to Bolshevik Russia and under the tutelage of Britain"[3]. The British Indian government despatched several military cum political expeditions to Caucasia, Transcaspia and Central Asia with an avowed object of forestalling any possible Turko-German advance towards the Indian frontier but implicitly to stall the establishment of Soviet power in Central Asia.[4] But the allied intervention did not deter Soviet Russia from continuing with its propaganda offensive against the British. A centre was established in Tashkent to train young Asians for stirring up the revolutionary activity in India and neighbouring countries.[5] The emigration of a number of Indian Muslims to Soviet Central Asia via Kabul, Chitral and Kashgar came as a rude shock to the British who began to see the Bolshevik hand behind every advance of the national liberation struggle.[6] To insulate India from any Bolshevik influence became the cornerstone of the new British policy.

Lenin's declaration to grant the right of self-determination and the Soviet appeals to the toiling masses of Russia and the East including the Persians, Turks, Arabs and the Indians exhorting them to "rise and

2. *Ibid*. p. 74.
3. See Curzon's draft memo. to the War Cabinet, 21 August 1919. Cited in Zafar Imam, *Colonialism in East-West relations*. N.Delhi, 1969. p. 113.
4. According to a report, the British had supplied the Amir of Bukhara with 20,000 rifles in April 1919 and 8000 rifles in May 1919. Similarly, the number of British instructors in the Emirate of Bukhara had reached 600 by the spring of 1919. See D.Kaushik, *Central Asia in modern times*. p. 157.
5. In early 1919 the Territorial Committee of the Russian Communist Party(Bolshevik), Tashkent had an agency for conducting propaganda work among Persians, Turks, Afghans Chinese, Uighurs and Indians. Later on a separate council for International Propaganda(Sovienterprop) was established in Turkestan with the object of uniting all the available revolutionary organisations of contiguious countries operating both in and outside Turkestan. The Council strove to train clear and able agitators and organisers in the East.
   See M.A. Persits, *Revolutionaries of India in Soviet Russia*. p. 100.
   Early in 1920, a special training school for Indian revolutionaries was set up in Tashkent by the Tashkent branch of the Soviet Commissariat for Foreign Affairs. The school was soon taken over by the Tashkent Bureau of the Communist International, headed by M.N. Roy. Several Inidian *muhajirs* were provided training in the school. But following the Anglo-Soviet Accord, the Tashkent School was closed.
   See James W.Spain, *The Pathan borderland*. Hague, Mouton, 1963. p. 250.
6. The mass protest against the passage of Rowlatt Bill of 1919 was described by *Times*, London dated 20 March 1919 as part of the "Bolshevik plans to raise revolution in India".

free themselves from yoke of alien capitalists"[7], was regarded by Britain as the Soviet ideological challenge to the British power in Asia. They feared about its repercussions upon their colonial rule in India. Bolshevism came to be dreaded like a most contagious disease, which, if allowed to filter within India would trigger off an anti-British revolution there. A series of anti-Bolshevik measures were initiated both in and outside India. Inside India, the entry of Bolshevik literature was not only censored but a section of the Indian press was also used to circulate anti-Communist propaganda just to develop hostility among the Indian masses towards the Soviet Union. Outside India, the British embassies in Peking, Tokyo, Washington and even Batavia (Netherlands East Indies) were used to prevent the publication of the Soviet proclamation within their host countries[8] so that the possibility of its transmission to India from those countries was averted. That the whole British imperial system failed in achieving a total success in its object, becomes clear from a report about an Indian delegation having informed President Sverdlov on 25 November 1918 that "in spite of all efforts of Britain to check it, the slogan of self-determination of peoples has penetrated India"[9]. Their memorandum highlighted the "enormous psychological impression of the Russian revolution on the Indian people. It ended with an expression of confidence that "the days of England are numbered, that the Indians will rise and drive out the foreign domination, and that free Russia will stretch out a fraternal hand to them"[10]. So when the Secretary of State in a bid to neutralise the anti-British feelings among the Caucasian Muslims, asked the Viceroy of India to extract written statements from leading Indian Muslims claiming participation in the war alongside the Allies and also a better treatment from the British

---

7. Telegram from G. Buchanan, British Amabassador at Petrograd to the Foreign office, London 5 Dec. 1917
   Foreign. War B(Secret). Oct. 1918. 1-82.
   For a translation of the Soviet appeal, December 3, 1917 to the Muslims of Russia and the East, see Appendix IV.
8. *Foreign. War B (Secret)* .Oct. 1918 . 1-82.
9. *Izvestia Turk Ts Ika* 13 April 1919, cited in D.Kaushik: *op cit*. p. 133.
10. Cited in Subodh Roy, *Ed, Communism in India, with unpublished documents 1919-24*. Calcutta, Editions Indian, 1971. p.123.
    The British were fully conversant with the activities of Indian revolutionaries in Soviet Russia. They had intercepted the Soviet Radio message about the meeting of Indian delegation with Sverdlov on 25 Nov. 1918 and and their presenting a memorandum to him.

rulers, the Government of India was unable to secure any such declarations.[11] This was a period when the anti-British feelings were high more particularly among the Indian Muslims for a variety of reasons such as the Home Rule movement, Bihar riots, fall of Jerusalem and pro-Turkish Sentiments. The British Indian authorities found it useless to get such declarations from the leading Muslims, who in their opinion carried little or no weight with the Muslim masses in India[12].

On the Central Asian front, the British Consul General at Meshed, Maj. Gen. W. Malleson had in 1918 opened a front in Trans-Caspia fighting desperately alongside the anti-revolutionary forces[13] to stop Bolsheviks from taking control over the whole of Central Asia. The British attached such a great importance to checking the progress of socialist revolution in Central Asia that they despatched yet another mission under the leadership of Lt. Col. F.M. Bailey from India to organise and operate the anti-Bolshevik forces there. As in the past, Kashmir again came in handy as a base for organising this expedition. Bailey left Srinagar on 22 April 1918.[14] taking the shorter route via Gilgit-Mintaka pass-Tashkurghan-Yangi Hissar to reach Kashgar on June 7, 1918.[15] Kashmiri coolies numbering about one hundred sixty[16] were used as carriers of loads of the English Sahibs over the snowy peaks upto the Chinese frontier. Bailey was also authorised to draw an advance of 29,500 rupees at Simla, Lahore or Srinagar treasuries[17] and the British Resident in Kashmir was to provide all the necessary assistance in this regard. Since the Red Guards had not yet extended their control over the frontier posts on the Russo-Chinese border or

11. *Foreign. War B (Secret)* Oct. 1918. 1-82. See Secretary of State's telegram to the Vicerory 29 Dec. 1917.
12. *Ibid.* Vicerory to the Secretary of State 1 January 1918.
13. The "Order of Star of Bukhara" "presented to General Malleson by the Amir of Bukhara in appreciation of his service for preventing all of Turkestan being overrun by Bolsheviks in ending 1918, naturally lost its relevance when Soviet People's Republic was established in Bukhara in late 1920.
See *Foreign Int. B.* June 1919. 296.
14. F.M.Bailey, *Mission to Tashkent*. p. 15.
15. *Ibid.* p. 22 Other route, a longer one, from India to Kashgar was via Srinagar, Leh, Nobra, Karakoram pass, Shahidullah and Yarkand.
16. *Ibid.* p. 15.
17. *Foreign Est B.* July 1918. 53 -58.
During the year 1918-19, the Bailey mission spent about 1,16,225 rupees, which was far in excess of the original sanctioned provision of rupees one lakh for the purpose. See *Foreign. Est. B.* May 1921. 240-261.

even in the Kashgar Consulate, Bailey's task was facilitated by the willing cooperation provided by the Russian officials manning these posts who were the adherents of old regime.

Though Bailey reached Tashkent on August 14, 1918 quite safely, his arrival at the capital of Soviet Turkestan synchronised with the attack by a British force upon the Bolsheviks in Ashkabad (Trans-Caspia)[18], creating unfavourable conditions for his proposed operations. He not only found it difficult to move freely within Tashkent, but also to communicate with either Malleson at Meshed or Etherton at Kashgar. The carrier pigeons brought over by him from Srinagar to meet such an eventuality had already fallen prey to the falcons of the Hunza valley and the Pamirs.[19] Though Bailey had already taken a loan of sixty thousand rubles from the Andijan branch of the Russo-Asiatic Bank[20] (through the good offices of G.Stephanovitch, Secretary of the Russian Consulate General at Kashgar), he could not strike a bargain with the Hindu Shikarpuri traders in Andijan for fiftythousand rubles by offering them a draft on India. Notwithstanding his wit and resources including the fruitful cooperation received from Tredwell, the American Consul at Tashkent and other anti-Bolshevik elements, Bailey could do nothing more than fritter away his energies in seeking safe hide-outs till he found a chance to escape to India via Bukhara and Meshed[21]. Both Malleson and Bailey failed in destabilising the Soviet power in Turkestan, Trans-Caspia, Bukhara and Khiva. But Bailey's experiences in Soviet Central Asia brought him glory at home and he was appointed as Political Officer in Sikkim, with the rank of second class Resident. In 1932, Bailey was posted as the British Resident at Kashmir[22] which was then considered a prestigious job amongst the second class Residencies in India.

---

18. Bailey, *Report of Kashgar mission*, 1918-20.
    Foreign. Sec. *Exl*. Aug. 1920. 253-256.
19. *Ibid.*
20. *Foreign. Est B*. Dec. 1918. 2-3.
    This amount was simultaneously refunded by the British Consul at Kashgar to his Russian counterpart.
21. Bailey arrived at Delhi on 9 Feb. 1920.
22. Bailey, *Mission to Tashkent*. p. 15.
    A. Swinson, *Beyond the frontiers: the biography of Colonel F M. Bailey explorer and special agent*. London, Hutchinson, 1971. p 226.

When the British sensed that the Soviet power in Central Asia was too firmly established to be destabilised, they took a number of steps for insulating India from any possible Bolshevik influence. A special cell was created in the foreign department of the British Indian government to "receive, collate, digest and disseminate information regarding Bolshevik activities outside India".[23] Another Officer on Special Duty on the staff of the Director, Central Intelligence was entrusted with the "duty of searching for and detecting Bolshevik activities in the provinces".[24] Weekly and monthly reports about the activities of Indian revolutionaries in India or abroad and also about their contacts with the Bolsheviks were now regularly circulated among the British officers posted at the frontier stations in Kashmir, Gilgit, Chitral, Kashgar and the North-West Frontier Province. They were especially alerted to check the possible infiltration of Bolshevik emissaries and India revolutionaries from the Soviet Central Asia into India. Meanwhile the Resident in Kashmir apprised the State government of the policy of the British Indian government to combat Bolshevik propaganda. He pointed out that the Boslhevik agents who might have already entered India in the guise of traders would play upon "the feeling of Muhammadans in regard to the partition of Turkey"[25]. The Resident summed up the steps decided to be taken by the Government of India in this regard as under:

(a) the collection of better information both from the sources outside as well as within India itself.

(b) the prevention of the ingress into India of Bolshevik emissaries or the detection and prevention of their activities in the case of any agents who may have already gained access to the country.

(c) The prohibition of the circulation of Bolshevik literature[26].

The Resident therefore desired the Kashmir Durbar to cooperate with the British authorities by taking all such measures within the State[27]. He advised the State government to depute special officers for

23. *Foreign. Secret. Internal.* Aug. 1920. 8-26.
24. *Ibid.*
25. C.B.J. Glancy, First Assistant to the Resident in Kashmir to the Chief Minister, J & K Dated 23 Dec. 1919.
O.E.R. 31/31-C .1919. (JKA).
26. *Ibid.*
27. *Ibid.*

making enquiries if any Bolshevik agents had already entered the State. The Durbar was also asked to proscribe all types of Bolshevik literature, if found in circulation within the State.[28] In order to prevent any possible influx of Bolshevik agents into India via Kashgar-Gilgit-Srinagar or Yarkand-Leh-Srinagar routes, the British agents posted at Gilgit and Leh were empowered to turn back all those travellers coming from Chinese Turkestan who did not possess the credentials bearing the signatures of British Consul General at Kashgar [29].

Soon after the receipt of Resident's directives the Kashmir Durbar decided to take immediately the following measures for preventing the spread of Bolshevism in the State:[30]

1. A careful watch will be kept by the State police for any Bolshevik literature which if found in circulation will be forthwith proscribed to prevent its smuggling into the State.
2. A special C.I.D. officer will be deputed to make enquiries and report as to whether any Bolshevik agents have found their way into the State and local officers will be warned of the forms which Bolshevik propaganda is likely to assume; and
3. Any person suspected of Bolshevik tendencies will be very carefully watched.

Maharaja Pratap Singh was particularly anxious that the Special C.I.D. officer proposed to be appointed should have some experience of this work and be competent enough to handle this duty.[31] In pursuance of Durbar's decision all the State administrative machinery was geared to prevent any type of Bolshevik activity in the State. All the Revenue officials like Governors, Wazir Wazarats, Tehsildars, Kanungos, Patwaris, Zaildars, Headmen and village Chokidars and also the Police personnel were enjoined to work in close coordination so that any signs of

---

28. *Ibid.*
29. *Ibid.*
30. Chief Minister, J & K to the First Assistant to the Resident in Kashmir. Dated 3 Jan. 1920.
31. For Pratap Singh's order dated 2 Jan. 1920. See *O.E.R.* 31/31-C. 1919. JKA.

Bolshevik propanganda in the State were promptly reported and curbed[32]. Any complacency on the part of these officials in this regard was to invite punishment.[33]

Special care was taken to prevent the entry of Bolshevik literature and agents into India from Soviet Central Asia via Wakhan and the frontiers of Kashmir. The Political Agent in Gilgit acted as a watchdog throughout this frontier belt[34]. Similarly the State government took steps to watch and search all strangers coming to Kashmir from the direction of Central Asia. For this purpose, additional police force was created to be deployed at Ganderbal, Bandipora and Uttarmachipura-the gateways to Kashmir from Ladakh and Gilgit[35]. As if this was not enough, the Resident in Kashmir asked the State administration to plug the gap at Skardu as well, so that any Bolshevik agents entering Kashmir via Mustagh pass could be interrupted[36]. Following this fresh directive the Wazir Wazarat, Ladakh was instructed to keep a strict watch over any such suspected arrivals at Skardu. The Kashmir ruler, Maharaja Pratap Singh, was even prepared to raise the Wazarat of Ladakh to Governorship with headquarters at Skardu, so that such an emergency situation could be handled adequately[37].

Since the import of Russian rubles into India formed an important item in the traditional Indo-Central Asian trade, it was feared that these rubles would be used to further the revolutionary activity in India. So the British Indian authorities issued two Ordinances in December 1919 and June 1920 prohibiting the circulation of this currency into India and also providing for its confiscation from any possessor[38]. Trade in the Russian rubles was rendered profitless in India and their value also depreciated in the outside markets. Since Kashmir occupied a key position in facilitating the import of Russian rubles and entry of Bolshevik emissaries and literature via Leh-Yarkand-Kashgar-Ferghana or Srinagar-Gilgit-Pamirs route into India, special care was taken to empower the

---

32. *Ibid.*
33. *Ibid.*
34. See telegram from Chief of General Staff, Simla to General Officer Commanding, Northern Command, Murree 11 May 1920. *Foreign. Pol.* 48 (III) M. 1924.
35. *O.E.R.* 31/31-C. 1919. JKA.
36. B.J. Glancy, First Asstt. to Resident to the Chief Minister, 29. Feb. 1920. See *Ibid.*
37. See *Ibid.*
38. *Foreign. Frontr. B.* August 1920. 4-11.

British agents stationed in Kashmir and Gilgit to meet such an eventuality. It was the Resident in Kashmir, who acting under the directions of the Imperial government prevailed upon the Kashmir Durbar to issue the Ordinance prohibiting the possession of ruble notes by any person within the Jammu and Kashmir State [39]. As a result of this measure about three million Russian ruble notes were voluntarily deposited at the Leh and Srinagar treasuries by various traders and individuals during a short period of three months (January to March 1920)[40]. Besides, about one thousand ruble notes were forcibly confiscated from a Khotani trader at Leh under the State Ordinance 3 of Samwat 1976 [41]. When the trade between India and Central Asia was largely diverted to the Leh-Yarkand route as a natural sequel to the disturbed conditions in Soviet Central Asia, the British Indian government took steps to stop the export of dyes, dye-stuffs, leather, cotton, woollen and silken goods from India[42], contrary to their professed policy of developing the Indo-Central Asian trade. Such a commercial blockade was not only designed to prevent essential commodities like cloth, leather, etc. from reaching the Bolsheviks in Soviet Central Asia, but also to check import of Russian currency into Indian in exchange thereof.

Kashmir was painted as a sensitive spot in the intelligence reports of the British Indian government which mentioned about the smuggling of Bolshevik propaganda material directed against the British rule in India from Soviet Central Asia via Afghanistan, Pamirs or Kashgar[43]. The circulation of Communist literature was, therefore, banned.Whenever the British Indian authorities suspected about the arrival of Bolshevik literature into India, the Resident asked the State administration to look out for such publications as were supposed to have been sent overland from Soviet Central Asia to India. Simultaneously censorship was

39. Lt. Col. A.D.A. Bannerman, Resident in Kashmir to Major G. D. Ogilvie, Deputy Secretary, Foreign Department, GOI 19 January 1920.
40. See *Ladakh Trade Report* 1919-20.
Due to this prohibition, the import of Russian ruble notes into India via Chinese Turkestan and Kashmir dropped to an insignificant number of 750 (valuing only seventy Indian rupees) in the year 1920-21 from an impressive figure of 58, 44, 439, (valuing 8,10,484 Indian rupees) during the year 1919-20.
41. *Foreign. Sec. Intl*. August 1920. 8-26.
42. *Foreign. Frontr. B*. Feb. 1919. 69-71.
43. One such report was circulated in March 1919.
Cited in Subodh Roy, *Communism in India, unpublished documents 1919-24*. p. 127.

introduced in Kashmir in early June 1919 when the Resident was authorized under Section 26 of the Post Office Act VI of 1898 to intercept any postal articles entering the territories of Jammu and Kashmir[44]. Following this, the Resident directed that all the postal articles mailed in any post office within the Gilgit Agency were to be delivered to the Political Agent there[45]. Such a censorship was enforced on a mere hearsay report that the Bolsheviks were receiving regular intelligence from Gilgit. When this suspicion was found to be baseless, the order was withdrawn soon after one month of trial.

The Soviet annulment of the secret Anglo-Russian treaties on Turkey and Persia not only created a favorable impression of Bolshevism among the Indian Muslims but also exposed the British imperialist aims in Asia. Ajmal Khan, the President of the All-India Muslim League openly arised his admiration for Russia in his presidential address at the 1919 annual session of the League[46]. Naturally the British became more particular to prevent the revolutionary ideas from making any impression upon the Indian Muslims. To achieve this end they secured *fatwas* (declarations) from the Grand Mufti, Cairo and the Sheikh-ul-Islam, Constantinople denouncing Bolshevism as "contrary to Islamic law and to the order, peace and progress of Muslims" [47]. Apart from getting the said *fatwas* suitably highlighted in a section of the Indian press,[48] a sufficient number of their Persian and Urdu versions was circulated among the Muslims in Kashmir [49] and Kashgar. The British feared that the Bolsheviks would play up the hurt sentiments of Indian Muslims consequent upon the dismemberment of Turkey. The big dent made by the Khilafat movement that was launched in India in early 1920, in far-flung areas like Jammu and Kashmir prompted the British Indian authorities to take adequate precautionary measures for keeping Kashmiri Muslims away from any Bolshevik influence. Urdu copies of

44. *Foreign. Frontr. B.* July 1919. 25-28.
45. *Foreign. Frontr. B.* July 1920. 30.
    This order was issued by Col. A.D.Bannerman on 25 May 1920.
46. Zafar Imam, *Colonialism in East-West relations*. New Delhi, 1969. p. 60.
47. *Foreign. Frontr B.* Secret. July 1920. 82-90.
48. *Pioneer* in its issue dated 8 Feb. 1920 described the *fatwa* as " a suitable commentary on the efforts of Lenin and Trotsky and their associates, to exploit the pan-Islamic movement for their own base ends".
49. It was on 23 April 1920 that the British Residency in Kashmir forwarded forty copies of an Urdu translation of the said *Fatwa* to Raja Daljit Singh, the State Chief Minister, for purpose of wide publicity in the State. *O.E.R.* 31/31-C. 1919. (JKA).

anti-Bolshevik literature such as Edmund Candler's pamphlet on Bolshevism were got distributed throughout the State.[50] The Muslims in Jammu and Kashmir organized several meetings to register their protest against the British excesses in Turkey and special prayers were held in numerous mosques to pray for the success and stability of the Caliphate.[51] Keeping in line with the decision of the Central Khilafat Committee in India, fast and hartal was observed by a broad section of the people in Jammu and Kashmir on 19 March 1920[52]. Though the movement had attained a mass character[53], it petered out by the end of 1920. This was a result of several factors such as the preventive measures taken jointly by the State administration and the British Resident to suppress the movement, conspiratorial role of certain leading Kashmiri Muslims[54] and also the impact of anti-Bolshevik and anti-Khilafat propaganda.

In the year 1919 the British Indian government was perturbed at the reported departure of two Kashgarians namely Yusuf Akhoon and his brother Ibrahim for Leh (from Chinese Turkestan) carrying alongwith huge quantities of Russian rubles, gold and silver, with the alleged objective of promoting Bolshevik activity in India[55]. The British Consul General stationed at Kashgar who shadowed their movements upon Yarkand, promptly informed the Resident in Kashmir advising him to keep a strict water over the two Kashgarians soon after they entered the territories of Jammu and Kashmir[56]. The British Consul in Kashgar alleged that these Kashgarians were in touch with the Bolsheviks and had left for India ostensible for trade but actually to forge a contact with the Indian revolutionary party[57]. However, the two Kashgarians arrived in Kashmir and left Srinagar for Rawalpindi by car on 20 August 1919[58].

---

50. *Ibid.*
51. *O.E.R.* 200. 1920. (JKA)
    G. H. Khan, *Freedom movement in Kashmir* 1931. 10. pp. 81-82.
52. *Ibid.*
53. First mass meeting was held at Idgah in Srinagar on 1 August 1920 which was participated by about twenty thousand people.
54. *Ibid.* pp. 86, 111.
    See also *O.E.R.* 209/45-C. JKA.
55. British Consul General, Kashgar to Resident in Kashmir, Telegram dated 27 June 1919. *Foreign and Political.* 48 M. 1924. 86.
56. *Ibid.*
57. *Ibid.*
58. *Foreign & Political.* 48-M. 1924. 132.

They were detained by the Punjab police at Rawalpindi and about eight lakh ruble notes lying in their possession were confiscated from them[59]. They also had with them 240 tolas of gold and 20,996 tolas of silver.[60] This circumstance coupled with the intention of this party to put up with one Imam-Din of Amritsar, who had been noticed by Calcutta Special Branch on 5 July 1919 as guiding a party of suspected Russian Tartars arriving there from Amritsar[61], led the British to suspect their motives. But the British Indian authorities failed in laying their hands upon any direct incriminating evidence. The British Consul General at Kashgar pursued the matter hard and wired the Government of India on 1 September 1919 informing about Yusuf's connection with the local Bolshevik organization at Tashkent and his visit to that place in the spring of 1919[62]. With this background in view the Consul General advised the Government of India to refuse permission to those travellers who came overland from Chinese Turkestan to India via Leh-Srinagar route if unprovided with credentials of the British Consulate at Kashgar[63]. While endorsing this proposal the Resident in Kashmir advised the Foreign Department to turn back all those travellers coming from the direction of Chinese Turkestan within the jurisdiction of the Gilgit Agency and Kashmir State, who did not possess any credentials from the British Consul General at Kashgar[64]. The government of India not only approved this proposal but even went a step ahead by asking the Resident in Kashmir to appoint a Special Officer to deal with the problems arising out of the influx of Bolshevik emissaries into India.[65]

British fears about the possibility of Kashmir being turned into a base for spreading Bolshevism in the neighbouring tribal areas of the North West Frontier Province and other places in India which were already in ferment against the British rule, were not altogether imaginary. On 10 April 1920 one M.Alexiev, who claimed to be the Chief Agent to Bolshevik Bureau for Northern India, sent three identical letters to

59. *Ibid.*
60. *Ibid.*
61. *Ibid.*
62. *Ibid.* No. 118.
63. *Ibid.*
64. Resident in Kashmir to Secretary, Foreign Department, GOI, Telegram dated 30 October 1919. *Foreign & Political*. 48-M. 1924. 173.
65. Deputy Secretary, Foreign Department, GOI to Resident in Kashmir, 22 November 1919. *Foreign & Political*. 48-M. 1924. 200.

the editors of "Englishman", "Amrita Bazar Patrika" and "Democrat", in which he, among other things, clearly stated his intention to go to Kashmir [66]. The British Indian intelligence authorities suspected that Bolshevik emissaries and Indian revolutionaries were also travelling to Russia via Kashmir [67]. The intelligence reports coming from British and certain 'friendly' embassies in Western Europe indicated the serious nature of anti-British activities of Indian revolutionaries who operated in Western Europe. By intercepting the letters exchanged by such revolutionaries (in this case from Bhupendranath in Berlin to Birendranath Das Gupta in Zurich), the British learnt about the activities of the Indian Committee in Kabul and "their efforts to utilize Kashmir as a secret jumping - off place for work in India"[68]. Hardayal, who had already established contacts in Srinagar, was reported to have "urged the desirability of making use of Kashmir, particularly for importing arms into India"[69].

Soviet support to the national liberation movements of the East had already proved a strong attraction to thousands of Indian Muslim emigrees (*Muhajirs*) who were disillusioned with the British due to overthrow of the Caliphate. These *Muhajirs* travelled on foot long and hazardous distances over the Hindu Kush and Karakoram mountain ranges to reach Soviet Central Asia, where they were kindly received and trained in Bolshevik ideology and also given military training. That Srinagar-Leh-Kashgar-Ferghana route was also taken by some *Muhajirs* comes clear from a report sent by the Comintern's Turkestan Branch in Andijan to Tashkent on 18 May 1921. It stated that 36 Indians who had left India for Russia via Yarkand and Kashgar had been detained in April 1921 and escorted back to India by the British Consul General in Kashgar [70]. Cecil Kaye, Director of the British Indian Intelligence, was keeping track of almost every activity of the Indian *muhajirs* in Soviet Russia and Central Asia. He was not unware of the formation of Indian Communist group by M.N.Roy at Tashkent and also the establishment of a school for training Indians in revolutionary work.[71] When a letter from Evelyn Roy (M.N.Roy's American wife) to someone in Paris was

66. Subodh Roy *Ed, Communism in India with unpublished documents 1919-1924*. p. 147.
67. Cecil Kaye, *Communism in India*. Cited in *Ibid*. p. 88.
68. Subodh Roy *Ed, Communism in India with unpublished documents 1919-24*. p. 154.
69. *Ibid.*
70. M.A. Persits, *op cit*. 78.
71. Cecil Kaye, *Communism in India*. Cited in S.Roy, *op cit*. p 4.

intercepted, the British intelligence came to know that 17 Indians had already been taken to Moscow to get trained at the Communist University of the Toilers of the East, after which they were to be sent to India for building up Communist organization there [72]. There is little doubt that the British had planted a spy named Masood Ali Shah amongst the Indians who had left for *hijrat* to Central Asia in 1920 [73]. Masood Ali must have been reporting the exact details about the activities of Indians in Soviet Russia. In fact when in 1922 a party of Indian revolutionaries arrived at Chitral via Osh, Marghilan, Kharog, and the Pamirs route, they were soon after arrested and later convicted on the charge of conspiracy against the British crown [74]. A young and educated Kashmiri, Mir Abdul Majid, who was residing in Lahore was one of them. He had come to India for doing revolutionary work and was subsequently arrested and sentenced to rigorous imprisonment [75]. The British intelligence network in the North-West Frontier Province, Chitral, Gilgit, Ladakh and Kashmir was so alert that almost all the visiting Indians from Central Asia were easily exposed and trapped, rendering it difficult for the Indian revolutionaries to gain any foothold in India.

Obviously, Kashmir was once again drawn into sharp focus of the new British strategy towards Soviet Central Asia. The strong British reaction to the success of the Soviet revolutionary movement had its roots in the British colonial policy in India. Their hold over India was already getting weak and the Soviet stand on the right of nations to self-rule was seen in the context of the Indian liberation movement. When in July 1920 intelligence regarding the overland journey of Raja

---

72. *Ibid.* p. 5.
73. For further details see Muzaffar Ahmad, *Myself and the Communist Party of India 1920-1929*. Calcutta, 1970. pp. 444-46.
74. Rafiq Ahmad, who was one among this group of Indians, has narrated his experiences of travel through difficult mountainous regions and later his conviction at Peshawar. See Muzaffar Ahmad, *Communist Party of India and its formation abroad*. Calcutta, 1962. pp. 12-55.
75. Between 1921 and 1924 four successive Communist Conspiracy cases were launched under Section 121-A of the Indian Penal code in Peshawar and another was launched in Meerut in 1927. All those Indian revolutionaries who had come to India from Central Asia, were arrested and later sentenced to rigorous imprisonment for a period ranging from one to seven years.
For additional details about the Peshawar Conspiracy cases See Subodh Roy, *Ed. Communism in India with unpublished documents 1919-24*.
Muzzaffar Ahmad, *Myself and the Communist Party of India* 1920, 29.

Mehendra Pratap through Tashkurghan reached the British authorities in India, a special detachment of Gilgit Scouts comprising a Subedar Major, one Havildar, two Naiks and thirteen sepoys was deputed by the Political Agent in Gilgit to the Kilik pass for the purpose of intercepting the Raja during his wandering on the Pamirs [76]. There in Kashgar, the British Consul General too launched combing operations in the frontier areas of Sarikol, Raskam, Yarkand and Khotan to apprehend Mehendra Pratap and his party. But the Raja escaped all these traps and retreated to Afghnistan finding that the Chinese authorities in Sinkiang were hindering his forward movement from Tashkurghan [77]. In his autobiography Raja Mehendra Pratap has revealed that this time he was on an Afghan mission carrying Royal Afghan letters addressed to seven rulers of different countries and to fulfill this mission he had travelled through steep and snowy mountain tracts of Afghanistan and Pamirs towards China [78]. The arrival of Mahendra Pratap at Tashkurghan and his grand entertainment by the local Chinese *Amban*, (Magistrate) and also the Muslim Qazi did not escape the notice of the British Indian agent posted there [79], who must have alerted the British authorities in Kashgar and Gilgit.

On 2 April 1927 a local newspaper of Amritsar named Akali published an article by Mahendra Pratap about his travels in Afghanistan, Pamirs and Chinese frontiers in Sinkiang [80]. Mahendra Pratap disclosed in this article that when in early 1920 he reached Tashkurghan, he was given a sympathetic reception by the Chinese authorities there. But they were unable to help in the fulfilment of Raja's mission for fear of the British. The British Consul General at Kashgar was the source of all the trouble. So Mehendra Pratap could not proceed with his contemplated journey to China through Sinkiang. He handed over the letter from King of Afghanistan addressed to the President of Chinese Republic to the Chinese frontier officer in Tashkurghan. After a year, when Mahendra

76. *Foreign. Frontr B.* July 1921. 139-140.
77. Raja Mahendra Pratap, *My life story of fifty five years* (December 1886 to December 1941). Dehradun, 1947. pp. 63-64.
78. *Ibid.*
79. *Ibid.*
80. An abstract of this article was forwarded by the Director, Information Bureau, Punjab to the Secretary, Foreign and Political Deptt., GOI on 19 April 1927. See Subodh Roy, *Ed. Communism in India: unpublished documents 1925-1934*. pp. 12-24.

Pratap recrossed the Pamirs with a view to go to Tibet, he was prewarned by the Chinese authorities in Sinkiang about the dispatch of British troops to arrest him. So Mahendra Pratap was obliged to retreat and this time he went to Soviet Central Asia via the Kara Kul Pamirs.

The British over-reaction to Mahendra Pratap's journey through the Pamirs was not only due to their apprehension about his possible entry into India through the Kashmir frontiers but a logical corollary to their colonial policy of liquidating all nuclei of opposition to their imperial authority over India. Even as late as 1924, the British Consul General at Kashgar, C.P. Skrine, was at pains to apprehend Raja Mahendra Pratap. In the course of his travels through Khotan, Keria, Polu and Sanju, Skrine took extra steps both at Polu and Sanju which commanded the passes towards Ladakh to keep track of and to intercept Mahendra Pratap in the event of him using these routes for his journey from Kabul to Tibet or Nepal [81]. The British forces stationed in Gilgit remained constantly watchful on the borders to prevent any crossing over of Indian revolutionaries from Soviet Central Asia towards Kashmir and India. Every possible step was taken to ensure that Kashmir did not become a transit station for the Indian revolutionaries in their attempted passage to India overland from Central Asia via the Pamirs.

In this imperialist game the Kashmir Durbar extended all possible assistance acting solely under the instructions of the British Resident. The resistance offered by the Kashmir ruler during the peak period of Anglo-Russian rivalry was no longer to be encountered now. Whereas the British hesitated in enforcing a commercial blockade upon the Afghan ruler[83], they easily did it in Kashmir to check the import of Russian money and export of Indian goods to Central Asia. On the whole the anti-Bolshevik measures implemented by the British jointly through the agencies of their Political Agents stationed in Kashmir, Gilgit, Chitral and Kashgar and also by using the influence of the Agha Khan over his Ismaili followers in the frontier belt, appear to have swung some anti-revolutionary tribal chiefs in the Russian Pamirs to their favour. Ironically a request made in the name of residents of Roshan, Bartang, Parshins, Kharogh, Ghand, Sochan, Shakhdara, Ash Kash and Wakhan, for British aid and protection was forwarded by

81. *Kashgar Diary* April -May 1924.
82. For details see *Foreign. Extl B.* Decemeber 1920. 447.

the erstwhile Russian officer of the Pamirs detachment at Kharogh, Col. Timaviev when he personally handed over the written petitions containing such a request to the British Agent in Chitral on his arrival there enroute to India [83]. Timaviev while at Kharogh and the British Consul General at Kashgar operated jointly to check the spread of Bolshevik influence in the Pamirs. He destroyed the Bolshevik literature in Persian language which had been brought to Kharogh by some Kirghizs from Tashkent for onward transmission to India via Faizabad and Kabul. [84] Had not the Red Guards succeeded in estabilishing themselves swiftly at the frontier posts in the Pamirs, the erstwhile Russian officers could have created some trouble for the Bolsheviks in conjunction with the British agents.

The problem of Soviet propaganda [85] against British colonialism in the East proved to be an important factor in the course of Anglo-Soviet negotiations which stretched for about a year from May 1920 upto March 1921 when the trade agreement was finally signed. Both powers displayed their mistrust and suspicion of each other's intentions. Whereas the Soviet side was skillful in using the anti-British propaganda in the East as a diplomatic weapon for combating the British pressures, the British Prime Minister Lloyd George employed all his diplomatic prowess to keep the revolutionary essence of Soviet Russia confined within her boundaries. Britain agreed to lift commercial blockade against Soviet Russia in 1921 only after the latter had agreed to refrain from hostile propaganda against the British interests in Asia, especially in India and

83. Foreign. Extl B. Secret. August 1920. 538-539. For a translation of this letter see Appendix V.
84. British Consul General, Kashgar to Foreign / Deptt Secretry, GOI. Telegram dated 12 May 1920. *Foreign Political*. 48(III) M. 1924.
85. It was as early as 27 March 1920 that the Director of British Intelligence, London informed his government about the stoppage of Indian propaganda by the Bolsheviks. In his opinion the Soviet government intended to use it as a great concession to England in the course of future negotiations. Cited in Subodh Roy, *Ed, Communism in India, unpublished documents 1919-24*. p. 133.

Afghanistan.[86] This agreement accorded the Soviet Union "de facto recognition" and also brought to an end the allied intervention against the Bolsheviks. Though the bilateral tension was relieved as a result of this mutual agreement, Britain continued to harbour fears about the Soviets abetting the Indian revolutionary activity from an advanced military post in the Pamirs[87]. When the Turkish question was being deliberated at the Lausanne Conference on 6 December 1922, Chicherin used the occasion to reiterate the Soviet policy of "friendship and brotherhood towards the propels of the East"[88]. In his speech Chicherin sought to dispel British fears about the appearance of the Soviet troops at the Pamirs, in these words:

> You are uneasy because our horsemen have reappeared on the heights of the Pamirs, and because you no longer have to deal wityh the half-witted Tsar who ceded the ridge of the Hindu Kush to you in 1895. But it is not war that we offer you, it is peace, based on the principles of a partition wall between us and on the principle of the freedom and ;sovereignty of Turkey.[89]

---

86. The fulfilment of the Anglo-Soviet Accord of 16 March 1921 was subject to the following pre-condition:
"That each party refrains from hostile action or undertakings against the other and from conducting outside of its own borders any official propaganda direct or indirect against the institutions of the British Empire or the Russian Soviet Republic respectively, and more particularly that the Russian Soviet government refrains from any attempt by military or diplomatic or any other form of action or propaganda to encourage any of the peoples of Asia in any form of hostile action against British interests or the British Empire, especially in India and in the independent State of Afghanistan. The British Government gives a similar particular undertaking to the Russian Soviet Government in respect of the countries which formed part of the former Russian Empire and which have now become independent". Cited in R.H. Ullman,*TheAnglo-Soviet Accord*. Princeton University Press, 1972. p. 474
87. These fears were officially conveyed by Robert Horne in his letter dated 16 March 1921 to L.B. Krassin, simultaneously with the signature of the Anglo-Soviet Accord on the same day in the following words :
"It is known that Indian revolutionaries have urged the formation of a military centre on the Chitral-Pamirs frontier. An Army Order issued by the Soviet authorities has announced the unfurling of the Red Flag on the Pamirs as an indication to the people of India that their deliverance is at hand ; and there is reason to believe that a project for action in these regions is now under consideration". Cited in R.H. Ullman, *op cit*.. p. 482.
88. *Lausanne Conference on Near Eastern Affairs 1922-23: Records of proceedings and draft terms of peace*. London,His Majesty's Stationery Office, 1923. p. 148.
89. *Ibid*. p. 149.

But Chicherin's assurance given to Curzon did not impress the great Russophobe in any way. New schemes for the defence of Indian northern frontier in and around Gilgit were initiated. These included the construction of air-landing facilities, installation of wireless sets and strengthening of the British force in these strategic pickets. But what proved to be catastrophic for independent India, was the taking over of complete political and administrative control of Gilgit Agency from the Maharaja of Kashmir on lease in 1935 by which the Maharaja's grip over this frontier area was lossened for all practical purposes.

7

Conclusion

Notwithstanding the great mountain barriers of the Himalayas and Hindu Kush, Central Asia maintained throughout history political, cultural and commercial contacts with Kashmir. These contacts, however, received a setback in the wake of the Anglo-Russian colonial rivalry in the region. In modern times, the earliest Russian interest in Kashmir affairs can be traced back to the travels of numerous Russian, Georgian and Central Asian travellers like Yefremov, Danibegov and Abdul Karim, all of whom visited Kashmir in the late eighteenth and the early nineteenth centuries. They were pioneers in exploring the three main overland routes from Central Asia to Inida, viz., (i) Bukhara-Kokand - Kashgar-Yarkand-Leh (ii) Semipalatinsk-Ili-Aksu-Kashgar-Yarkand-Leh and (iii) Bukhara-Kabul-Peshawar-Muzaffarabad-Srinagar. Their travelogues assume additional importance as they shed interesting light on the political and socio-economic conditions in Kashmir during the Afghan rule. Presenting a Russian and Central Asian view of Kashmir, these narratives form a valuable source for the study of Kashmir history during this period. The elaborate description of shawl industry and its problems in the accounts of these foreign visitors shows the great attraction Kashmir shawls held for the people in Central Asia and Russia.

In fact, it were the shawl goods of Kashmir and the *pashm* (fine wool) yielding goats of Ladakh that stimulated the Russian interest in developing commercial relations with Kashmir and the Punjab during the first quarter of the nineteenth centrury. This interest in developing overland trade with adjacent countries was particularly intensified in the wake of enforcement of the continental blockade by Napoleon in Europe. Tsarist Russia sent several missions to the Khanates of Bukhara and Kokand to secure their consent in the free movement of Russo-Chinese trading caravans from Russia to Kashgar via Bukhara and Kokand and vice versa. Once this was achieved, Russia could and did think of extending her commercial relations with Ladakh, Kashmir and the Punjab. Agha Mehdi Rafailov who did establish himself as a shawl trader, was instrumental in arousing Russian interest in Kashmir and its shawl goods. He visited Ladakh on an official mission in 1808 and later attained the position of court Counsellor in Russia due to his efforts for opening up Russian commerce with Kashmir. The despatch of Rafailov in 1820 as the Russian emissary carrying Nesselrode's letter addressed to the Raja of Ladakh and Maharaja Ranjit Singh of Punjab was a step directed towards the establishment of direct diplomatic relations between Russia and Kashmir. The Choice of Rafailov as head of this mission was but natural as he was fully conversant with the local milieu. But Rafailov was not destined to fulfil this mission as he died near the Karakoram pass, possible due to treason by some of his followers.

The Agha Mehdi mission to Ladakh throws important light on the convergence of Anglo-Russian commercial activities in this region from the two opposite directions as far back as the early nineteenth century. Whereas Agha Mehdi was despatched by the Russian Foreign Minister in 1808 to examine the trade routes to India via Kashmir, Izzet Ullah was sent by the British to Central Asia in 1812 on a fact-finding mission. There is a striking similarity in the manner in which the two powers launched their efforts to secure pashm-yielding goats from Ladakh for the purpose of rearing them in Britain and Siberia. It had become necessary to give practical shape to their plan to manufacture shawls in British and Russian factories, thereby reducing their dependence on the hand-woven shawls of Kashmir. It was in pursuit of shawl-wool goats that the British sent Moorcroft to Tibet in 1812 and the Russians sent Agha Mehdi to Ladakh in 1820. Both powers were quite unwittingly following the same object but from two opposite directions. The commercial factor in the Anglo-Russian rivalry in Central Asia was coming into prominence.

That Agha Mehdi had been trained in the art of dyeing and had also been entrusted with several pony-loads of dyes meant to be used in the Kashmir shawl industry, shows that the Russian object in sending this mission to Ladakh was mainly commercial. Since Ladakh and Kashmir happened to be dependencies of Maharaja Ranjit Singh of Punjab, it was imperative for Nesselrode to send a warm and friendly letter inscribed in gold ink and accompanied by costly presents to the Sikh ruler. However, Agha Mehdi's complicity in instigating the rebel Muslim Chiefs of Kashgar against the Chinese authorities there, as was alleged by Izzet Ullah, requires further inquiry. As the intervening Central Asian Khanates and also the Chinese possessions in Eastern Turkestan stood as a formidable barrier to any possible Russian move towards Kashmir, it would not be correct to infer any aggressive design of Russia from the despatch of Agha Mehdi's missions. Russia was obviously exploring the possibility of establishing friendly political relations with the Indian frontier states to pave the way for a regular commercial intercourse.

The growing Russian threat to the Central Asian Khanates of Kokand resulted in the despatch of Kokandi emissaries to India for seeking British support. Since the Kashgar-Yarkand-Leh route was practically free from robbers, Central Asians preferred this to the troublesome Kabul route for coming to India. It was in 1837 that an envoy from Kokand arrived at Ladakh but he got scared on seeing a native of Yarkand being maltreated by Dogra official in Ladakh for his direct dealings with a British visitor. The Kokand envoy did not pursue his object and retreated for fear of facing a similar treatment. Another Kokandi envoy, Shahzada Sultan Muhammad Khan, who travelled to Peshawar via Oxus-Zebak-Chitral route in August 1854 with a request for British arms returned to Kokand via Kashmir. Maharaja Gulab Singh, who received the Kokandi envoy very well, saw to it that the British Indian surveyor accompanying the envoy, did not proceed beyond Kashmir. The Dogra Chief wanted to prevent any direct contact between his Central Asian neighbours and the British agents or visitors. Obviously Gulab Singh was motivated by a desire to extend his direct friendly relations with the neighbouring Central Asian Khanates. He was keen to restrict the British activity in his frontier territories in order to maintain his high political stock in Central Asia and to prevent its erosion in the face of British paramountcy in India.

After the mid-nineteenth century when the Anglo-Russian rivalry gained its intensity, Britain became restive to use Kashmir as a listening post for monitoring the Russian movements in Central Asia. With this end in view, sustained pressure was brought upon Maharaja Gulab Singh and his successor Ranbir Singh to secure a foot-hold in this frontier outpost. Whereas the British were bent upon acquiring firmer control over the conduct of domestic and external politics of the State, the Dogra rulers were not prepared to allow any erosion of their authority over their subjects or to see their prestige wane in the eyes of their Central Asian neighbours. Yet the Dogras continued to play it safe by lending armed assistance to the British Indian Government during the secondAnglo-Sikh war and the 1857 uprising. At the same time, both Gulab Singh and his successor Ranbir Singh permitted such staunch anti-British fighters as Bhai Maharaj and Kukas to operate covertly from their territory. The Dogra strategy was focussed on the aim of keeping the British at an arm's length from Kashmir. But the British could not bear that Kashmir being their subsidiary ally, should prove to be a bottleneck in their policy of extending commercial and thereby political influence in Central Asia. They mounted pressure on Ranbir Singh to allow free movement of Indian trade to Central Asia. Further to keep a vigil on the Central Asian developments British officers were stationed in Kashmir. The growing British interference in Kashmir made the Dogra rulers bitter.

When the Russians occupied Tashkent in 1865, Maharaja Ranbir Singh was the first Indian prince to send secret emissaries to convey his greetings to the Russian General Cherniaev on his success. He also extended a hand of friendship to the Russians. Judging from the conditions existing in India during the period of British paramountcy Ranbir Singh's attempt to move away from the British stranglehold was daring and unique when compared to the meek servility displayed by other Indian princes. His success in maintaining a friendly liaison with the Russians in Central Asia by means of regular exchange of emissaries thus outwitting the alert British intelligence network, speaks of Ranbir singh's acumen in diplomatic manoeuvring. The first such mission comprised Abdul Rahman Khan and Sarfaraz Khan arrived at Tashkent in November 1865 and met Cherniaev there. The Kashmir ruler was careful to enter into oral rather than any written communications with the Russian to avoid detection by and consequent involvement with the British Indian government. All these emissaries invariably took Sringar-Muzaffarabad-Peshawar-Kạbul-Central Asia route rather than the Leh-Yarkand-Kashgar-Kokand route, in order to escape detection by the British agent posted in Leh. So the story floated by Abdul Rehman Khan and Sarfaraz Khan at Tashkent that their leader had been murdered and the Maharaja's letter stolen, was a sheer fabrication and the assumption of Soviet scholars that the British Indian authorities were reponsible for this murder and the theft of Maharaja's message is not correct. The Kashmir Government records mention the despatch in July 1866 by Maharaja Ranbir Singh of an agent named Mehta Sher Singh to Central Asia on a fact-finding mission. In 1869 another trusted emissary, Baba Karam Prakash, was sent on a secret mission to Central Asia. The Kashmir ruler had desired Karam Prakash to enquire from the Russian authorities at Samarkand as to when they would be advancing towards India, in which case he was reported to have offered his full support and asked for Lahore State in return.

The Russians are reported to have informed Ranbir Singh through Karam Prakash that they would not make any move until the rulers of Nepal, Gwalior and Kabul offered similar support. That the Kashmir ruler later employed Karam Prakash in secret missions to Nepal and Gwalior and also maintained secret communications with the Amir of Kabul, shows that he stood firm by his offer. It was during the Ili crisis when Russia and China were on the brink of war, that Ranbir Singh reiterated his support to the Russians if they succeeded in taking Kashgar from China and thus came close to the borders of Kashmir. Ranbir Singh maintained direct and regular contacts with the Russian authorities in Central Asia throughout his reign. These contacts had turned into frank and friendly relationship. For instance, ignoring the British presence in Kashmir, General Kaufmann, the Russian Governor General of Turkestan, sought in 1877 Ranbir Singh's help in recovering the treasure of the dethroned chief of Kashgar, Beg Kuli Beg, who had taken refuge in Russian Central Asia. Kaufmann's successor, General Rosenbach maintained this liaison and was prompt in sending his condolences to Maharaja Pratap Singh on hearing the news of the death of Ranbir Singh in 1885.

Kashmir's overtures to the Russians in Central Asia can be better explained in the context of the Anglo-Russian rivalry in Asia. Russian successes in Central Asia created a deep psychological impact on the Indian princely rulers who were already annoyed with the increasing British interference in their domains. Consequently their anti-British aspirations got stimulated. The Kashmir ruler thought it wise to cautiously develop friendly relations with the Russian power in Central Asia.

On their part the Russians reciprocated Ranbir Singh's friendly sentiments but they steered clear of any active involvement in the internal affairs of British India which could have led them to a direct conflict with the British. The entire Tsarist administration, from the Governor General of Orenburg to the Foreign Minister, Gortchakov, or even to the Tsar Emperor himself, was unanimous in the view that Russia should not use the opportunity provided by Kashmir ruler's offer of friendship for making any hostile gesture towards the British. This was also due to the Russians being not sure of their capacity to offer any help to remote countries lying beyond the Himalayas. The Russian response to Kashmir evertures can easliy be compared to the British response to similar overture from the Khans of Kokand and Bukhara. Both powers, though competing with each other over ascendancy in this region, did not want to run the risk of a direct military confrontation. They confined themselves to playing the game by means of diplomacy and other peaceful means.

If Ranbir Singh's attempt to forge diplomatic links with the Russians in Central Asia did not bear political fruit, it helped in gaining the Russian consent to the free import of Kashmir shawls into the Russian territory. The Russian offer of protection to Kashmiri merchants stood in marked contrast to their policy of curbing imports from British India. Tsarist Russia also reciprocated by sending some envoys in disguise to meet the Kashmir ruler. Pachino, an officer in the Russian foreign service, made two attempts in 1870s to meet Maharaja Ranbir Singh in Kashmir. Each time he failed to penetrate the fence of British intelligence network and had to return without having attained his object. Similarly when in mid-1872 a high-power Russian embassy headed by General Kaulbars was negotiating a treaty with Yakub Beg in Kashgar, one of its members tried to establish contact with the Kashmir ruler through the medium of some Kashmiri traders residing in Yarkand. The said Russian officer had come from Kashgar, the venue of negotiations, to Yarkand to find out if the Indian exports to Yarkand via Kashmir included arms and ammunition. During this visit, the said officer contacted a Kashmiri trader, Khaliq Dar, who was also the trusted agent of the Maharaja in Yarkand and sent through him the Russian offer of a secret alliance with Kashmir. Next year in 1873, Khaliq Dar proceeded to Kashmir and informed the Maharaja accordingly. But Ranbir Singh leaked to the British Indian authorities the information regarding Russian interest in Kashmir which was received from Khalik Dar. It appears that Ranbir Singh wanted to reaffirm his loyalty to the British, as he was not impressed by the Russian response to his ambitions. But this proved counter-productive for him as the British became increasingly alarmed over the prospects of Russo-Kashmir alliance. This time the British decided to mount their squeeze on Kashmir by having a full-fledged Residency which could put a check to Ranbir Singh's flirtations with the Russians. Even though the India Office refused to accept the proposal, the British Indian authorities went ahead unilaterally in coercing the Maharaja of Kashmir to accept the stay of British officers in Srinagar and Leh for eight months and one year respectively.

Hunza's coterminous border with the Pamirs and the cultural affinity of its Ismaili inhabitants with their co-religionists residing in Wakhan, Russian Pamirs and Sarikol area were two important factors that facilitated the percolation of Russian influence in this frontier dependency of Kashmir. But the first direct Russian contact with Hunza was forged officially in 1888 when Safdar Ali, the Chief of Hunza, hosted a reception for the visiting Russian explorer, Captain Grombchevsky and both exchanged presents. These links were fostered by Petrovsky, the Russian Consul at Kashgar, who lost no opportunity of making 'friendly' enquiries from any Hunza visitors to Kashgar. Safdar Ali was so much impressed by Russian power that he sent two emissaries to Russian Turkestan in 1891 to seek Russian support against the feared British attack. Russians received the envoys well and advised Safdar Ali to play it cool with the British until Russia consolidated her position in the Pamirs. While moving forward in the Pamirs, the Russians did not burn their fingers in the military confrontation between the British and Safdar Ali in late 1891, following which the Hunza chieftain fled to Chinese Turkestan But there too Safdar Ali's movements were curbed by the Chinese under British pressure. This was because the British had become restive on seeing that a section of Hunza population was still entertaining an exalted image of Russian power, thereby becoming a potential source of strength to the pro-Russian Safdar Ali.

The establishment of Russian political connection with the Hunza chieftain in the late nineteenth century was a logical sequel to the Anglo-Russian rivalry which had now shifted its focus to the Pamirs. The reconnaissance missions by British officers in and around the Pamirs had attracted Russian attention. In fact both Grombchevsky and Younghusband were proceeding to reconnoiter the Pamirs area in 1888 from two opposite directions. Their encounter at Bozai Gumbaz was a clear indication of the convergence of the Anglo-Russian movements in the Pamirs. Whereas Grombchevsky became alarmed at the British intentions to keep Russia away from the Pamirs, the British became worried over the prospects of Russian inroads into Hunza. This resulted in the extension by military force of British control over Hunza in 1891 and a simultaneous assumption of Russian control over a greater part of the Pamirs. The British occupation of Hunza caused a flutter in Russian government, which became now seriously interested in the formal delimitation of frontiers at the Pamirs, so as to prevent the possible extension of British influence from Hunza into the Pamirs. This resulted in the conclusion of the Pamirs Boundary Agreement in 1895, which ensured a neutral buffer between the British in India and the Russians in Central Asia.

Kashmir's trade connection with Russian Central Asia was indirect as the two sides had no common border. Whatever commerce was conducted through circuitous and difficult mountainous trade routes which passed through Leh and Chinese Turkestan on the one side and Chitral and Pamirs on the other. Leh-Yarkand route was much frequented by the traders who conducted business in Chinese Turkestan. The safety of this route can be gauged by the fact that the traders would usually abandon their goods on the snowy Karakoram mountains in the event of unfavourable weather or breakdown of transport arrangements. Other routes like Ferghana-Kashgar-Tashkurghan-Hunza-Gilgit, Bukhara-Kabul-Chitral-Peshawar, Ferghana-Pamirs-Wakhan-Chitral, were usually thronged by such traders as traded between Punjab and Central Asia or between the frontier dependencies of Kashmir and Central Asia, thus bypassing the valley of Kashmir. Due to its geographical location, Kashmir acted as a transit emporium for Indian trade with Central Asia. The Tsarist policy of curbing the import of British Indian goods into Central Asia caused a great setback to this traditional trade. But still Kashmir shawls, Indian tea, muslins, brocades, spices, medicines, Indigo and coral filtered into Central Asia through these channels, as these goods were strongly liked by Central Asians. The Central Asian exports to India via Kashmir were comparatively fewer and these comprised mainly gold coins, rubles and coarse cotton goods. Kashmir's trade with Russian Central Asia was thus insignificant in quantitative terms when compared to that passing through Bukhara-Afghanistan and Punjab.

Since this trade was mainly routed through Chinese Turkestan, the state of diplomatic relations existing between the Chinese in Sinkiang and the Russians in Central Asia conditioned the extent and pattern of Kashmir's commercial relations with Russian Central Asia particularly after the mid-nineteenth century. Thus when the relations between Russia and China became smooth after the conclusion of St. Petersburg Treaty in 1881, Indian exports of coral to Russian Central Asia through Kashmir and Kashgar increased manifold. The imposition of heavy duties on this item by the Russian customs authorities only encouraged large scale smuggling of coral into Russian Central Asia from Kashgar which received its supplies from India via Kashmir. Coral worth about 27 lakh rupees was imported into Chinese Turkestan from India via Kashmir during the period from 1881 to 1918, half of which can safely be said to have found its way into Russian Central Asia.

Russian cotton goods being cheap, coarse and durable were popular amongst the Buddhists of Ladakh and the tribal population in Hunza, Gilgit and Chitral. There is reason to believe that *Shaitan Tari*, a drill cloth used by Kashmiris during winter even upto mid-twentieth century, originated from Russia.

Bukharan and Kokandi gold coins used to be imported into Kashmir regularly till these Khanates came under the Tsarist administration . However, in the late nineteenth century when a large number of Indian traders closed their business in Russian Central Asia as a result of the restrictive policies of the Russian authorities, a considerable amount of gold coins was brought into India by these traders as a forced medium for bringing back their capital into India. They also brought in some quantity of Russian gold thread. Towards the close of the nineteenth century, such imports were substituted by those of Russian gold and paper rubles. Ruble import, which was predominant feature of the Indo-Central Asian trade from 1897 till 1919, was resorted to by the Indian traders in Chinese Turkestan only as a forced medium for sending back their sale proceeds to India since Kashgar markets did not provide alternative means. Russian rubles worth about 80 lakh rupees were imported into India through Kashmir during this period. This trade dropped to the lowest point in 1920 as a result of the British prohibition on such trading. The British feared that Russian rubles could be used in fomenting anti-British agitations in India.

The disturbed conditions in Central Asia in the post-Bolshevik revolution period affected adversely the movement of trade between Russian Central Asia and Kashmir, which was already irregular and insignificant. With the State take-over of the private trade in Soviet Rusia, little scope was left for Indian trade with Soviet Central Asia which was solely operated through the medium of private traders. The restrictions imposed by the British on export of essential commodities like cloth, leather etc. from India to Central Asia during the height of Anglo-Soviet tensions, also inhibited the development of this trade. In short whatever little commercial connection existed between Russian Central Asia and Kashmir dwindled to a small trickle in the wake of the October revolution in Russia. These relations, however, got revived on a national plane after the attainment of independence by India.

Geographical proximity and cultural affinity in terms of religion, customs, dress, food and drinking habits provided a strong base for the continuation of the socio-cultural links between the peoples of Central Asia and Kashmir even after the two regions had become parts of the two rival empires-Russia and Britain-respectively in mid-nineteenth century. These soical ties were further nourished by the existence of common ecological and environmental factors in the two regions.

Kashmir shawls continued to be a favourite apparel of the Central Asian and Russian elite. The Persian and Arabic literary texts copied by Kashmiri calligraphists occupied an honoured position in the personal libraries of the Central Asian nobility. That works of Central Asian history like *Matla-as-Sadin* which was authored by Abdur-Rahman-Samarkandi, a Central Asian himself, were copied in Kashmir testifies to the existence of close links between the two regions even up to the eighteenth century. Persian literary classics were narrated and heard both in Central Asia and Kashmir with great enthusiasm.

Kashmiri families bearing surnames like *Akhoon, Beg, Kashgari, Turki, Bukhari, Nakshbandi* etc. are a living example of the cultural assimilation that took place as a result of immigration of Central Asian refugees and traders into Kashmir in the past. During the nineteenth century, the Nakshbandi family of Kashmir came in handy both to the Dogra rulers and the British Indian authorities for obtaining political information about Central Asian Khanates. The Nakshbandis still commanded a large following in Turkestan.

The movement of men and their ideas between Russian Central Asia and Kashmir did not cease altogether, though it became subdued during the nineteenth century on account of the inhibiting influences of Anglo-Russian rivalry in the region. Kashmir was a special attraction for the Central Asians who braved all hazards to travel by a circuitous and mountainous overland route to Bombay for making a Haj pilgrimage. This was mainly due to Kashmir being a cool hill resort free from political turmoil and banditry. The same factors were responsible for the desire of numerous Central Asian princes to seek refuge in Kashmir after they were deprived of authority in their native places. In this connection the unsuccessful attempts made by Beg Kuli Beg, the ex-ruler of Kashgaria in 1878, Yakub Khan Tora, ex-envoy of Yakub Beg of Kashgaria in 1878 and Abdul Malik Tora, a Bukharan prince in 1880 to settle in Kashmir are noteworthy. A Kokandi fugitive prince, Abdul Karim Khan succeeded in developing matrimonial relations with the Mehtar of Chitral.

Whereas both Britain and Russia imposed stringent curbs on the free movement of the people from India into Central Asia and vice versa, the two powers found it expedient to use the Indians including Kashmiris and Central Asians as pawns in their 'great game'. The success of these native agents in collecting intelligence for use of their respective European masters was due to the existence of traditional social relations between the two regions. Thus they could easily escape detection while moving around and conversing freely with the local people.

It was during the rule of Maharaja Ranbir Singh of Kashmir that relations with Central Asia were strengthened. His emissaries and agents used to stay in Russian Central Asia for years together learning Russian and Uzbek languages and even conducting business. One such agent, Mehta Sher Singh prepared a report of his experiences. Ranbir Singh even established a Russian language school, which was obviously aimed at training his agents in that language with a view to communicate freely with the Russians in Central Asia. Russian officers posted in Central Asia also evinced keen interest in the life and culture of Kashmir. Pachino took pains to collect tales about Kashmir by interviewing numerous Kashmiri visitors in Central Asia. He published them in Russian language.

The Ismaili inhabitants of Gilgit, Hunza and Chitral maintained close social relations including matrimonial, with their co-religionists in

Sarikol, Wakhan and the Russian Pamirs, as both the peoples were followers of the Agha Khan. Russian made cotton goods were freely available in the markets of Hunza, Gilgit and Chitral even up to late 1930s.

The whole pattern and context of the cultural interaction between Central Asia and Kashmir changed after the establishment of Soviet power in Russia. In a bid to prevent the influx of Bolshevik ideas into India through Kashmir, Britain imposed stringent curbs on the movements of men and materials from Central Asia overland into Kashmir and its frontier territories. But some anti-Bolshevik erstwhile Russian officers were allowed to come to India via the Pamirs-Gilgit route. Besides, some Bukharan refugees including the representatives of the ex-Amir of Bukhara entered India via Chitral. The Bukhara Amir was himself keen to seek refuge in Kashmir, but he could not make his way upto Gilgit before the arrival of Red Army at the Pamirs. As would have been normally expected, the October revolution did not result in large scale migration of Central Asians into India via Chitral, Gilgit or Leh routes. However, some tribal chiefs of Russian Pamirs who sought British protection against the Bolsheviks under the advice of their spiritual master--the Agha Khan, were an exception. This stands in total contrast with the mass migration of Muslim Uighur and Tungan refugees to Kashmir right from 1937 onwards due to political disturbances in Chinese Turkestan. But after the 1930s, some Central Asian and Russian refugees though their number was not so large, did come to India via Afghanistan-Chitral, Pamirs-Gilgit and Kashgar-Leh routes. They were forced to migrate largely because of the hardships caused due to famine and collectivisation campaign in Soviet Central Asia.

From the side of Kashmir there was no such emigration to Central Asia as was the case in North West Frontier Province and Punjab in the wake of Hijrat movement. But the case of a Kashmiri, Mir Abdul Majid, who was working in Lahore, having emigrated to Soviet Central Asia along with a group of Indian revolutionaries in 1920 is historic in character. Abdul Majid not only received training in arms at Tashkent but also studied at the Communist University of the Toilers of the East in Moscow. He returned to India via Kharogh-Pamirs-Chitral route in 1921 to organise the revolutionary movement in India. Even though he faced several trials by British authorities, Abdul Majid fought relentlessly against the British colonial rule in India.

The Anglo-Russian rivalry, which was constantly alive throughout the nineteenth century but for brief pauses put many restraints on the conduct of normal political, commercial and cultural intercourse between Central Asia and Kashmir. The existence of such traditional relations did have a cumulative impact on the future shaping of the Anglo-Russian strategies to promote their imperialist designs in this region. Thus Maharaja Ranbir Singh's flirtations with the Russians in Central Asia only activised the British determination to enforce their paramountcy in Kashmir through the establishment of a full-fledged Residency to supervise the internal administration and conduct the external relations of the State. If the British were interested in promoting Indian trade with Central Asia through the Srinagar-Leh-Kashgar route with a view to extending their influence in Central Asia, the Russian authorities were equally determined to keep the Indian trade out of Russian Turkestan and the protectorates of Khiva and Bukhara. The Russians even undersold their goods in the Chinese Turkestan in a bid to keep the British Indian goods out of its markets. It was usual for both Britain and Russia to despatch the native agents to Central Asia and India including Kashmir respectively for obtaining information of commercial, political or military value. In order to prevent the entry of such agents, each power imposed stringent curbs on the overland journey of strangers from Central Asia to India and vice versa.

The Anglo-Russian rivalry in Asia had its roots in the conflict of their strategic interests in Europe. In the first quarter of the nineteenth century the British concerned themselves with creating a friendly buffer in distant Persia, so as to secure their position in Asia against any rival European power. But with the defeat of Persia in 1827-28 at the hands of Russia, this strategy broke down. Now the British perceived a direct Russian threat to their hegemony in Asia. The very thought of a Russian advance in West and Central Asia scared the British who now feared its possible psychological repercussions on the Indian people. Moreover, Britain did not want Russia to advance further into the weak and unstable Central Asian Khanates which offered good market for its goods. Thus from 1830 onwards the British became serious about the extension of their commerce and through it the political influence into the Central Asian Khanates that intervened between British India and Russia. To achieve this end, British control over the Indus which was a vital link with Afghanistan and Central Asia, became imperative. British Indian missions were despatched to Sind and Punjab to conclude treatie[illegible] these

States. Once the right of British forces to pass through the Indus and Punjab was acquired, the British launched their offensive against Afghanistan which was important as a spring-board for penetration into Central Asia. But with the eventual reverses in Kabul in 1842 when British forces left that country, British attention once again fell back on Sind and Punjab. By 1849 Britain had secured control of both these territories and had also created a subsidiary ally in the person of Maharaja Gulab Singh whose family ruled the northernmost territory of Jammu and Kashmir up to 1947.

Whereas Britain was busy launching diplomatic and war offensive against numerous Asian States in the first half of the nineteenth century, Russia remained generally pre-occupied with securing its ends elsewhere in Europe. But this preoccupation of Russia with Europe did not prevent her from consolidating her hold on the Kazakh Steppes and from maintaining regular touch with the affairs in the Central Asian Khanates by despatching missions. It was only after her defeat in the Crimean War (1854-56), which exposed her weakness in Europe, that Russia focussed her attention on Central Asia. By 1867 Russia had established firm control over western Turkestan. She began to realise the commercial and political advantages of her occupation of Central Asia. Russia could now pose a direct threat to the British possessions in India to divert British pressure in Europe. On their part the British were more concerned over the possible adverse psychological impact of the emergence of a powerful European rival on the borders of India on the disaffected Indians.

The British were quick to realise the strategic importance of Kashmir and its frontier territories in Ladakh, Gilgit, Hunza and Chitral as a convenient listening post to monitor Russian movements in Central Asia. Since the native agents could not collect the vital political intelligence the British required and as British officers were too scared to travel in Central Asia after the murder of Stoddart and Connolly in Bukhara, the only alternative left was to post experineced British officers on the frontiers of Kashmir. However, the Kashmir ruler could not afford to see his prestige and authority among his subjects and the neighbouring Central Asian peoples eroded by the presence of British officers in his territory. Though the conflict of British and Kashmir interests embittered their mutual relations, the Kashmir ruler could do little more than making vain protests against the increasing British interference. In 1852 the Dogra ruler of Kashmir agreed to the presence of a British officer in Kashmir during summer season only. In course of time this temporary arrangement was converted into a permanent British Residency in Kashmir (in 1885).

The urgency of exerting a firmer control over Kashmir's trade with Central Asia and also of posting an officer at Leh, which was the entreport of trade between India and Central Asia, dawned upon the British Indian authorities soon after Russia had made considerable advance into western Turkestan. It was in 1867 that a British officer was posted at Leh, the main town of Ladakh, ostensibly to look after the interests of the traders but actually to monitor developments in Central Asia. Though Lawrence had envisaged this as a temporary arrangement his successor, Mayo, turned it into a permanent British Agency at Leh. The British officer at Leh played a key role in developing a direct rapport between the British Indian authorities and the visiting Central Asian emissaries in order to undermine Kashmir's influence in that region.

When reports about Ranbir Singh's overtures to Russians in Central Asia assumed seriousness in 1873, Northbrook decided to impose a British Resident on Kashmir. The implementation of this decision was, however, deferred on the advice of the Home government. It was after Ranbir Singh's death in 1885 that the British Residency was established in Kashmir. The new British move in Kashmir was described as virtual annexation in a section of the Russian press. Again in 1889, the deposition of Maharaja Pratap Singh was procured by the British Resident on the pretext of the Kashmir ruler's intrigues with Russia. Now the British Resident was in virtual control of the State's administration which paved the way for future British moves in this region. The re-establishment of Gilgit Agency in 1889 was soon followed by starting work on projects like construction of Srinagar-Gilgit military road, Jhelum valley cart road, Jammu-Sialkot railway etc. at Kashmir government's expense. Thus Kashmir was made to pay for the projects intended to serve the imperial interests. Forced labour (*begar*) which earned notoriety in Kashmir for the miseries it inflicted on the Kashmiri peasants and coolies in transporting the baggage of British travellers, officers and soldiers along the slippery mountain tracks from Srinagar to Gilgit, and which is commonly ascribed to the Dogra ruler's indifference to the welfare of Kashmiris, in reality owed its wide prevalence to the imperial British requirements. The maintenance pf a garrison at Gilgit, which was vital as a base for future British action right up to the Hindu Kush imposed a big socio-economic burden on the poor Kashmiris. The British action in tightening up their control over Kashmir was not dissimilar to their treatment of other Indian princely states. But their forward policy in Kashmir acquired an added significance in view of their strategy of consolidating their foothold over the frontier territory in and around Hunza, Nagar and Chitral, in the context of the Anglo-Russian rivalry. By 1895 all these territories had been brought under the effective control of Kashmir by the use of military force, which left no chance of their flirting with the Russians.

In order to offset any possible Russian advance on India through the Hindu Kush passes, the British plugged the gaps on the north-western frontiers of Kashmir up to the foot of the Hindu Kush, which was the natural stable frontier. But the British strategy in the northern frontiers of Kashmir skirting the Pamirs and Sinkiang was diametrically opposite to this. This was motivated by the British desire to keep Russia away from the Pamirs. Since neither the Afghans nor the Chinese exercised any effective control in the Pamirs, the area lay open for Russian penetration. So the British priority was for joining the two ends of the Afghan and Chinese frontiers at the Pamirs in a bid to create a wedge to separate the British and Russian empires. To achieve this end the reluctant Chinese authorities in Sinkiang were induced to expand in the Pamirs. As part of this appeasement policy towards China the British Indian authorities turned a deaf ear to the Kashmir ruler's pleadings for stopping the Chinese from occupying Shahidulla and Suget, which were once in the possession of Kashmir. Such a British stand resulted in the non-settlement of the Indian northern boundary with China in Sinkiang. In 1895 the British eventually achieved their object of creating a buffer at the Pamirs which eliminated for ever the coterminity of the Indian and Russian frontiers in this region.

The conclusion of Pamir Boundary Agreement of 1895 did not, however, bring an end to the 'great game'. Now the focus of Anglo-Russian rivalry shifted to the Kashmir frontiers. Russia, which was disgruntled at the extension of British authority up to Hunza in 1891, objected to the British support of Hunza claims on Raskam lands. Russia feared that Britain would use Raskam and Taghdumbash as a base for further expansion in Sinkiang by outflanking the Russian position in the Pamirs. When in 1898 the Chinese authorities in Sinkiang acknowledged Hunza's right to cultivate these lands, Russia threatened Peking with the occupation of Sarikol. The British, who were now masters of Hunza adopted a lukewarm attitude and preferred to let the matter be resolved through direct negotiations between Hunza and China. This was due to their pre-occupation with the negotiations with China over Tibet. A tough British stance on the Hunza claims would have not only jeopardized their bargaining position with China, but also provoked Russian incursions into Sinkiang. Obviously the British gave higher priority to make some gains in Tibet and Burma at the cost of Kashmir's rights and claims in the area lying beyond the Karakoram and the Taghdumbash Pamirs. Notwithstanding the Russian opposition and lukewarm British support to Hunza, the Chiefs of Hunza continued to levy grazing taxes on the Kirghizs in Taghdumbash Pamirs throughout this period with the assistance of local Chinese officials. The Hunza Chief also used to depute his men to Raskam annually to cultivate the lands there brushing aside the Chinese objections. It was only between 1898 and 1914 that Hunza could not exercise its rights in Raskam due to persistent Russian pressures on China. However, after 1914 Hunza resumed the cultivation of Raskam lands. The big-power rivalry in this area only helped China in deferring the formal delimitation of its frontiers in Sinkiang with Hunza and Kashmir.

By 1895 Britain had completed its expansion upto the foot of the Hindu Kush and this activity had not gone unnoticed by the Russians. From 1890s onwards the Russian desire to explore the strategic overland routes to India via Leh, Gilgit, Hunza and Chitral became irresistable. Numerous Russian military officers like Novitsky, Snesarev, Polotsov, Shersky, Kuznetsov, Kornilov and other specialists succeeded in obtaining British permission to travel down to India via the Karakoram, Mintaka and Kilik passes. Since the British too were keen to send their officers to restricted zones in Russian Central Asia on similar pursuits, they utilized the Russian requests for obtaining a reciprocal permission for British officers. Despatch of such reconnaissance missions on the part of both Russia and Britain was an essential feature of their mutual conflict in this region. Whereas Britain wanted to know about the Russian weak spots in Central Asia, Russians still regarded India as the sensitive nerve of the British empire which when touched would force Britian to ease its pressure on Russia in Europe. Hence the need for the Russians to know the up-to-date details about the British defence arrangements at the north-western frontier and also about the practicability of numerous mountainous overland routes. However, with Germany emerging as a common threat to Russia and Britain in Europe, both powers were bound to act in cooperation in the changed circumstances. In fact, Russia categorically declared to the British in 1912 that she had no desire to have any foothold in Chinese Turkestan or in the neighbourhood of the Kashmir frontiers. The Russian and British agents posted in remote listening posts in Tashkurghan and Kashgar (both inside Chinese Turkestan) who were hitherto playing antagonistic roles, now acted in unison during the period of the first World War. But this brief period of cordiality came to an abrupt end soon after the Bolsheviks came to power in Russia.

The Soviet withdrawal from the war against Germany and their support to the liberation of the peoples of the East from the alien colonial rule were directly aimed against the British imperial interests. Soviet appeals to the peoples of the East exhorting them to rise against the alien imperialist rule came at a time when the British policy towards Turkey and their harsh measures to suppress the Indian national movement had alienated a large section of Indian population against them. The Hijrat movement of thousands of Indian Muslims to Afghanistan and Soviet Central Asia came as a rude shock to the British. They now began to see the Bolshevik hand behind every movement in India which was already simmering with discontent. British anxiety to insulate India from any Bolshevik influence became more intense due to the Soviets launching a propaganda crusade against British imperialism in the East and also by their open support to Indian revolutionaries who operated from Soviet territory. In the British eyes the whole northern frontier region comprising the North-West Frontier Province, Punjab and Kashmir including its frontier territories in Chitral, Hunza, Yasin, Gilgit etc. were potential bases for spreading Bolshevism in India as these areas were geographically and culturally close to Central Asia. Consequently Kashmir and the area around its frontiers, which commanded numerous routes from Central Asia into India, came into the sharp focus of the new British strategy against Soviet power in Central Asia. This meant an increasing British control over the frontier dependencies of Kashmir, wherefrom they could better monitor the Soviet movements.

Numerous precautionary steps like closing the borders at Gilgit, Hunza and Chitral in order to prevent any possible entry of Bolshevik emissaries and Indian revolutionaries from Soviet Central Asia into India, censorship of Bolshevik literature, imposing a ban on the import of rubles into India, curbing the export of essential commodities from India to Central Asia and the circulation of anti-Bolshevik propaganda literature amongst the Muslims in Kashmir, Gilgit, Hunza, Chitral, North West Frontier Province and Chinese Turkestan were taken. Every activity of the Soviets and the Indian revolutionaries in Central Asia was closely monitored. As a result of such measures, more than three million rubles were deposited in the Kashmir government treasuries of Leh and Srinagar in the first quarter of the year 1920. In addition the movement of people from the Chinese Turkestan into Kashmir via Gilgit or Ladakh routes was restricted. The British officers at Gilgit and Kashgar worked jointly to apprehend Raja Mahendra Pratap while on his overland journey through the Pamirs. Although the Kashmir ruler cooperated with the British in all these measures, the British did not desist from undermining the Maharaja's authority in his frontier territories of Gilgit, Hunza, Chitral etc. Even after the signing of the Anglo-Soviet Accord in 1921, Britain continued with its imperialist policy on the Kashmir frontier. Though they continued to recognise Kashmir's jurisdiction over these frontier districts, the British wanted to have a more direct role there. Numerous defence projects like installation of wireless sets and air-landing facilities in Gilgit, Chitral, Hunza, Chilas, etc., improvement of road and telephonic communications were launched in this area. What irked the British was Maharaja Hari Singh's sustained effort to exert his direct control over these frontier dependencies. The circumstance of Kashmiris' agitation against the Dogra ruler which took a violent turn in 1931, provided the British with a favourable opportunity to wrest direct administration of Gilgit agency from Maharaja Hari Singh in 1935 though they continued to recognise his sovereignty over this area. It was the British commandant of the Gilgit Scouts, Major Brown, who hoisted Pakistan's flag in the Gilgit Agency soon after India became independent in 1947.

Thus Kashmir played a significant role in India's relations with Central Asia on account of its geographical proximity and cultural affinities with the region. Kashmir assumed a new importance in the context of the Anglo-Russian rivalry over Central Asia. The shadow of this rivalry continued to lurk even after the establishment of the Soviet power in Central Asia. The Anglo-Russian rivalry which lost its intensity with the conclusion of the 1907 convention and in the face of the emergence of a common threat from Germany, was again revived in the wake of the October revolution in Russia. The British felt tempted to interfere in Central Asia owing to the chaotic conditions of civil war there. The Soviets tried to embarrass the British by giving encouragement to anti-British activities of the Indian revolutionaries, which in turn resulted in the further tightening of British stranglehold over Kashmir and its frontier dependencies.

The emergence of an independent India in 1947 alone terminated the Anglo-Russian tug of war in this strategic region. Independent India freed herself from the old hangovers of British imperialist policy in Central Asia and established close friendly relations with the Soviet Union.

Appendix I

SUBSTANCE OF THE LETTER* FROM A RUSSIAN MINISTER TO THE RAJA OF LADAKH SENT TROUGH AGHA MEHDI.

Akibat Mahmood Khan Nazim of Thibet

My master the great Emperor of all the Russias is the soveriegn of many realms and countless nations, and is no less found for the benevolence and liberality of his disposition than for the vast extent of his Empire.

Travellers and strangers from all quarters of the Globe rest to the Russian Empire and are there treated with kindness and distinction. The bearer of this letter Aga Mehdi, the son of Rafael, a native of Kabul will fully apprize you of the encouragement afforded by our customs and regulations to the resort of merchants and visitors from all quarters of the Imperial dominions.

---

* This letter appears to have been delivered by Agha Mehdi to the Raja of Ladakh during his first mission. Moorcroft claims to have seen this letter in original by courtesy of the *Kahlon* (Prime Minister) of Ladakh. Accordingly he forwarded its copy to Charles Metcalfe, the then Political Secretary, GOI from Leh on 1 January 1821. Whereas George Trebeck made an exact facsimile copy of the Russian original, Mir Izzet Ullah translated the Turki version of the letter into Persian.

See Moorcroft, *Travels*. Vol. 1, p. 383
Foreign. Political. 10 Oct. 1823. 23-24.

Aga Mehdi has reported to us the respectable character of your Government and the wise policy which you pursue of affording every facility to commercial dealings in your country. We are therefore extremely anxious to establish a friendly intercourse between the people of Russia and Thibet and to open a trade with your part of the world and it is to promote these objects that we have written a letter and despatched an Envoy. We trust that you will consider it and will send an agent to confer regarding the best means of establishing a commercial intercourse. The country of Gezim Khan, that is to say the Emperor of China lies between us but all obstacles may be removed if goodwill and friendly disposition exist on both sides. We are now thinking of despatching caravans to Kokan (Ferghana) and request your opinion on the subject.

If you will depute an Elchee we engage that he shall obtain an audience in His Imperial Majesty, that a person shall be sent to meet him on the frontier and that he shall be received with the utmost respect and consideration. Our Envoy will make known all further particulars to you and will offer the fullest assurance of our amicable purposes and disposition.

Appendix II

TRANSLATION OF A LETTER* FROM COUNT NESSELRODE, RUSSIAN FOREIGN MINISTER TO RAJA RANJIT SINGH OF PUNJAB, JANUARY 1820.

To

The Illustrious
Rajah Ranjeet Singh
Ruler of the Punjab and Chief of the Sikh nation.

At this time the respectable Aga Mehdi, son of Rafail the Agent(or Counsellor) for the affairs of the merchants of Persia and Tartary trading to Russia who is an old and attached friend of yours, has arrived here and has made frequent mention of your excellent qualities and disposition, the justice and wisdom of your administration, your friendly conduct towards neighbouring states and travellers visiting your country and more especially your attention to all merchants subjects of Russia who made to that quarter.

---

* Moorcroft claims to have seen this letter in Russian original written in golden ink and also its Persian version. After having got it copied exactly at the hands of G. Trebeck, Moorcroft forwarded the same to C.T. Metcalfe, Political Secretary, GOI on 6 May 1821, from Leh.
See *Foreign. Political*. 10 Oct. 1823. 25-26.

The above favourable reports of your character and government have afforded me the most lively satisfaction and have inspired me with a sincere desire to cultivate a correspondence with you. I further communicated the substance of what I have heard regarding you to my Imperial Master Alexander Ist Emperor of all the Russias who has been graciously pleased to express his wishes for the increase of your power and reputation and the continual prosperity of your dominions.

So much indeed is High Imperial Majesty gratified by the rumours which reach him from all quarters of your love of justice and benevolent disposition that he has instructed me to despatch to your Courts an Envoy charged with letters in order that the gates of friendly intercourse may be thrown open and the road of traffic between the merchants of Russia and the Punjab cleared from all impediments.

In compliance therefore with the orders of my Imperial Master I address to you this letter of compliment and congratulation which I have entrusted to the respectabie Aga Mehdi one of the aulic Counsellors of the State of Russia. I feel satisfied that on his arrival in your dominions you will receive him with the attention and consideration befitting his rank and circumstances and will afford him every assistance in the prosecution of his commercial speculations.

In conclusion I beg to offer you an assurance that when any people of business, merchants or travellers of whatever description belonging to your native may visit Russia they will be received in the most friendly manner and will experience a degree of consideration exactly proportioned to their rank and station.

St. Petersburgh, 1820.
Sd/-
(Nesselrode)
Minister for Foreign Affairs

Appendix III

TRANSLATION OF AN IMPERIAL DECREE ISSUED BY THE CHINESE EMPEROR ON THE KENG-YIN DAY OF THE IST MOON(FEBRUARY 1860).

We have this day received the report in which Cha-la-feu-tai (the Military Governor of Ili) gives an account of what he has gathered in respect of the affairs and disposition of the barbarians, and requests that advantage be taken of the opportunity to strike a blow in a vital point, as an accessory to the measures conducive toward keeping the adversary in check.

It is stated that the Russian headman Kwang-Su-leh(Consul) has entered into conversation with Colonel Ha-pu-Ch' i-hsien and others of the Ili garrison, remarking that as the English barbarians are intending to go to Tientsin to take vengeance for the past, the best thing to do would be to send a force to harass them by an attack on the Indian frontier. This might, it was added, compel them to desist from their warlike intentions. The Military Governor reports a general outline of what he has gathered on the subject of the affairs and intentions of the barbarians and with the idea that there is an opportunity offered of which it would be worthwhile to take advantage; he proposes that the Russian barbarians should be induced(lit. stirred up, instigated) to make a flank attack on India from the south-east, while at the same time the Nipalese barbarians should be encouraged to invade the country from the north-west. He further requests that an officer may be deputed from the Mongolian Superintendency(Li Fau Yuan) by confidential decree, with instructions to lay the needful commands upon the Russian barbarians, the Nipalese barbarians being simultaneously summoned into activity.

The report thus laid before us, dealing as it does with the entire question of relations with the barbarians, is undoubtedly the result of careful consideration. The writer however has been long away from Pekin and he is not in a position thoroughly to understand the policy at present pursued in the treatment of barbarian affairs. He observes, for instance, that "the Russian barbarians are twice as friendly in their disposition towards us as they formerly were". He is unaware, when saying this, that Envoy of the Russian barbarians now at Pekin, I-Keh-ma-ti-yeh-fuh(iquatiew),. has sent despatch after despatch, insisting with violent language upon a demarcation of the frontier in the territories appertaining to the province of Kirin. His designs are of the most insidious nature and it is far from being true that a greater degree of friendliness exists, in comparison with the past, as a consequence of an agent being in residence at Pekin.

It has, moreover, to be considered that, in point of fact, the Russians, English, and French are united by a common understanding. As regards the proposed attack upon India, not only is the army required for such undertaking not forthcoming, but even suppose a successful result obtained, it is Russia who would take possession of the country, leaving China in the enjoyment of no advantage. There is reason besides to fear that if any proposal of this kind were to be offered on the side of China, the first step taken by Russian barbarians would be to give information of it to the English representing us as the mischief-makers, so that in actual fact we should simply be made fools of by the barbarians. Nipal is a small country and a poor one. More than this, it is subject to the English barbarians. Were we to propose that it should place its resources at our disposal for an attack upon India, it would be certain to decline giving offence to the English, and the only result would be to open a door to their demands and reclamations. On this side also, there is nothing to be gained.

Let Cha-la-feu-tai give instructions confidentially to the officers above named to refrain from broaching this subject in future conversation with the Consul.

In case the Consul should himself introduce the question, the officers above-named may be instructed to inform him that the policy of the Celestial Dynasty, in the exercise of its control over outer nations is based upon good faith and uprightness; and that it stands altogether aloof from insidious acts of treachery, the result of which must be to give rise to war. As for the defensive preparations that have now been instituted at Tientsin, these are not due to apprehensions of vindictive reprisals on their part, but are designed to prevent the barbarians in question from treating China with contempt.

Appendix IV

APPEAL OF THE COUNCIL OF PEOPLE'S COMMISSARS TO THE MOSLEMS OF RUSSIA AND THE EAST.

3 December 1917

Comrades ! Brothers !

Great events are taking place in Russia ! An end is drawing near to the murderous war, started by the bargainings of foreign powers. The rule of the plunderers who exploit the peoples of the world is tottering. The ancient citadel of slavery and serfdom is crumbling under the blows of the Russian revolution. The world of violence and oppression is approaching its last days. A new world is being born, a world of the toilers and the liberated. At the head of this revolution stands the workers' and peasants' Government of Russia, the Council of People's Commissars.

Revolutionary Councils of workers', soldiers', and peasants' deputies are scattered over the whole of Russia. Power in the country is in the hands of the people. The labouring masses of Russia burn with the single desire to achieve an honourable peace and to help the oppressed peoples of the world to win their freedom.

Russia is not alone in this sacred cause. The mighty call to freedom sounded by the Russian revolution has been taken up by all the toilers in the East and West. The peoples of Europe, exhausted by war, are already stretching out their hands to us, in our work for peace. The workers and soldiers of the West are already rallying under the banner of socialism, storming the strongholds of imperialism. Even far off India, that land which has been oppressed by the 'enlightened' European robbers for so many centuries, has raised the standard of revolt, organizing its councils of deputies, throwing the hated yoke of slavery from its shoulders, and summoning the peoples of the East to the struggle and to freedom.

The empire of capitalist plunder and violence is falling in ruins. The ground is slipping from under the feet of the imperialist robbers.

In the face of these great events, we turn to you, toiling and disinherited Moslems of Russia and the East.

Moslems of Russia, Tatars of Volga and the Crimea, Kirghiz and Sarts of Siberia and Turkestan, Turks and Tatars of Trans-Caucasia, Chechens and mountain Cossacks ! All you, whose mosques and shrines have been destroyed, whose faith and customs, have been violated by the Tsars and oppressors of Russia ! Henceforward your beliefs and customs, your national cultural institutions, are declared free and inviolable ! Build your national life freely and without hindrance. It is your right. Know that your rights, like hose of all the peoples of Russia, will be protected by the might of the revolution, by the Council of Workers', Soldiers', and Peasants' Deputies !

Support this revolution and its authorized Government.

Moslems of the East ! Persians, Turks, Arabs and Hindus. All you in whose lives and property, in whose freedom and native land the rapacious European plunderers have for centuries traded ! All you whose countries the robbers who began the war now desire to share among themselves ! We declare that the secret treaties of the dethroned Tsar regarding the annexation of Constantinople confirmed by the deposed Kerensky, are now null and void. The Russian Republic and its Government, the Council of People's Commissars, are opposed to the seizure of foreign territory; Constantinople must remain in the hands of the Moslems.

We declare that the treaty for the partition of Persia is null and void. Immediately after the cessation of military operations the troops will be withdrawn from Persia and the Persians will be guaranteed the right freely to determine their own destiny.

We declare that the treaty for the partition of Turkey, which was to despoil it of Armenia, is null and void. Immediately after the cessation of military operations, the Armenians will be guaranteed the right freely to determine their political destiny.

It is not from Russia and its revolutionary Government that you have to fear enslavement, but from the European imperialist robbers, from those who laid waste your native lands and converted them into their colonies.

Overthrow these robbers and enslavers of your country ! Now, when war and desolation are demolishing the pillars of the old order, when the entire world is blazing with indignation against the imperialist brigands, when the least spark of discontent bursts out in a mighty flame of revolution, when even the Indian Moslems, oppressed and tormented by the foreign yoke, are rising in revolt against their slave drivers-now it is impossible to keep silent. Lose no time in throwing off the yoke of the ancient oppressors of your land ! Let them no longer violate your hearths ! You must yourselves be masters in your own land ! You yourselves must arrange your life as you yourselves see fit ! You have the right to do this, for your fate is in your own hands !

Comrades ! Brothers !

Advance firmly and resolutely towards a just and democratic peace !

We inscribe the liberation of the oppressed peoples of the world in our banners !

Moslems of Russia !

Moslems of East !

We look to you for sympathy and support in the work of regenerating the world.

Appendix V

TRANSLATION OF A PETITION FROM THE INHABITANTS OF SHIGHNAN(ROSHAN, BARTANG, SHAKHDARA, GHAND, SOCHAN AND WAKHAN) TO THE POLITICAL OFFICER, CHITRAL DATED 19 RAJAB 1338 (AH)

As Russia, under whose defence we have been living since 30 years, has left our country to itself, that is, the few Russians who protected us have left this place, we therefore hope that you will very kindly extend your protection over us so that this small party of helpless people may not be ruined because foreign powers who resemble borrowed states encroach upon our possessions and we being unequipped with modern weapons are unable to defend ourselves. It has therefore been considered necessary to request you to come to our help expeditiously in order that the string of these relations may not be broken or entangled. In this very year we received a letter from Aga Khan Sahib on behalf of the Government that whenever any disturbance appears on the northern border we should request the British government for help. On account of these two reasons we do not look upon any other power for assistance. We emphasise the request that timely help should soon be sent because encroachments have already begun on our possessions from all sides. Rather on account of the lack of activity on the part of the subjects and the scarcity of weapons thieves even can take over the control of our region.

(Signatures and Seals)

Bibliography

PRIMARY SOURCES

(A) National Archives of India, New Delhi.

Official records/proceedings of the Foreign and Political Department, Government of India from 1808 to 1935. Following series have been consulted:

A Pol. E.
B Genl. E.
B Pol. E.
Est. A, B.
Extl. A, B.
F. C.
Frontr.
Frontr. A, B.
Genl.
Genl. A, B.
Intl. A, B.
Intl. Deposit
Poltl. A, B.
P. C.
Rev. A.
Sec.

S. C.
Sec. E.
Sec. G.
S. H.
S. I.
S. M.
S. S.
War.B(Secret)

(B) State Archives Repository, Jammu and Kashmir Government, Jammu.

(a) Persian Records 1724-1892.
(b) Old English Records 1868-1921.

(C) Official Publications and Contemporary Accounts

Aitchison, C. U. *Comp*	A Collection of treaties, engagements and sanads relating to India and neighbouring countries. Calcutta, 1931. (Volume 12:Treaties relating to Jammu and Kashmir).
Aitchison, J.E.T.	Handbook of the trade products of Leh with the statistics of the trade from 1867 to 1872 inclusive. Calcutta, Wyman, 1874.
Bailey, F.M.	Mission to Tashkent. London, Jonathan Cape, 1946.
Bates, Charles Ellison.	A Gazetteer of Kashmir. Calcutta, 1873.
Blacker, L.V.S.	On secret patrol in High Asia. London, 1922.
Bonvalot, G.	Through the Heart of Asia, over the Pamirs to India. London, 1889. 2 Volumes.
Burnes, Alexander.	Cabool being a personal narrative of a journey to and residence in that city in the year 1836-1838. London, John Murray, 1842.

---------------------- Travels into Bukhara (1831-33) together with a narrative of a voyage on the Indus. London, 1835. Reprinted by Oxford University Press, Karachi, 1973. 3 Volumes.

Cobbold, Ralph P. Innermost Asia:Travel and sport in the Pamirs. London, W. Hutchinson, 1900.

Cumberland, C.S. Sport in the Pamirs and Turkestan Steppes. London, W. Blackwood, 1895.

Davies, R.H. Report on the trade and resources of the countries on the north western boundary of British India. Lahore, 1862.

De Bourbel, Le Marquis. *Comp.* Routes in Jammu and Kashmir. Calcutta, Thacker Spink, 1897.

Degras, Jane. *Ed.* Soviet documents on foreign policy. London, Oxford University Press, 1951. Volume 1: 1917-24.

Douie, James. The Panjab, North-West frontier province and Kashmir. Cambridge University Press, 1916.

Drew, Frederic. The Jummoo and Kashmir territories, a geographical account. London, Edward Stanford, 1875.

Dughlat, Mirza Hyder. Tarikh-i-Rashidi : a history of the Moghuls of Central Asia. Translated from Persian by E. D. Ross. Edited by N.Elias. London, 1895.

Duke, Joshua. Ince's Kashmir handbook, a guide for visitors. Calcutta, Thacker Spink, 1888.

Durand, Algernon. Making of a frontier. London, 1899.

Dumore, Earl of (C.A.Murray). The Pamirs, being a narrative of a year's expedition on horseback and on foot through Kashmir, Western Tibet, Chinese Tartary and Russian Central Asia. London, John Murray, 1893. 2 Volumes.

Elias, N. — Confidential report of a mission to Chinese Turkestan and Badakhshan in 1885-86. Calcutta, 1886.

Ellis, C.H. — The Transcaspian episode. London, 1953.

Elphinstone, Mountstuart. — Account of the kingdom of Kabul, and its dependencies in Hunza, Tartary and India, comprising a view of the Afghan nation. Second edition. London. Longmans, 1819. 2 Volumes.

Etherton, P.T. — Across the roof of the world: a record of sport and travel through Kashmir, Gilgit, Hunza, the Pamirs, Chinese Turkestan, Mongolia and Siberia. London, Constable, 1911.

Faiz Buksh(F.B.) — Translation of a report on Badakhshan, Balkh and Bokhara. Lahore, Civil Sectt. Press, 1871. (Confidential).

Forster, George. — A Journey from Bengal to England through the northern part of India, Kashmir, Afghanistan, and Persia and into Russia by the Caspian sea. London, R. Foulder, 1798. 2 Volumes.

Forsyth, T.D. — Autobiography and reminiscences. Edited by Ethel Forsyth. London, R. Bentley, 1887.

--------------------- — A Memorandum of trade with Central Asia. Calcutta, Foreign Deptt. Press, 1870.

--------------------- — Report of a mission to Yarkand in 1873. Calcutta, Foreign Deptt. Press, 1875.

Fraser, David. — Marches of Hindustan: the record of a journey in Thibet, Trans-Himalayan India, Chinese Turkestan, Russian Turkestan and Persia. Edinburgh, 1907.

Gerard, M.G and Holdich.T.H. Report on the proceedings of the Pamir Boundary Commission. Calcutta, Supdt. Govt. Printing, 1897.

Girdlestone, Charles. Memorandum on Cashmere and some adjacent countries during 1871. Calcutta, Foreign Deptt. Press, 1874.

Godfrey, S.H. The trade of Ladakh with China and Thibet. In *A Summer in high Asia*. by F.E.S. Adair. London. W.Thacker, 1899. pp. 255-75.

Gordon, T.E. Roof of the world:being the narrative of a journey over the high plateau of Tibet to the Russian frontier and the Oxus sources on Pamir. Edinburgh, Edmonston, 1876.

--------------------- A Varied life : a record of military and civil service of sport and of travel in India, Central Asia and Persia 1849-1902. London, John Murray 1906.

Hedin, Sven Anders. Central Asia and Tibet. London, 1903. 2 Volumes.

---------------------- Through Asia. London, Methuen, 1898.2 Volumes.

Henderson, George and Hume, Allen O. Lahore to Yarkand:incidents of the route and natural history of the countries traversed by the expedition of 1870 under T.D. Forsyth. London, L. Reeve, 1873.

Honigberger, J.M. Thirty five years in the East, London, 1852.

Hugel, Baron Charles. Travels in Kashmir and the Panjab. Translated into English by T.B. Jervis. London, John Petheram, 1845.

Imperial Gazetteer of India. Oxford, Clarendon Press, 1908. Volume 15.

Imperial Gazetteer of India. Provincial Series-Kashmir. Calcutta, Supdt.Govt. Printing, 1909.

India, Army Headquarters. Intelligence Branch. Frontier overseas expeditions from India. (First published, 1907) Reprint by Mittal Publications, Delhi in 1983. Volume 1. Part I.

India, General Staff. Military report on Russian Turkistan.Simla, Govt. Press. 1914.

India,Home Deptt. Intelligence Bureau. India and Communism, Simla, GOI Press, 1935.

India, Quarter Master General. Gazetteer of Kashmir and Ladakh. Calcutta, 1890.

Izzet Ullah, Mir. Travels beyond the Himalayas. "*Journal of Royal Asiatic Society of Great Britain and Ireland* Volume 7. 1842-43. pp. 283-342".

J&K Administration Reports.(Select years).

J&K Govt. Ain-i-Dharmarth, regulation for Dharmarth trust fund, J&K State. Jammu, n.d.

J&K, Sericulture Department. Report on the investigation into the conditions of the sericulture industry in Jammu and Kashmir State. Srinagar 1942.

Kalhana. Rajatarangini : a chronicle of the kings of Kashmir. Translated into English with introduction and notes by Aurel Stein. Westminster, A. Constable, 1900. 2 Volumes.

Karam Prakash, Baba. Report of a journey to Nepal, Samvat 1931.(Persian MS, JKA).

Kashmir Census Report, 1891. By Pandit Bhag Ram. Lahore, 1893, (Census of India, 1891 Series. Volume 28)

Kashmir Census Report, 1901. By Guhlam Ahmad Khan. Lahore 1902. 2 parts.(Census of India, 1901 Series. Volume 23).

Kashmir Census Report, 1911. By Matin-uz-Zaman Khan. Lucknow, 1912, 2 parts.(Census of India, 1911 Series. Volume 20).

Kashmir Census Report, 1921. By Chaudhari Khusi Mohammad. Lahore, 1923. 2 Parts. (Census of India, 1921 Series. Volume 22).

Kemp, P.M.*Tr* and *Ed*. Russian travellers to India and Persia 1624-1798(Kotov,Yefremov, Danibegov). Delhi, Jiwan Prakashan, 1959.

Knight, E.F. — Where three empires meet : a narrative of recent travel in Kashmir, Western Tibet, Gilgit and the adjoining countries. London, Longmans, 1893.

Kostenko, L.F. — The Turkistan region : being a military statistical review of the Turkistan military district of Russia. (St.Petersburgh, 1880). Translated from Russian into English by Intelligence Branch, GOI. Simla, 1882, 3 Volumes.

Kuropatkin, A.N. — Kashgaria. Translated from Russian into English by W.E. Gowan. Calcutta, 1882.

Ladakh Trade Reports, 1867-1935.

Lansdell, Henry. — Russian Central Asia, including Kuldja, Bokhara, Khiva and Merv. London, S. Low, 1885. 2 Volumes.

Lockhart, W.S.A and Woodthorpe, R.G. — Gilgit mission, 1885-86. London, 1889.

Mason, Kenneth. — Routes in the Western Himalaya, Kashmir and C. Second edition. Calcutta, 1929. Volume 1-Punch, Kashmir and Ladakh.

Mohan Lal. — Travels in the Punjab, Afghanistan and Turkistan to Balk, Bokhara and Herat and a visit to Great Britain and Germany. London, 1846. (Reprinted by Calcutta, K.P. Bagchi, 1977).

Montgomerie, T.G. — Routes in the Western Himalayas: Kashmir. Third edition. Dehradun, Survey of India, 1909.

Moorcroft, William and Trebeck, George. — Travels in the Himalayan provinces of Hindustan and the Punjab, in Ladakh and Kashmir, in Peshawar, Kabul, Kunduz and Bokhara, 1819-1825. Edited by H. H. Wilson. London, 1841. 2 Volumes.

Nakshbandee, Khwajah Ahmed Shah. — Narrative of travels. *Journal of Asiatic Society of Bengal*" Volume 25, 1856, pp. 344-58.

Nazaroff, P.S. — Moved on, from Kashgar to Kashmir. Translated from Russian into English by Malcom Burr. London, 1935.

Plowden, T.C. — Confidential precis of correspondence regarding to affairs in Central Asia, 1875-77. Calcutta, 1878.

Punjab Administration Reports (Select years).

Raina, J.L. — Means of communication in the last century in Kashmir and how the control passed into British hands. Jammu, 1926.

Robertson, George S. — Chitral: the story of a minor siege. London, Methuen, 1899.

Schefer, Charles. *Ed* and *Tr*. — Histoire de L'Asie Centrale par Mir Abdoul Kerim Boukhary : Afghanistan, Boukhara, Khiva, Khokand depuis les dernieres annees du regne de Nadir Shah 1153, jusquen 1233 de 1 'Hegire 1740-1818 A.D. Paris, 1876.(Reprint at Philo Press Amsterdam, 1970).

Schuyler, E. — Turkistan:notes of a journey in Russian Turkestan, Khokand, Bokhara and Kuldja. London, 1882. 2 volumes.

Scott, I.D. — Notes on Chitral. Simla, GOI Press, 1937.

Sher Singh, Mehta. — Safar nama. (Urdu MS in JKA, RDL).

Strachey, Henry. — Report on geographical and statistical information and commerce of Ladakh. Simla, 1851.(Confidential).

Subodh Roy . *Ed*. — Communism in India, with unpublished documents from National Archives of India:1919-24. Calcutta, 1971.

------------------------ — Communism in India; unpublished documents, 1925-34. Calcutta,1972.

Temple, H.M. *Comp.* Precis of information regarding lower and upper Chitral, Hunza and Nagar. Simla, Govt. Press, 1877. Part I.

Torrens, H.D. Travels in Ladakh, Tartary and Kashmir. London, 1862.

Turkestanskiye Vidomosti dated 9(21), 13(25) and 16(28). October 1894.

Valikhanov. Account of a journey from the Zauku pass to Kashgar and back again(in 1858). Translated from Russian into English by Robert Mitchell.

------------------------------ The Russians in Central Asia. Translated from Russian by John and Robert Mitchell. London, E.Stanford, 1865.

Vambery, Arminius. Sketches of Central Asia: additional chapters on my travels, adventures and on the ethnology of Central Asia. London, W.H. Allen, 1868.

------------------------------ Travels in Central Asia, being the account of a journey from Teheran across the Turkoman desert on the eastern shore of the Caspian to Khiva, Bokhara and Samarkand, performed in 1863. London, John Murray, 1864.

Vigne, G.T. Travels in Kashmir, Ladakh, Iskardoo. London, H.Colburn, 1842. 2 Volumes.

Wolff, Joseph. Narrative of a mission to Bokhara in the years 1843-1845. Third edition. London, J.W. Parker, 1846.

Wynne, H.Lepoer, Comp. Confidential precis of papers regarding affairs in Central Asia, 1867-72. Simla, Govt. Central Press, 1872.

Younghusband, F.E. The Heart of a continent: a narrative of tavels in Manchuria across the Gobi desert, through the Himalayas, the Pamirs and Chitral, 1884-1894. Third edition. Lahore, London, John Murray, 1896.

------------------------	Kashmir.London, A&C Black, 1917.
------------------------	Report of a mission to the northern frontier of Kashmir in 1889. Calcutta, 1890.
--------------------------- and Younghusband, F.E.	The Relief of Chitral. London, Macmillan, 1897.
Young, W.M.	Report of the Indian Hemp drugs Commission. Calcutta, 1894.

SECONDARY SOURCES

Adamova, A and Greck, T.	Miniatures from Kashmirian Paintings. Translated from Russian into English by Yu E. Borshchevsky. Leningrad, 1976.
Alder, G. J.	British India's northern frontier 1865-95: a study in Imperial policy. London, 1963.
Allworth.E.*Ed.*	Central Asia : a century of Russian rule. New York, Columbia University Press, 1967.
Arora, R.C.	In the land of Kashmir, Ladakh and Gilgit. Agra, 1940.
Bajpai, S.C.	The Northern frontier of India. Bombay, Allied, 1970.
Bamzai, P.N.K.	Kashmir and Central Asia. New Delhi, Light and Life, 1980.
Bellew, H.W.	Kashmir and Kashgar : a narrative of the journey of the Embassy to Kashgar in 1873-74. London, 1875.
Bernier, Francois.	Travels in India, 1665-1668 A.D. containing a series of letters concerning his journey to Kashmir in Aurangzeb's suite. Edited by A. Constable. London, 1914.
Biddulph, John.	Tribes of the Hindoo Kush. Calcutta, Supdt. Govt. Printing,1880.

Bisheshwar Prasad. The Foundations of India's foreign policy 1860-82. Calcutta, 1955.

Bongard-Levin, G and Vigasin, A. The Image of India: The study of ancient Indian civilization in the USSR. Moscow, Progress, 1984.

Boulger, D.C. England and Russia in Central Asia. London, W.H Allen, 1879. 2 Volumes.

Caroe, Olaf. Soviet empire, the Turks of Central Asia and Stalinism. London, Macmillan, 1967.

Carr, E.H. The Bolshevik revolution, 1917-1923. Penguin, 1983. 3 Volumes.

Charak, S.S. Life and times of Maharaja Ranbir Singh of Jammu, Jay Kay, 1985.

Chavda, V.K. India, Britain and Russia: a study in British opinion 1838-78. Delhi, Sterling, 1967.

Christie, Ella K. Through Khiva to golden Samarkand. London, Seeley, Service, 1925.

Clark, J. Hunza : lost kingdom of the Himalayas. London, 1957.

Clubb, O. Edmund. China and Russia; the great game. New York, 1971.

Coates, W.P. and Coates, Z.K. Soviets in Central Asia. London, Lawrence, 1951.

Colebrook, T.E. Life of Honourable Mountstuart Elphinstone. London, John Murray, 1884. 2 volumes.

Curzon, George, N. The Pamirs and the source of the Oxus. London, 1896.

---------------------------- Russia in Central Asia in 1889 and the Anglo-Russian question. London, Longmans, 1889.

Datta, C.L. Ladakh and Western Himalayan politics 1819-1848. Delhi, Munshiram Manoharlal, 1973.

Davies, C. Collin. The problems of the north-west frontier 1890-1908. With a survey of policy since 1849. Second edition. London, Curzon Press, 1975.

Didamari, Muhammad Azam. Tarikh-i-Kashmir Azami. Srinagar. 1936.(in Persian).

Digby, William. Condemned unheard : the government of India and His Highness the Maharaja of Kashmir, a letter to U.K.Shuttle Worth. London, 1890.

Dmitriev, G.L. Iz istorii Sredneziatsko-Indiskikh otnoshenii vtori poloviny IX-nachala - XX veka. Tashkent, 1965.

Druhe, David N. Russo-Indian relations 1466-1917. New York, Vantage Press, 1970.

------------------------ Soviet Russia and Indian communism 1917-1947, with an epilogue. New York, Bookman Associates, 1959.

Dumasia, Naoroji, W. The Aga Khan and his ancestors : a biographical and historical sketch. Bombay, Times of India Press, 1939.

Fauq, Muhammad ud Din. Mukamal Tarikh-i-Kashmir. Lahore, 1912. 3 Volumes. (In Urdu).

------------------------ Tarikh-i-aqwami Kashmir. Lahore, Zaffar Brothers, 1934. (In Urdu).

Fisher, Margaret W, Rose, Leo E and Huttenback, Robert A. Himalayan battleground: Sino-Indian rivalry in Ladakh. New York, 1963.

Forrest, George W. Ed. Selections from the minutes and other official writings of Mountsuart Elphinstone. London, R.Bentley,1884.

Francke, A.H. Antiquities of Indian Tibet. (First published in 1914,1926). Reprint by S.Chand, Delhi in 1972. 2 Volumes.

------------------------ Ladakh, the mysterious land. (First published in 1907). Reprint by Cosmo, Delhi, 1978.

Frechtling, Louis E. Anglo-Russian rivalry in Eastern Turkestan, 1863-1881. *Journal of Royal Central Asian Society* Vol. 26, Part III, July 1939,pp 471-89.

Fraser-Tytler, W.K. Afghanistan : a study of political developments in Central Asia. London, Oxford University Press, 1950.

Gadru, S. N. Ed. — Kashmir papers: British intervention in Kashmir. Srinagar, 1973.

Ganju, M. — Textile industries in Kashmir. Delhi, Premier, 1945.

Ganpat. *Pseud.* — Magic Ladakh: an intimate picture of a land of topsy-turvy customs and great natural beauty. London, Seeley, Service, 1928.

Ghose, D.K. — Kashmir in transition, 1885-93. Calcutta, World Press, 1975.

Gillard, David — The Struggle for Asia, 1828-1914: a study in British and Russian imperialism. London, Methuen, 1977.

Gopal, Surendra — Indians in Russia in the 17th and 18th century. New Delhi, 1988.

Graham, Stephen. — Impressions of seven rivers land and Russian Central Asia. *Journal of Central Asian Society* Volume 2, Part III, 1915, PP.113-126.

Griffiths, Percival. — The History of Indian tea industry. London, Weidenfeld, 1967.

Guha, Amalendu. *Ed.* — Central Asia: movements of Peoples and ideas from times prehistoric to modern. Delhi, Vikas, 1970.

Gupta, Hari Ram. — Life and work of Mohan Lal Kashmiri 1812-1877. Lahore, Minerva, 1943.

Hamilton, Angus. — Afghanistan. London, W.Heinemann, 1906.

Hasrat, Bikram Jit. — Anglo-Sikh relations 1799-1849. Hoshiarpur, 1968.

------------------------ — The Punjab papers. Hoshiarpur, 1970.

Hassnain, F.M. — British policy towards Kashmir, 1846-1921. New Delhi, Sterling, 1974.

------------------------ — Gilgit, the northern gate of India. New Delhi, Sterling. 1978.

Higgens, Humphrey. — Khanykov on Bukhara in 1841. *Central Asian Review* Volume 15, No. 2, 1967. pp. 114-122.

Hukm Singh Sodhi. *Comp.* History of Kokand, from the commencement of Russian intercourse until the final subjugation of the country by that power. Translated into English by C.E. Bates. Lahore, Govt. Press, 1878.

Huttenback, Robert A. Gulab Singh and the creation of the Dogra State of Jammu, Kashmir and Ladakh. *Journal of Asian Studies* Vol. 20. No. 4, August 1961, pp. 477-88.

Indian Officer. *Pseud.* Russia's march towards India. London, S.Low, 1894. 2 Volumes.

Indra Krishan. An Historical interpretation of the correspondence of Sir George Russel Clark, 1841-43. Delhi, 1952.

Irving, B.A. Commerce of India, being a view of the routes successively taken up by the commerce between Europe and the East. London, Smith, Elder, 1858.

Irwin, John. Shawls : a study in Indo-Iranian influences. London, 1955.

Kalla, Badrinath. Influence of the Central Asian languages upon the Kashmiri language. *Neelja* No. 7, 1981-82, pp. 79-87. (In Hindi).

Kapur, M.L. Kashmir sold and snatched. Jammu, 1968.

Kaul, Anand. Geography of the Jammu and Kashmir State. New Delhi, Light & Life, n.d.

Kaul, Har Gopal. Tarikh-i-Kashmir. Lahore. (In Urdu).

Kaul, Jayalal. Studies in Kashmiri. Srinagar, Kapur, 1968.

Kaul, Saligram. The Biography of Maharaja Gulab Singh, founder of Jammu & Kashmir State. Srinagar, 1923.

Kaushik, Devendra. Central Asia in modern times : a history from the early 19th century. Moscow, 1970.

---------------------- India and Central Asia in modern times. Delhi, 1985.

---------------------- Indian revolutionaries in Soviet Asia. *Link* 26 January 1966.

Keay, John. The Gilgit game: the explorers of the Western Himalayas, 1865-95. London, John Murray, n.d.

Khalfin, N.A. Angliskaya kolonialnaya politika na srednem vostoke (70-e gody XIX v).Tashkent,1957.

---------------------- Russia's policy in Central Asia 1857-1868. Translated from Russian into English by Hubert Evans. London, 1964.

Khan, Ghulam Hassan. Freedom movement in Kashmir 1931-40. Delhi, Light & Life, 1980.

Kemp, P.M. Bharat-Rus: an introduction to Indo-Russian contacts and travels from mediaeval times to the October Revolution. Delhi, 1958.

Khan, Hasmat Ullah. Tarikh-i-Jammu. Lucknow, 1939.

Khuihama, Hassan Shah. Tarikh-i-Kashmir (political part). Translated from Persian into Urdu by Maulavi Mohammad Ibrahim. Srinagar, 1957.

Klimburg-Salter, D.E. The Silk route and the diamond path. Los Angeles, 1982.

Krist, Gustav. Alone through the forbidden land: journeys in disguise through Soviet Central Asia. Translated by E.O. Lorimer. London, Reader's Union, 1939.

Kuhn, Alexander von. The Province of Ferghana, formerly Khanate of Kokand. Translated from German by F.Henvey. Simla, Govt. Press, 1876.

Kuznetsov, V.S. British and Russian trade in Sinkiang 1819-1851. *Central Asian Review* Volume 13, No. 2. 1965, pp. 149-156.

Lamb, Alastair.	The Sino-Indian border in Ladakh. Canberra, 1973.
Lattimore, Owen.	Pivot of Asia. Boston, 1950.
Lydolph, Paul C.	Geography of the USSR. London, John Wiley, 1970.
Mac Gregor, C.M. *Comp.*	Topography, ethnology, resources and history of Afghanistan. Calcutta, Supdt. Govt. Printing, 1871.
Mitrokhin, L.	Failure of three missions. Moscow, Progress, 1987.
Mohibbul Hassan.	Kashmir under the Sultans. Calcutta, Iran society, 1959.
Morgan, Gerald.	Ney Elias: Explorer and Envoy Extraordinary in High Asia. London, 1971.
Morozova, A.C. etc.	Folk art of Uzbekistan. Tashkent, 1979.
Muzaffar Ahmad.	The Communist Party of India and its formation abroad. Translated from Bengali into English by Hirendranath Mukerjee. Calcutta, 1962.
---------------------	Myself and the Communist Party of India : 1920-1929. Translated from Bengali by Prabhas Kumar Sinha. Calcutta, 1970.
Neve, Arthur.	Thirty years in Kashmir. London, Edward Arnold, 1913.
Nevill, H. L.	Campaigns on the north-western frontier. London, John Murray, 1912.
Pandit, K. N.	My Tajik friends. N. Delhi, 1985.
Panikkar, K.M.	Gulab Singh 1792-1858: founder of Kashmir. London, M. Hopkinson, 1930.
Park, A.G.	Bolshevism in Turkestan, 1917-23. New York, 1957.
Parmu, R.K.	A History of Muslim rule in Kashmir, 1320-1819. Delhi, People's Publishing House, 1969.
---------------------	A History of Sikh rule in Kashmir 1819-1846. Srinagar, Govt. Press, 1977.

Persits, M.A. — Revolutionaries of India in Soviet Russia. Moscow, Progress, 1983.

Pierce , R.A. — Russian Central Asia, 1867-1917. Berkeley 1960.

Ponomaryou, B., Gromyko, A. and Khvostov, V. — History of Seviet foreign Policy; 1917-1945. Moscow, Progress, 1969.

Rafiqi, Abdul Qaiyum. — Sufism in Kashmir from the fourteenth to the sixteenth century. Varanasi, n.d.

Rothermund, Dietmer. — Asian trade and European expansion in the age of mercantilism. Delhi, 1981.

Samra, C.S. — India and Anglo-Soviet relations 1917-47. Bombay, 1959.

Sankrityayana, Rahul. — History of Central Asia: Bronze Age (2000 BC) to Chengiz Khan (1227AD). New Delhi, 1964.

Schomberg, R.C.F. — Between the Oxus and the Indus. London, 1935.

Sethi, R.R. — The Lahore Darbar in the light of the correspondence of Sir C.M. Wade, 1823-40. Delhi, 1950.

Sharma, D.C. — Kashmir under the Sikhs. Delhi, Seema, 1983.

Sharma, B.P. — Ranbir Singh: a princely freedom fighter. *Hindustan Times* 9 March 1969.

Singh, Bawa Satinder. — The Jammu Fox: a biography of Maharaja Gulab Singh 1792-1857. Southern Illinois University Press, 1974.

Skrine, C.P. and Nightingale, Pamela — Macartney at Kashgar: new light on British, Chinese and Russian activities in Sinkiang 1890-1918. London, Methuen, 1973.

Skrine F.H. — The Expansion of Russia 1815-1900. Second edition. Cambridge University Press, 1904.

Skrine, F.H. and Ross, E.D. — Heart of Asia. London, 1889.

Sladkovsky, M.I. The Long road: Sino-Russian economic contacts from ancient times to 1917. Moscow, Progress, 1981.

Solovyev, O.F. K voprosu ob otnoshenii tsarskoy Rossii k Indii v XIX nachale XX veka. *Voprosy Istorri*, 1958, No. 6, pp. 96-109. (For English translation see *Central Asian Review* Volume 6, No. 4. 1958 pp. 448-64.)

Srivastava, M.P. British diplomacy in Asia: Persian Gulf, Soviet Central Asia, Tibet, China, India and Burma, New Delhi, Ess Ess, 1978.

Staal, Frits. The Stamps of Jammu and Kashmir. New York, Collectors Club, 1983.

Stanwood, F. War, revolution and British imperialism in Central Asia. London, 1983.

Teng, M.K. etc. Kashmir: constitutional history and documents. New Delhi, Light and Life, 1977.

Terentyff, M.A. Russia and England in Central Asia. (St. Petersburgh, 1875). Translated from Russian by F.C. Daukes. Calcutta, Foreign Department Press, 1876.

Ullman, Richard H. Anglo-Soviet relations 1917-21. New Jersey, Princeton University Press. Volume 1-Intervention and the War. 1961. Volume 2-Britain and the Russian Civil War. 1968. Volume 3-The Anglo-Soviet accord. 1972.

Ulyanovsky, R. National liberation. Moscow, Progress, 1978.

USSR Academy of Sciences. Lenin and national liberation in the East. Moscow, Progress, 1978.

Vaidyanath, R. The Formation of the Soviet Central Asian republics: a study in Soviet nationalities policy 1917-1936. New Delhi, People's Publishing House, 1967.

Vambery, Arminius. History of Bokhara. London, H.S. King, 1873.

Warikoo, K. Jammu, Kashmir and Ladakh:a classified and comprehensive bibliography. New Delhi, Sterling, 1976.

Wheeler, G. Modern history of Soviet Central Asia. London, 1964.

Williams, D.S.M. Taxation in Tsarist Central Asia. *Central Asian Review* Volume 16, No. 1, 1968, pp. 51-63.

Wyllie, J.W.S. The External policy of India during the nineteenth century. Edited by W.W. Hunter. (First published in 1875). Reprint by Neeraj Publishing House, Delhi in 1984.

Yapp, M.E. Strategies of British India: Britain, Iran, and Afghanistan, 1798-1850. Oxford, Clarendon Press, 1980.

Zafar Imam. Colonialism in East-West relations. New Delhi, 1969.

Zelinskiy, A.N. Ancient routes through the Pamirs. *Central Asian Review* Volume 13, No. 1, 1965, pp. 44-54.

Zutshi, N.K. Sultan Zain-ul-Abidin of Kashmir: an age of enlightenment. Jammu, 1976.

Journals

Central Asian Review, London.
Central Asian Survey, Oxford.
Central Asiatic Journal.
Journal of Asian Studies.
Journal of Royal Asiatic Society of Great Britain and Ireland.
Journal of Royal Central Asian Society.
Proceedings of the Royal Geographical Society.

INDEX